P9-CMW-077

The Venezuelan Democratic Revolution

Other Books by ROBERT J. ALEXANDER

The Perón Era, 1951

Communism in Latin America, 1957

The Bolivian National Revolution, 1958

The Struggle for Democracy in Latin America
(with Charles O. Porter), 1961

Prophets of the Revolution, 1962

Labor Relations in Argentina, Brazil and Chile, 1962

A Primer of Economic Development, 1962

Today's Latin America, 1962

The Venezuelan Democratic Revolution

A Profile of the Regime of Rómulo Betancourt

by
ROBERT J. ALEXANDER

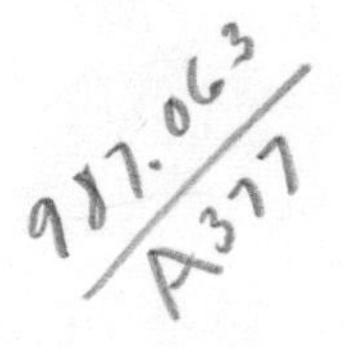

Rutgers University Press
New Brunswick *New Jersey*

Library of Congress Catalogue Card Number: 64-19176
Manufactured in the United States of America
by Quinn & Boden Company, Inc., Rahway, New Jersey

Dedicated to LEOPOLD KOHR

Preface

It is only fair to the reader that an author state explicitly the preconceptions and prejudices with which he approaches a subject about which he is writing. This is particularly relevant in the discussion of such a controversial subject as the Venezuelan Democratic Revolution.

I do not approach this theme without a point of view or personal sympathies. Quite frankly, I am favorably disposed to the efforts of the leaders of the democratic regime which came to power in 1959 in Venezuela. As a firm believer in democracy, I laud their attempts to establish political democracy as a permanent form of government in Venezuela. As one who believes in a society with a high degree of social mobility and relatively small disparities of wealth and income, I cannot but be sympathetic with the program of social reform being undertaken there. Since I share the belief of most Latin Americans in the need for rapid economic development in their area, I cannot but admire the efforts of contemporary Venezuelan leaders to achieve this in the face of enormous difficulties.

Since I feel that in modern society there is need for a wide degree of social planning, without destroying the ability of private enterprisers to make the utmost contribution in sectors of the economy where that is appropriate, I look with interest and sympathy upon the efforts of the Venezuelan leaders to develop a mixed economy. Finally, I regard what is going on in Venezuela to be of key importance to the fate of democracy and social progress in the whole hemisphere.

Once my preconceptions are stated, however, I would add that I have tried to allow for them and to be objective. I hope that I have been able to see and evaluate the weaknesses of the Rómulo Betancourt regime, as well as its strong points. To the degree that I have been able to do so, this book should be of value to students of Latin American affairs.

In a sense, this book is the result of a decade and a half of research. For more than fifteen years I have been following the trend of events in Venezuela through frequent visits to the country and acquaintance with Venezuelans who were forced during the Pérez Jiménez dictatorship to live abroad. Of the twelve trips that I have been able to make to the country, two took place during the Acción Democrática party's first government, in the late 1940's. Three others were made during the dictatorship, one during the provisional government of 1958, and the last six under the second administration of President Rómulo Betancourt.

Much of the detailed material that the reader will find in this book was collected during a nine-week visit to Venezuela that I made during the summer of 1961. At that time I was able to travel widely throughout the country, visiting fifteen of Venezuela's twenty states, going through the central region, and visiting the mountain areas of the west and the Orinoco–Caroní Valley section in the east.

During this visit I was able to talk to a wide variety of people, including government officials, leaders and rank and file members of all of the country's political parties, trade union and peasant leaders, businessmen, university students and professors, and foreign diplomatic personnel of various countries. I was able to see for myself much of the agrarian reform, the new industries, the Caroní hydroelectric project, the oil fields around Lake Maracaibo, as well as schools, housing projects, and new water supply and sewerage systems.

A good deal of the background sections at the beginning of the book is derived from earlier acquaintance with Venezuela and Venezuelans. Of particular importance were my experiences in the country during the first Acción Democrática period in power, and lengthy conversations with exiles during the long years of the dictatorship.

As a result of all of these contacts, I owe many debts of gratitude for what is in these pages, though of course no one is responsible for what appears here except me. I owe much to the hundreds of people who submitted to my interrogation over the years. I could not possibly mention them all, but special thanks should certainly go to President Rómulo Betancourt, Dr. Rafael Caldera, leader of the Copei party, Drs. Jóvito Villalba and Ignacio Luis Arcaya of the Unión Republicana Democrática, Jesús Farías, secretary-general of the Communist party, and Domingo Alberto Rangel, leader of the Movimiento de Izquierda Revolucionaria.

I also owe very much to Professor Alejandro Yabrudy, President Betancourt's private secretary, who greatly facilitated my studies in the summer of 1961. The governors of all states that I visited also aided me a great deal in my researches in their areas. Likewise I owe a large debt of gratitude to José González, who accompanied me on my trips to the interior during this same period and was of untold help in breaking through red tape and in tracing down people whom I was to interview.

Here at home, I must mention with gratitude the work of Mrs. Emma Wenz in typing the manuscript twice over. Katherine Morgan of the Rutgers University Press thoroughly edited the manuscript. Likewise, my wife, Joan Alexander, who accompanied me to Venezuela in 1961, has contributed much in ideas and comments on what we saw, and has been very patient with the rattle of the typewriter night after night while this was being written.

ROBERT J. ALEXANDER

New Brunswick, New Jersey
January, 1964

Contents

Tables

Part One

The Background of the Democratic Revolution

Introduction

Venezuela is a large and underpopulated country. It is a land of contradictions and unresolved conflicts. It has vast potentialities in the qualities of its people and in natural resources, but only now after a century and a half of independent national existence are these potentialities even beginning to be realized.

Were it not for the Venezuelan Democratic Revolution, the situation of Venezuela in the middle of the twentieth century would be tragic. Although it is famous as a land of riches in petroleum and minerals, the majority of the people have benefited little from these, and continue to live in abject poverty. They scratch a miserable existence from the soil, or earn a pittance in the cities and towns.

Although the country has produced literary figures of world-wide renown, a high percentage of the people remain illiterate. Although the country has not fought an international war since it gained its independence during the first quarter of the nineteenth century, the military have dominated the civic and political life of the nation during most of the country's independent life.

This situation has been very slow to change in spite of one of the most spectacular oil booms that the world has seen. For most of the forty-five years or so that Venezuela's great subsoil wealth has been under exploitation, much of the income from it has been wasted. Until the overthrow of a nine-year dictatorship in 1958, if national revenue did not go into the pockets of the self-selected few who ruled the country, it was spent in building public works which are grandiose, and impress the visiting foreigner, but do little to raise the standards of living of the great majority of the people. When the great mass of the people benefited, it was usually in spite of not because of the actions of their rulers.

The parts of the economy not connected with the oil industry or the government's gigantic public works projects were largely ignored, except during short periods. Agriculture, which was the basis of the country's economic life before 1920, tended for long years to decline. The peasants, most of whom did not own land, fled from the countryside to the vicinity of the oil centers, or to the capital city, Caracas, where successive dictatorships concentrated their huge building projects. As a result, the rural areas in some parts of the country were all but abandoned, the traditional agricultural exports declined, and the country became a large importer of agricultural products that it could quite well produce for itself.

These things are what the Venezuelan Democratic Revolution is all about. It is a valiant attempt to reverse the trend of Venezuelan political and economic history. It is an effort at one and the same time to substitute a system of representative democracy for the traditional rule by *coup d'état* and military command, and to turn the income from the exploitation of the nation's natural resources to the broadening of the economy and raising the standards of living of the mass of the population.

There is a tremendous feeling of urgency about all of this. This sense of haste arises not only from the fact that everything has to be done at once but also from the existence in the hemisphere of an example of an alternate way to achieve economic diversification, education, health services, and the like: that of Fidel Castro and his associates in Cuba.

There is no doubt that the rivalry between the Cuban Totalitarian Revolution and the Venezuelan Democratic Revolution will go far to determine the future of the whole of Latin America. Leaders of governments, political parties, labor movements, the business communities of other Latin American countries, are observing very closely the results that are being achieved in the two republics.

This feeeling that the whole hemisphere is watching them undoubtedly increases the feeling of urgency with which the leaders of the Venezuelan government conduct their revolution. This feeling would be there even if Fidel Castro had never existed, however. As many Venezuelans have remarked, "everything remains to be done" in Venezuela. Even the substantial financial resources of the Venezuelan state are sorely taxed by the growing and insistent demands for new schools, new hospitals, new rural roads, funds for financing the agrarian reform, funds for developing the country's manufacturing industries, funds for expanding the nation's electrical power resources, funds for irrigating or draining land for new agricultural colonies.

The situation was made more difficult by the fact that the constitutional democratic regime that came to power on February 13, 1959, was faced with a first-rate financial and economic crisis, such as had not occurred in four decades. The economic crisis made it impossible to initiate as many projects and programs as the democratic government would have liked. It also made necessary measures of retrenchment and of conservation of financial resources which were unpopular and which raised further doubts in the minds of the businessmen concerning the ability of the government to survive the tremendous buffeting that it was receiving.

The pressures upon President Rómulo Betancourt and his government were also increased by a factor in the national psychology of the Venezuelans, the tendency to look to the government for everything. The pioneer spirit is not characteristic of the people of Venezuela. This is true not only of the humble peasant or worker but also of the businessman, whose tendency is to want a government guarantee of the profitability of his enterprise before he is willing to take a risk in a new field. Happily, there has developed during recent decades a type of businessman who does not conform to the old pattern, and is more willing to strike out for himself.

One of the most important contributions of the democratic regime of President Betancourt was its attempt to inspire in the rank and file of the people a willingness to do things for themselves. This was particularly notable in the rural areas, where the government's community development organization and the leaders of the Peasants Federation of Venezuela cooperated in getting the peasants to help themselves in building schools, water systems, rural roads, and a variety of other public works.

One other factor made the work of the democratic regime exceptionally difficult. This was the constant menace to its stability arising both from elements among the military and civilians associated with the old order who sought to apply the age-old formula of an Army *coup d'état* to reverse the current situation, and from elements of the extreme Left, who, though not able themselves to carry out a coup, sought to create conditions that would be propitious to such a military movement against the regime.

The armed forces as a whole showed themselves loyal to the

regime on numerous occasions, attributable in no small part to the ability of President Rómulo Betancourt to convince them that it was in their own best interests to do so. The military men also feared the repetition in Venezuela of a Castro type of movement that would do away with the traditional armed forces. Nonetheless, small elements of disgruntled officers, many of them on the retired list, continued to plot and conspire against the democratic regime. They found some support among civilians who had profited from the previous dictatorships, and were reported to have received considerable financial aid from the exiled dictator, General Pérez Jiménez.

The willingness of most of the military to support a constitutional government was not the only positive factor working on behalf of the success of the Venezuelan Democratic Revolution. Of great importance, too, was the basic financial soundness of the Venezuelan economy. The country is still the world's largest exporter of oil and the third largest petroleum producer. The government's share of the profits from the oil industry was raised late in 1958 to approximately 70 per cent, thus providing the Venezuelan regime with very large resources, not enough to do all that the government would have liked to do, but enough to carry out a very substantial program.

Even more important as a factor in favor of the success of the regime was the quality of its leadership. Starting with the President, and going down through the executive branch and the various parts of the legislative, Venezuela was fortunate to have an exceptionally talented and selfless group of leaders for its effort to establish a democratic, economically sound and socially just form of society.

Rómulo Betancourt is undoubtedly the finest politician in Latin America today. He is a man of long experience in the political life of his country, is of undisputable personal honesty, has a physical resistance and ability to work which are the despair of his associates. Furthermore, he has a political acumen and an ability to maneuver, to balance one situation or one group against another, which is the essence of a successful politician. Likewise, he has a pecularily strong hold on the loyalty of those who work with him, and upon the masses of the workers and peasants of Venezuela.

Below the President, too, there was an unusually able group of individuals. In Congress, the leaders of the government forces included Carlos D'Ascoli, one of Latin America's leading economists, and Luis Beltrán Prieto Figueroa, one of the great educators of the hemisphere. Of the principal leaders of the organized labor and peasant movement, most were people of great sagacity and long experience. In the executive branch the regime had the services as Minister of Mines and Petroleum of Juan Pablo Pérez Alfonso, who probably is the best informed man in the country on the oil industry, and is the architect of the Acción Democrática party's oil policies. In charge of general economic planning was Manuel Pérez Guerrero, also a leading Latin American economist, who during the years of exile worked for the Technical Assistance Board of the United Nations and helped establish the planning mechanisms of half a dozen of the newer nations of the world.

Among the government leaders who were more politicians than technicians, there also was a very capable group. These included Raúl Leoni, in his middle fifties the "old man" of the Acción Democrática party, who presided over Congress between February, 1959 and March, 1962, and is a man who is a thorough student of his country's problems, and an astute politician. In the Chamber of Deputies, the presiding officer during the same period was Dr. Rafael Caldera, the leader of the Partido Social Cristiano Copei, which collaborated with the majority Acción Democrática party as a coalition partner from the first day of the constitutional regime. He is one of the principal spokesmen for Christian Democracy in the Western Hemisphere, and is a student of and has published his researches on various aspects of Venezuelan social and economic problems.

These were only a few of the principal figures in the constitutional government. The leaders of the 1959 to 1964 Venezuelan regime were probably the most capable, the most studious, and the most cosmopolitan-minded group of national leaders to be found any place in Latin America.

What were these men trying to accomplish? Their objectives can be summed up under six headings: agrarian reform, diversification of the economy, establishment of a greater degree of Venezuelan control over the Venezuelan economy, the development of a modern educational system, the provision of the social amenities in terms of housing, electricity, water supply, sewerage, for both the rural and urban population; and most important of all, the consolidation of a democratic society and form of government.

The agrarian reform undoubtedly constitutes the cornerstone of the economic and social policy of the Venezuelan Democratic Revolution. The aim is to provide the majority of the population, which still lives in the countryside, with its own means of making a decent living. This requires not only giving the peasants land but also providing them with credit, technical assistance, equipment, and all of the other things necessary for a profitable agricultural enterprise. Through the agrarian reform, not only can the standards of living and income of the rural people be raised but also there can be developed a source of raw materials and a market for the industries of the cities and towns.

The agrarian reform was closely connected with the Betancourt government's efforts to diversify the economy. It was anticipated that the new small landowners would produce a variety of agricultural products that Venezuela had hitherto had to import. At the same time, however, the government made a strenuous effort to develop manufacturing industries in the cities. Through the Corporación Venezolano de Fomento it extended sizable financial aid to private entrepreneurs, and at the same time proceeded with the development of government-owned petrochemical and steel industries and the establishment of a large "mixed" enterprise together with the Reynolds Aluminum Company to produce aluminum in the Orinoco Valley. It also energetically pushed geological surveys, particularly in the Orinoco area, to discover new mineral resources.

The democratic regime further sought to lessen the degree of foreign control which has characterized the Venezuelan economy since the beginning of the oil boom in the 1920's. The establishment of a government oil company had as its objective the entry of Venezuelan interests into the country's basic industry, which previously had been completely in the hands of foreign firms. The regime also pushed energetically the establishment under government ownership of a national electricity network, which ultimately would absorb the foreign-owned electric companies that serve some of the country's largest cities.

Nevertheless, the Betancourt regime did not discourage further foreign investment, except in the oil industry. Rather, it sought to encourage the establishment of branches of foreign manufacturing companies in the country, feeling that in time these would be "nationalized" in the sense of being run by Venezuelans and having Venezuelan capital invested in them. Meanwhile they would serve to strengthen and broaden the general Venezuelan economy, giving rise, undoubtedly, to many new native firms to provide parts and to process many of the products made in foreign-owned firms.

The democratic regime put great emphasis on the development of education, and at least from the quantitive standpoint did as much as any other country in the world in so short a time. The government's education program involved much more than just providing sufficient classrooms and teachers, important as that was. It set out to develop an educational system that would be adapted to Venezuelan needs and could reinforce and promote the other programs of the regime in the fields of agriculture and industry.

The democratic government also expended great efforts on providing the country with adequate health services, water and sewerage facilities, and similar services. The fact was that when the regime came to power early in 1959, most of the people of the country did not enjoy any of these services, which are generally thought of as basic to a modern civilized society. Remarkable progress was made after 1959 in bringing them even to the people in isolated parts of the country.

Finally, the whole orientation of the regime was toward establishing a firm base for political democracy in Venezuela. Essentially, this meant three things: First, the government proposed to accomplish enough in the economic, educational, and social fields to prevent the people from becoming doubtful about the ability of a democratic regime to provide for their welfare. Second, it made every effort to convince the armed forces of the necessity of supporting a democratic, constitutional regime. Third, it set out to convince the political parties of the value of functioning in a democratic manner, and to prevent opposition political elements from succeeding in attempts to overthrow the regime.

Obviously, it is too early to pass final judgment on the Venezuelan Democratic Revolution, but surely, anyone reading what follows will appreciate the vastness of the effort that is under way to transform a nation, to make up for time lost during a century and a half. The author is convinced of its significance not only for Venezuela but for the democratic future of Latin America, the Western Hemisphere as a whole, and the world at large. If the Venezuelan effort succeeds, the possibility that political democracy, economic progress, and social justice will become general throughout Latin America is very good. If it fails, totalitarian forces may well sweep over the rest of Latin America. With Latin America in the totalitarian camp, the chances for the success of the world-wide struggle for democracy would be greatly reduced.

Chapter One
Venezuela and Its People

Venezuela lies in the tropics. At its southernmost point in the Federal Territory of Amazonas it comes within a few miles of the equator. The country nevertheless has a variety of climates and temperatures because the end of the eastern spur of the Andean range cuts across the northwestern states of Venezuela, leveling off in the central region and ending in a number of offshore islands, the largest of which is Trinidad, a member of the British Commonwealth.

It is in these western and central coastal parts of the country, characterized by mountains or steep hills and deep valleys, that most of the people of Venezuela live. Elsewhere the population is very sparse. Thus the majority of Venezuelans are concentrated within some two hundred miles of the ocean, except in the extreme west, where the comparatively heavily populated Andean states of Táchira, Mérida, and Trujillo reach further inland, and in the Orinoco River Valley at the eastern extremity of the country, where economic developments of the last two decades have brought rapidly increasing settlement.

South of the expiring Andean chain lie the great *llanos* or plains. These have been the favorite theme of Venezuelan novelists and poets, and the *llanero* is as romantic a figure in Venezuelan folklore and literature as is the late nineteenth century cowboy in the United States or the gaucho in Argentina. There have existed since colonial times enormous cattle ranches, and out of the llanos came some of the bravest and most brutal fighters for independence from

Spain. Their leader, General José Antonio Páez, himself the owner of a large hacienda, became the first President of Venezuela.

The cattle industry of the llanos, which had provided an important export before the beginning of the oil boom, was all but abandoned. Only now are serious efforts being made to improve the grazing areas and to encourage agriculture in those parts of the llanos which are suitable for it.

In the eastern part of the country is the vast Orinoco Valley, with its 1,600-mile-long meandering river. The tropical jungles of the Orinoco until recently were known best for their snakes, crocodiles, and other wild creatures, and for the mining of gold and diamonds and the production of Angostura bitters. The town of Angostura, near the delta of the Orinoco, was at one time the headquarters of Simón Bolívar in the wars of independence. It was rechristened Ciudad Bolívar. The Orinoco Delta is a maze of islands and swamps, for the most part uninhabited.

In the late 1940's iron ore of very high quality was discovered not far from Ciudad Bolívar, and the opening of several large iron mines there has given new life to the whole area. It is now planned to make this the center of heavy industry in Venezuela. The first stage in the construction of a large hydroelectric project on the Caroní River has already reached completion, and a steel plant has been completed at San Félix. In project is a whole new city, Santo Tomé de Guayana, which ultimately will house 250,000 people and will rival Brasilia as one of the wonders of the modern world.

In the southwestern part of the country rise the Guayana Highlands, which extend from Venezuela through the three Guianas and down into northeastern Brazil. The few inhabitants are principally Indians, many of whom are still uncivilized. Whatever mineral or other wealth there may be, remains largely unexplored.

It is in the narrow coastal strip and in the mountains in the west that 86 per cent of the people live.[1] Although Venezuela is a country of rapidly growing cities, almost half of the population still makes its living from agriculture. In the valleys there developed in colonial times large estates, where cacao and coffee trees, indigo, and maize were grown. The civil wars of the nineteenth century resulted in the destruction of the position of the aristocracy and the physical extermination of many of them. In the redistribution of their land, however, most of the valleys of central and western Venezuela were given to relatively large landowners associated with the victors in the civil wars.

Since then, however, sizable portions of the land in a number of the coastal states have come into the possession of the federal and municipal governments as a result of confiscations following the dictatorship of Juan Vicente Gómez (1909 to 1935), who had put much of the best land in the hands of his family and closest friends. Many agricultural laborers and share tenants were employed on the private estates in the valleys; however, since many peasants preferred to be their own masters, the typical Venezuelan phenomenon of the *conuquero* developed: the peasant who leaves the valley, goes up the moutainside where no one will bother him, and having burned off a piece of forest land, plants his corn and beans and bananas in rows running up and down hill. The first year his crop is acceptable, but by the second year much of the topsoil has run off and his crop is considerably smaller. The third year he merely gets enough to keep body and soul together. The fourth year he moves to a new part of the mountain to start the whole process all over again. Much of the land these squatters occupy belongs to the government, although some of it is private property. Neither the state nor the private owners usually bother to collect rent from the conuquero.

The *conuco* system, under which tens of thousands of peasants still live, has proved exceedingly detrimental for a number of reasons. For one thing, the peasant is able to make only the poorest kind of living. Isolated on the mountain, he can enjoy none of the benefits of schools, running water, electricity, or other modern amenities. For another, as the population grew the conuqueros destroyed more and more of the forest area, and disastrously reduced the water level in many of the lowland areas that had previously drawn their water supply from small streams protected by the forests of the mountains.

In recent years, however, thousands and thousands of the migratory farmers have moved to the urban areas, and the cities of Venezuela have grown with alarming rapidity. Caracas more than tripled its population in a dozen years in the late 1940's and the 1950's, and metropolitan Caracas now has about 1.2 million of the country's total population of 7 million. Other cities such as Maracay, Valencia, Barquisimeto, and Maracaibo grew with almost equal rapidity.

The swift urban population increase brought with it innumerable problems. With the exception of Valencia and one or two other towns, the increase in population was not accompanied by an increase in jobs. Particularly after the fall of the dictatorship of Marcos Pérez Jiménez in 1958 and the curtailing of his fantastic public works programs, the cities were faced with huge unemployment problems. Each year some 80,000 people come onto the labor market. For an economically underdeveloped nation such as Venezuela, it is exceedingly difficult to find new employment each year for more than 1 per cent of its total population.

Moreover, it has been impossible to build houses as fast as the number of people grew. As a result, every important city of Venezuela is infested with *ranchos,* whole wards where people have put up jerry-built houses of packing boxes, sticks, and mud, or anything they could lay their hands on. In cities like Caracas, where these are built on hills, every rain storm washes away hundreds if not thousands of these ranchos. Furthermore, the rancho communities have grown without rhyme or reason. They have no streets, no water supply, no sewerage system, and constitute a major health menace for the whole population of the city. Crime, promiscuity, and other vices thrive in these communities.

The rapid development of the cities also reflects one of the basic facts of the Venezuelan scene: the very high rate of population increase. It is estimated that the annual population growth is about 3 per cent, which puts Venezuela among the world's most rapidly growing nations in terms of population.

This rapid rate of population growth means that the average Venezuelan is very young. The 1961 census showed that more than 50 per cent of the population was under twenty years of age, and that 70 per cent of the population was under thirty. This fact is reflected in the rapid increase in the demand for schools and other children's services, which considerably complicates the problems of a government that is trying for the first time to provide its constituents with these services.

This population increase has its positive aspects, however. It is the result in large part of one of the most spectacular public health achievements of modern times—the almost complete control of malaria mosquitos. Starting at the end of World War II, the public health authorities of Venezuela, through a thorough campaign of regularly spraying with DDT virtually every building in the country, succeeded in dramatically cutting down the incidence of malaria and reducing it to a relatively minor cause of death.

From an economic point of view, too, the growth of population can have its positive results. With 7 million people, Venezuela does not have a sufficient home market for many kinds of industries that might otherwise be established in the country. Thus, although a rapid population growth complicates the problems of providing essential social services, it will make easier the development of certain other sectors of the national economy.

Venezuela's population is a mixture of three races: the white, the African, and the native American Indian. At the present time the last of these is the least important numerically. Only a very small proportion of the population is considered or considers itself to be Indian. There are some civilized tribes in the area of Lake Maracaibo, and in the eastern and southern parts of the country there are still unknown numbers of indigenous people who have had little contact with modern civilization. Although the original inhabitants of the area mixed their blood over the centuries with that of the European conqueror and the African slave, for the most part, the Indian contribution to the Venezuelan racial amalgam has been submerged. Except for the Andean area in the west, where the Indian strain is strong, the average Venezuelan is a mulatto, some of whose ancestors came from Europe, others from Africa.

One government official, himself of a very light complexion, explained the racial situation of Venezuela thus: "We are all café au lait; some a bit more café, others a bit more au lait." And this is a fair summary of the facts. Although one finds blue-eyed blondes or jet black Negroes, most of the population of Venezuela exhibits characteristics somewhere between these two extremes.

There is relatively little racial feeling. There certainly is no noticeable discrimination in public places, in employment, even among officers of the armed forces, on the basis of racial background. Venezuela has in recent times had Presidents, leaders of Congress, top officers of the armed forces, important figures in the business community, who were noticeably African in ancestry. And the important thing is that nothing has been made of this, no arguments have been offered either in support of or against their qualifications on racial grounds. Color is in general an irrelevant issue.

This attitude towards race is a reflection of one of the most important facts about contemporary Venezuela: the high degree of social democracy that exists in the country. It is striking that in a nation which has so little enjoyed the benefits of political democracy—freely elected governments respectful of the rights of minorities—there should be so little feeling of class or caste as in present-day Venezuela.

This social democracy is usually attributed to the Federal War of the 1860's. During this conflict, which was a class war as well as a political one, the position of the landed aristocracy which had its roots in the Spanish Conquest was largely destroyed. As a result, extreme class consciousness and snobbery, tinged with pretensions of racial superiority, is of little significance in Venezuela.[2] Whatever their racial heritage, sons of poor families who are able to go to secondary schools or the university mix with freedom with the scions of the nation's richest families. A person tends to be judged on his own merits, not on the basis of what his ancestry is. There is less servility evident on the part of members of the lower classes, and less haughtiness and superciliousness among members of the upper classes, than one finds in much of Latin America.

This same spirit has molded the religious life of the nation. Although the majority of the people of Venezuela are nominally Roman Catholics, the Church has learned to live at peace with those who are not. It largely lost in the nineteenth century the entrenched rights and wealth inherited from colonial times. As a result, the Church has not generally played the role of a violent defender of the *status quo,* as has often been the case in other Latin American countries.

There is complete freedom of worship in Venezuela. Although relations between Church and state are cordial, the ecclesiastical authorities do not try to use the government to force those of other beliefs to conform. There exist active though very small Protestant and Jewish minorities, and one sometimes sees even in remote parts of the country a peasant rancho displaying a sign "Iglesia Evangélica" (Protestant Church). A considerable part of the population is free thinking or more or less indifferent to matters religious, but there exists little of the violent anticlerical feeling that one finds in Latin American countries in which the Roman Catholic Church has been less tolerant.

In spite of these positive elements in the Venezuelan national character, there are great and even shocking social and economic contrasts in the republic. A visitor who sees only the capital cannot help but be impressed by the difference between the elegant and sometimes beautiful homes of the middle and wealthy classes in the valleys of Caracas and the miserable and primitive lean-tos of the poorest people in the hills overlooking the city. This disparity between the living conditions of the well-off minority and the abysmally poor majority is a standing challenge to the reigning political, social, and economic order in Venezuela.

The challenge is the greater because the oil boom and the extravagant building programs of successive dictatorial regimes in Caracas and one or two other centers have served to demonstrate the material benefits of modern industrial society to the poor population of the major urban areas. Within the limits of their small incomes, the urban poor have tried to participate in these benefits. Thus, many of the shacks in the hills of Caracas are furnished with television sets and electric refrigerators. These possessions but whet the appetite for better living conditions, and inability to achieve these conditions creates a kind of social and political pressure that constantly threatens internal strife.

Equally serious is the contrast between Caracas and one or two other major cities, on the one hand, and the interior of the country, on the other. Within some two decades the capital has been converted into a show place of modern architecture and has become a cultural and artistic center of importance. But in the provinces, a large part of the people live much as did their ancestors. The peasant population in particular has done without schooling, medical service, anything but the most primitive housing, sanitation facilities, and water supply, without electricity, or even roads to put country people in contact with the outside world.

Thus centuries have separated the major cities from the countryside. Mud huts, with thatched roofs and dirt floors and without any of the modern conveniences, are the homes of 800,000 Venezuelan peasant families. Medicine men are the nearest equivalent of doctors. Most rural folk live and die without the sanction of a legal marriage. They are born, grow up, and are buried without benefit of clergy. Few of the peasants learn to read and write.

These are the conditions that the government that came to power in February, 1959, set out to change in a very short span of years. However, both the conditions that this regime faced and the constitutional and democratic, but revolutionary, government itself are the result of a long historical development. They cannot be understood without at least some knowledge of this historical background.

Venezuela was a backwater of the Spanish colonial empire. Its subsoil contained no large deposits of precious metals, nor did it lend itself to the exploitation of sugar on a large scale, as did the islands of the Caribbean and the northeast coast of Brazil. As a result, it was never raised to the dignity of a viceroyalty but had the subordinate status of captaincy general.

Perhaps for the very reason that it was neglected by the Spanish authorities, Venezuela developed a strong feeling of identity and of separateness before many other parts of the Spanish Empire. The mixture of Spanish, African, and Indian peoples was more thorough than in many other parts of the empire. Thus, perhaps, the leading colonial families of the time feared the results of a separation from the mother country less than did their counterparts in Peru or Mexico. In any case, it was the Venezuelans who took the lead in liberating from Spanish rule the northern part of the South American continent. Francisco Miranda, the great prophet of independence, was a Venezuelan. So was Simón Bolívar, the Liberator, and so were most of his most trusted military lieutenants. Venezuela supplied much of the man power for the revolutionary armies, and a great deal of the actual fighting took place in Venezuela.

Although the wars of the early nineteenth century brought independence to Venezuela, they did not bring freedom for the people. When one of Bolívar's principal lieutenants, General Páez, proclaimed the separation of Venezuela from the Republic of Gran Colombia (which the Liberator had brought into being), and established himself as first President, he also set up the first of a long line of more or less brutal and tyrannical dictatorships.

Throughout the nineteenth century, Venezuela was ruled by military tyrants, most of whom came from the llanos of the southern part of the country and based their power on armed forces drawn largely from the llanero population of that region. Then at the turn of the century the balance of power shifted to the mountain states of the west, and particularly to the state of Táchira, which provided the nation with five dictators who dominated the country during most of the first half of the twentieth century. Generals Cipriano Castro and Juan Vicente Gómez, who ruled until 1935, were tyrants of the old school, whose power came from an untrained and illiterate volunteer army. Gómez' successor, General Eleazar López Contreras, began the process of democratizing the country, and was followed by General Isaías Medina Angarita, who continued this process. After the short interlude of 1945 to 1948, during which a democratic government was installed, however, came the nine-year-long dictatorship of Colonel Marcos Pérez Jiménez, another Táchira soldier, who returned to the violence and tyranny that had been traditional. He held power from November, 1948, to January, 1958.

Meanwhile, the economy of the country had changed drastically. Until the end of World War I, Venezuela was almost exclusively an agricultural and livestock raising country. It exported small but substantial quantities of coffee, cacao, and cattle. The country was nearly self-sufficient, almost completely so in agricultural products.

Then came the petroleum boom. During the first two decades of the century various companies had begun to show interest in Venezuela as a source of petroleum, but it was not until 1918 that the oil industry began to develop in earnest. In the course of the next two decades the government of Juan Vicente Gómez granted numerous concessions for exploration and exploitation of the nation's petroleum reserves, and two principal areas of production developed. The first was around Lake Maracaibo in the northwestern part of the country, the second in the east, near the Orinoco River Valley.

The conditions under which these concessions were granted were scandalous. Juan Vicente Gómez, members of his family, and close associates organized a series of phantom companies which were granted most of the concessions extended by the government. These companies, in turn, sold their concessions, which they had no intention of exploiting, to one or another of the great international petroleum concerns. As a result of these deals, leading members of the Gómez government profited personally on a grand scale in the establishment of the oil industry of Venezuela.

The advent of the petroleum industry brought a violent change in the nation's economy. Oil exports quickly eclipsed in volume and value the shipment of all other products put together. At the same time, although the direct return to the government from these exports was very modest in the beginning, the intensive activity of the oil companies in looking for and developing the country's petroleum resources resulted in a rapid increase in economic activity and national income. General Gómez, in addition to using this increased income to enrich himself, his family and friends, also took advantage of it to pay off the national debt, and to begin a modest program of road building and other public works. By the time Gómez died in 1935, petroleum production was firmly established as the most vital and sensitive part of the nation's economy.

As a result of the easy wealth that flowed into the nation from the petroleum industry, other parts of the economy began to suffer. Workers tended to stream to the vicinity of the oil fields, where comparatively high wages were offered. As time went on, and the government's income from the oil industry grew, a larger and larger part of the national income of the country came to depend on oil revenues. Moreover, except for the period between 1945 and 1948, all of the regimes between 1922 and 1959 concentrated their expenditures on Caracas and a few other major cities.

The development of the oil industry along with the government policy of favoring big cities in allocating its large income is to a large degree responsible for the contrasts between the large urban areas and the countryside. Whereas funds were lavished on grandiose projects in Caracas, the rural areas were all but ignored, except for the building of a network of trunk highways in various parts of the country. The movement of the peasantry to leave the land to seek urban employment and the higher standard of living that they thought they could attain in the big cities reached catastrophic proportions in the 1950's.

Caracas grew to monster size. It came to have about one fifth of the total population. It grew so rapidly, particularly during the dictatorship of 1948 to 1958, that it was impossible to provide essential sewers, water supplies, housing—even had the dictatorial government been interested in doing so, which it was not. At the same time, there was little for many of the migrants to Caracas to do, since the government's vast expenditures on public works did not generate industries that could provide permanent employment.

Meanwhile, with the death of General Juan Vicente Gómez on December 15, 1935, the political structure of the country began to change. As long as the dictator lived, he held an iron-bound control over the country. Absolutely no legal opposition was permitted, and the nation was treated much as if it were the personal hacienda of Gómez, his family, and his friends.

With Gómez' death, his son-in-law and Minister of War, General Eleazar López Contreras, succeeded to the presidency. In spite of his lifelong association with the Gómez regime, the new President moved rapidly to dismantle much of the structure built by the dictator. Within a few days of Gómez' death, López Contreras exiled most of the dictator's family, and within a few weeks the new government confiscated large portions of the fortune of the Gómez family, as well as of many others who had become rich under its protection.

As the result of a gigantic public meeting in Caracas on February 14, 1936, the first such meeting of the anti-Gómez opposition in many years, the López Contreras regime was also forced to relax the reins of the dictatorship. During the next eighteen months, exiles returned, political parties were formed, the press enjoyed a high degree of freedom, a labor movement was born, and in general the country began to breathe more easily and to establish the bases for a democratic life. Although General López Contreras cracked down again on the opposition in the middle of 1937, his regime never returned to the terrorism and the tyranny that had existed under his predecessor.

During the López Contreras regime there were established at least four factions, including two that developed into political parties in this period, and two others that were to do so a few years later. At first all anti-Gómez groups formed a somewhat amorphous group known as Organización Revolucionaria Venezolan (ORVE). Within a year and a half of the dictator's death, ORVE had disappeared, and there existed in its place two groups, the Partido Democrático Nacional (PDN), led by Rómulo Betancourt, and the Partido Comunista de Venezuela (PCV), led by Gustavo Machado. Two other groups, one of Social Catholic orientation and the other consisting of personal followers of the president of the Venezuelan Student Federation, Jóvito Villalba, were outside both the PDN and the PCV.

With the end of López Contreras' term of office in 1941, he chose as his successor, General Isaías Medina Angarita, another military man from the state of Táchira. Although the anti-Gómez elements had considerable suspicion of Medina Angarita in the beginning, his regime went very far indeed in permitting the establishment of civil liberties and in a modification of economic and social policies inherited from the days of Juan Vicente Gómez.

Both the PDN and the PCV were legalized by the Medina regime, the first under the name of Acción Democrática (AD), the second as Unión Popular. Although these opposition parties were not allowed to win elections, they were allowed to participate in them, and were allowed to publish and speak freely. The group around Jóvito Villalba became an open collaborator with the Medina government, and Villalba himself was chosen by the President as a senator.

In 1943 the Medina regime also undertook to modify the oil policy that had existed since the days of Juan Vicente Gómez. A new petroleum law put a halt to the granting of new concessions and substantially increased the government's participation in the profits of the oil industry. Furthermore, Medina developed a new social policy. He founded the nation's social security system and began a modest program of public housing, mostly in Caracas. The Medina government also encouraged the development of a trade union movement, which acquired considerable importance, particularly in the oil fields. During the Medina regime, control of the majority of the trade unions passed from the Communists to elements belonging to Acción Democrática.

In spite of its admirable record, which some people still insist was the best in the history of Venezuela, the Medina regime was overthrown by a military-civilian coup on October 18, 1945. The story of this coup, and of the three-year regime to which it gave rise, constitutes what may be called the prelude to the Venezuelan Democratic Revolution.

Chapter Two
The Forerunner of the Revolution, 1945 to 1948

The prelude to the Venezuelan Democratic Revolution took place during the period between 1945 and 1948. Acción Democrática was in power for the first time during this period, and Rómulo Betancourt served as President of the Republic. During the three years of this first AD regime many of the programs that are part of the Venezuelan Democratic Revolution were first undertaken. Although most of these programs were abandoned by the dictatorship of 1948 to 1958, they were renewed thereafter by many of the same people who had first launched them.

Acción Democrática came to power by means of a military coup, and the provisional government presided over by Rómulo Betancourt remained in power from October, 1945, until February, 1948. In the latter month it turned over power to Rómulo Gallegos, world-famed novelist, who had been elected Constitutional President of the Republic as AD's candidate in elections held two months before. The Gallegos regime, however, remained in office for only nine months, being overthrown by a new military *coup d'état* on November 24, 1948.

The Acción Democrática government of 1945 to 1948 was nationalist, democratic, and socially oriented. It sought to establish firm Venezuelan control over the country's principal source of income and foreign exchange, oil, while at the same time increasing the return to the nation from its exploitation. It sought to use this increased income to develop both the material and human resources of the nation. Above all, it sought to establish the bases for a democratic and civilian constitutional form of government.

Fundamental to the whole program of the Acción Democrática government of the 1940's was its policy with regard to the oil industry. This program had been elaborated by the party's leaders, notably Juan Pablo Pérez Alfonso, during nearly a decade before AD came to power. Pérez Alfonso, as Minister of Development, was directly in charge of carrying out the AD oil policy.

The AD oil program can be summed up under several headings:

1. Raising taxes on the foreign oil companies as high as the Venezuelan competitive position in the international petroleum market would permit.
2. Establishment of a government oil firm to which all future new concessions would be granted, to be exploited exclusively by this firm or through contracts with third parties.
3. Processing Venezuelan oil production within the country, and establishment of a national refinery, with state or mixed state-private capital.
4. Conservation of the nation's petroleum resources.
5. Reinvestment of profits of petroleum firms in development of other parts of the economy.
6. Improvement of the economic and social conditions of the oil workers.
7. Use of the increased tax resources from petroleum in diversifying the national economy.
8. Sale by the Venezuelan government in the international market of that part of the production payable to it as royalties.[1]

A sizable increase in taxes on the oil companies was carried out in various stages. The object of these tax increases was to put into effect a principle that the AD government frequently expressed, and that was embodied in a resolution passed by the National Constituent Assembly, to the effect that "in no cases should the petroleum companies receive a share of annual profits superior to that received by the state."[2]

The first year in which this famous "50-50 principle" (which became the standard for the whole petroleum-producing world in subsequent years) was applied was 1947. At the end of that year, the taxes on the companies did not reach the 50 per cent of profits provided for in the government policy, which the oil companies had accepted. As a result, the companies and the government conferred on the problem, and the former agreed to invest the remaining amount of money in "works of collective interest" indicated by the government.[3]

A second aspect of the AD government's oil policy was to have the state itself sell the 16⅔ per cent of total oil output that the oil companies turned over to the government; the government had hitherto turned royalty oil back to the companies to sell on its behalf. President Betancourt has described the reasons for this aspect of his regime's policy: "We found the warehouses empty of food items upon assuming responsibility for the administration. Meat, cereals, and fats were lacking. These were the critical postwar years, and money was not enough to acquire foodstuffs. It was necessary to barter certain urgently needed raw materials, none of which was of greater value than petroleum.

". . . In that form, the petroleum of the state was bartered for Argentine meat, Portuguese oleaginous products, babassu nuts from Brazil, to provide needed raw materials for our national vegetable oil factories.

"These operations proved that it was possible to obtain higher prices in international markets for crude oil than the companies operating in the country had estimated, and this fact was important in the relations of the government with these companies." [4]

A third part of the government's petroleum policy was the firm refusal to extend new concessions to the international companies. President Gallegos, in his message to Congress early in 1948, stated this policy as follows: "The decision of the government not to extend new concessions was also maintained, because the systems previously adopted did not fully protect the national interest, and it was not considered proper to continue those systems as a permanent method of disposing of our subsoil reserves." [5]

The leaders of the AD government insisted frequently that this no-concession policy was not intended to halt the growth and development of the oil industry. Instead, the government proposed to establish a nationally owned oil company, which would have the following attributes: "(a) to carry on directly the work of exploration and exploitation; (b) to contract out those tasks; (c) to sign such other contracts as might prove convenient." [6]

President Gallegos suggested to Congress the establishment of a national oil company early in 1948. Before this firm had actually been agreed to by the legislature, however, his government was overthrown; and in the succeeding nine years the dictatorship did not feel the matter of sufficient urgency to continue with the plans laid down by the Acción Democrática regime.

The Acción Democrática government of 1945 to 1948 set about to use the increased resources that it received from the oil industry to diversify the economy and raise general living standards. Fundamentally, the regime was seeking to end Venezuela's excessive dependence upon a single industry, oil. It wished to develop other parts of the economy, so that the country's agriculture, industry, mining, and trade would provide a healthy economy even when the petroleum industry was no longer bringing in the large income that it was then providing.

President Betancourt has discussed this aspect of the AD government's policy in the following terms: "In Venezuela, this 'jump,' in the Hegelian sense, from the colonial to the modern in the economic structure of society, was to be planned, regulated, by a government loyal to the social movement of our time, and consequent with the interests and aspirations of those strata which are the most solid base for its maintenance: the middle, professional, and technical classes, workers, artisans, and peasants, and groups of industrialists with a modern outlook. More concretely, there was not being repeated the 'Enrich yourself' of Guizot to the French bourgeoisie, but production was being oriented in three ways: (1) studying the characteristics of the economy, and stimulating its development in conformity with those technical studies; (2) undertaking those programs which, for their magnitude or lack of attraction for private investment, require active intervention of the state; and (3) stimulating liberally, with the aid of credit and technical assistance, businessmen who are dynamic and adventurous, but only when those businessmen channel their efforts to fields in which the nation needs production, adjusting their costs to what the consumer can rationally pay, and agreeing to provide a level of social welfare equivalent to that already acquired by Venezuelan workers."[7]

For this purpose, the Betancourt government established two institutions: the Consejo Económico Nacional (National Economic Council), a body provided for in the Constitution of 1936, but never established by intervening governments; and a new organization, the

Corporación Venezolana de Fomento (Venezuelan Development Corporation).

The Corporación de Fomento was of particular significance. The law that established it provided that it should receive at least 10 per cent of the government's annual budget. In conformity with this, the Corporación de Fomento received 372 million bolívares in 1948, and it was foreseen that it would receive 1 billion bolívares by the end of President Gallegos' constitutional term.

The Corporación had a five-man board of directors. One of these was chosen by the President of the Republic to preside over the organization. Two others were named by Congress, and the last two were chosen from a list presented by the Federation of Chambers of Commerce and Production. The president of the Corporación during the Acción Democrática regime was an independent but pro-AD businessman, Alejandro Oropeza Castillo.

Although the Corporación was empowered to invest in and aid both industry and agriculture, it concentrated principally on the latter during this period. It specialized in programs in the fields of meat, milk, and sugar production.

In addition to setting up the Corporación de Fomento, the AD regime gave additional funds to two pre-existing institutions, the Banco Agrícola y Pecuario and the Banco Industrial. The capital of the former was increased by the government by three and a half times between 1945 and 1947, while that of the latter rose 250 per cent in the same period.

The Banco Agrícola y Pecuario paid particular attention to small agriculturalists during the AD regime. Thus, though total credit extended by this bank rose a little more than 100 per cent between 1946 and 1948, the number of beneficiaries of the bank's operations rose almost 400 per cent during the same period.[8]

The AD government also spent considerable amounts of money on mechanization of Venezuelan agriculture and on irrigation. The former contributed significantly to increasing national agricultural output. Although several small irrigation projects were completed, many more were only in the planning stage at the time the AD regime was overthrown. Between 1945 and 1948 programs for irrigating some 400,000 hectares (about 1 million acres) were planned.[9]

The effects of the agricultural development policies of the Acción Democrática government were very positive. Rómulo Betancourt cites the 1949 annual report of the Banco Central in this regard: "National production has developed favorably. Agricultural output grew, because of the large area under cultivation. . . . Coffee output was estimated in the year 1946 to 1947 at 741,000 sacks of 60 kilograms; but the following year it was estimated at 890,000 sacks. Production of cacao was estimated for 1946 at 475,000 sacks of 50 kilograms, against 301,100 sacks in 1945. The harvest of corn underwent a notable increase . . . and though early estimates proved too optimistic, the harvest probably reached 400,000 metric tons, in a cultivated area which increased to 376,400 hectares. . . . The harvest of black beans is calculated by the Banco Agrícola y Pecuario at 54,000 metric tons; the estimates for previous years were substantially below these figures." [10]

Production of other crops also increased dramatically between 1945 and 1948. Sugar rose from 1.95 million metric tons to 2.37; peas from 8,000 metric tons to 16,000; potatoes from 9,185 metric tons to 16,000.[11]

Government aid also gave considerable impulse to manufacturing. The textile, shoemaking, and fertilizer industries in particular received aid from the Corporación Venezolana de Fomento. Perhaps most spectacular was the advance made in the cement industry; with government aid, production almost doubled between 1947 and 1948, and a program was got underway which soon made the country self-sufficient in this product. Between 1946 and 1948 the Corporación invested 58 million bolívares in loans to manufacturing firms, while the investments of the Banco Industrial increased sevenfold compared to the years before AD came to power.[12]

The Acción Democrática regime also took the first steps toward the establishment of an iron and steel industry. The Corporación de Fomento began studies to ascertain the most appropriate type of steel production for Venezuela, and these had been completed by the time the AD regime was overthrown. It took the Pérez Jiménez dictatorship half a decade more before the actual work of constructing a steel plant was under way.[13]

The Acción Democrática regime further undertook to develop the electric power resources of the country, an essential prerequisite for large-scale industrial growth. During the first two years of the AD government, the number of electric plants rose from 322 to 600, and the number of towns served by electricity rose from 319 to 616. Half a million Venezuelans were introduced to the use of electricity for the first time. In comparison, only five towns had been electrified during the decade previous to AD's coming to power.

In addition to these specific efforts, the AD regime developed a general plan for the electrification of the nation. This was elaborated by the electric energy section of the Ministry of Development and the electricity department of the Corporación de Fomento, with the technical assistance of the engineering consultant firm Burns and Roe, Inc., of New York City.

Complementing the program to diversify the economy was the AD government's effort to raise the standard of living and improve the social services of the Venezuelan people. The AD regime sought not only to stimulate popular consumption of key foodstuffs and other consumer goods but also to use some of the greatly augmented resources of the state to improve educational, medical, and other facilities available to the general public.

The first part of this program—increasing consumption of food and other key products—was undertaken in two ways. First of all, the government encouraged the increase in money income of the wage-earning portion of the population. The trade union movement, which grew substantially during the AD period, was encouraged to seek and obtain sizable wage increases. In the second place, the Betancourt and Gallegos administrations undertook to import large amounts of essential consumers' goods, defraying the cost both by bartering royalty oil and by allocating sizable sums from the general budget. In 1946 and 1947 the Betancourt government spent 100 million bolívares for this purpose, as compared with 450,000 spent by its predecessor in 1944. As a result, there were substantial increases in national consumption of sugar, meat, milk, and other products.[14]

The AD regime also made major efforts to provide an adequate educational system for the Venezuelan people. During the thirty-six months that the Acción Democrática governments were in power, the number of children in school rose from 131,000 to nearly 500,000. The number of elementary teachers rose from 8,520 in 1945 to 13,500 in 1948. The number of secondary schools rose from twenty-nine to forty-seven. As against 11,500 secondary school students, there were 22,000 at the time of the overthrow of President Rómulo Gallegos.

At the same time, the AD government sought to change the orientation of Venezuelan education, putting new emphasis on vocational training. A system of technical-industrial schools was planned, and two of these were constructed by the AD regime, with a capacity of approximately 1,000 students each. At the same time, the one existing crafts school was considerably expanded, and eight new schools of the same type were established.

The AD regime also began an all-out campaign to reduce adult illiteracy. The Ministry of Education officials in charge of this campaign reported that 10 per cent of the people were taught to read and write between 1945 and 1948. By the time President Gallegos was overthrown, there were some 3,000 illiteracy centers functioning throughout the country.

Finally, the income and working conditions of the teaching profession were considerably improved. Salaries were increased 75 per cent, and the training facilities were greatly expanded and improved.

The AD government was likewise concerned with increasing the medical facilities available to the people. During the single year 1947 hospitals with a capacity of 660 beds were completed, and hospitals and clinics with a 1,600-bed capacity were started.

Housing was the final aspect of the Acción Democrática's social policy. The government housing institution, the Banco Obrero, which was established in 1929, had produced 2,460 low-cost housing units for workers before 1946. During the first two years of the Acción Democrática regime, the Banco Obrero built more than double this number. The rate of construction was still higher in 1948.

There was a change in housing policy as well as an increase in number of units constructed. Previous regimes had concentrated the activities of the Banco Obrero on building huge apartment projects in Caracas. The AD regime, in contrast, centered its attention on the cities and towns of the interior, and built individual houses or small apartment units rather than "super-blocks."

The Betancourt and Gallegos administrations of 1945 to 1948 were revolutionary in the sense that they sought to bring about a fundamental alteration of the economic and social structure of the republic. The programs for the diversification of the economy, particularly the industrialization program, were essential elements of the whole; however, the most fundamental effort was the agrarian reform.

During the nine years after the death of Juan Vicente Gómez, much of the late dictator's landed property was seized by the state.

On it, the governments of López Contreras and Medina Angarita established seven agricultural colonies, settling 310 colonists on 2,730 hectares (6,800 acres) of land. The cost of these settlements was 27,942,670 bolívares.[15]

This exceedingly modest effort was the nearest thing to an agrarian reform that Venezuela had experienced prior to the seizure of power by Acción Democrática. The new government immediately made known its intention to carry out a thorough reorganization of the system of land tenure. President Betancourt announced the government policy in the following terms, on December 14, 1945:

"In order for the land to be productive, it is necessary that it be in the hands of those who make it produce. When I maintain this thesis—presenting it in the name of the revolutionary government, which has a definite concept of agrarian reform—I do not take a position on the radical extreme left. The thesis that the peasant should be owner of the land that he fertilizes with his sweat has its roots in the best national traditions. It was Bolívar who first advocated in Venezuela the need for an agrarian reform.

"It should not be feared that a government such as ours, which has been demonstrating that it has a sense of responsibility, is going to adopt a demagogic policy with regard to land distribution. The land will be redistributed, but at such time as the government has the plans and technical facilities that will permit rational and productive exploitation of those lands."[16]

On February 11, 1946, the Revolutionary Government Junta issued Decree No. 183, which authorized the Ministry of Agriculture to divide among peasants land belonging to the government. By the end of 1947, some 73,770 hectares (approximately 183,000 acres) had been divided among 6,000 peasant families. At the same time, the Ministry had established nine new agricultural colonies, on which were settled 2,000 peasant families, with each family possessing a minimum of 10 hectares (25 acres).

The Corporación Venezolana de Fomento also participated in this land redistribution program. It undertook to set up agrarian communities on government land, administered under the supervision of the Corporación, on which the most modern techniques and machinery would be used. By the end of 1946 fourteen such communities had been set up.[17]

The Acción Democrática regime took the position that the redistribution of privately owned land should be undertaken only by a constitutional and popularly elected regime. Meanwhile, the National Constituent Assembly, dominated by AD, wrote Article 69 into the new Constitution, which read as follows:

"The state will carry out a planned and systematic action, designed to transform the national agrarian structure, to rationalize agricultural and livestock production, to organize and distribute credit, to improve the conditions of life in the rural areas, and to effect the progressive economic and social emancipation of the peasant population. A special law will determine the technical and other conditions, in accordance with the national interest, by which will be made effective and efficacious the exercise of the right that the nation recognizes for peasant associations and individuals capable of agricultural and grazing work, and who lack workable land or do not have sufficient land, to be granted it, as well as the means necessary to put it in production."

After the establishment of the constitutional regime with the inauguration of President Rómulo Gallegos, a general agrarian reform law was introduced by the regime. It was discussed and passed by Congress during the early months of 1948, and was signed by President Gallegos only a month before he was overthrown by the military.

The 1948 Agrarian Reform Law provided for the expropriation of private land needed for the agrarian reform, and the compensation of the owners, partly in cash, partly in bonds. The Instituto Agrario Nacional (IAN), which was established to administer the law, was empowered to grant land to colonies of peasants, who would own their own land, but would not be empowered to sell it or alienate it without permission of the IAN; to cooperatives, in which land would be communally owned; and to individual peasants, who would enjoy full property rights. In the last case, the peasant would pay a small amount for his land.

Since this law was passed on the eve of the overthrow of the Gallegos regime, it did not become effective; however, in general terms it was the forerunner of the agrarian reform law that was to be enacted by the Betancourt government more than a decade later.

One of the principal objectives of the Acción Democrática regime of the 1940's was to establish a firm foundation for a stable democratic form of government in Venezuela. Fundamentally, this involved two things: the establishment of civilian organizations which could challenge the traditional military domination of the country's political life; and the installation of a democratically elected administration.

During the 1945 to 1948 period, civilian organizations and pressure groups proliferated. The most important of these were the trade unions and the political parties. The growth of both of these was encouraged by the Acción Democrática regime.

The development of the labor movement was dramatic. In 1945 there existed 252 legal trade unions in Venezuela. By the time of the fall of the Gallegos government, there were 1,014 such organizations in existence.[18] Over 450 of the new unions were organized among agricultural workers.[19] Not only did the number of local unions increase spectacularly, but the structure of the labor movement was strengthened. Seven national industrial unions or federations were established, as well as fifteen state labor federations. Finally, at the end of 1947, the first national central labor body, the Confederación de Trabajadores de Venezuela (CTV), was founded. It brought together the great majority of the organized workers of Venezuela, the only group outside being a small federation in the Distrito Federal under the control of the "Black" Communists of the Partido Revolucionario Proletario.

Collective bargaining was strongly encouraged by the government. By the time of the overthrow of Gallegos, there were some 575 collective agreements in effect, and industry-wide labor-management contracts existed in many fields, including petroleum, textiles, construction, and public services.

The potential importance of this rapid development of the trade union movement for the stability of the government should be emphasized. The labor movement, through its ability to call a general strike, presented the Venezuelan people's first challenge to the control of the military over national political life. Although when the crisis came in November, 1948, the potential force of the trade union movement was not used, this mistake was recognized and was not repeated after the fall of the Pérez Jiménez dictatorship on January 23, 1958.

Political parties also prospered during the AD regime. Until shortly before Acción Democrática took power in October, 1945, there were only two effective parties in the republic: Acción Democrática and the Communists. The latter split into the so-called Reds and Blacks less than a year before the October, 1945, revolution. The other party then existing, the Partido Democrático Venezolano, was little more than a part of the administrative apparatus of the Medina Angarita government, without life of its own.

Only four days after the October 18, 1945, revolution, the new government set up a commission, only one of whose members belonged to Acción Democrática, to draw up a new electoral law. On March 15, 1946, the Revolutionary Government Junta enacted this commission's recommendations into law.

Shortly afterwards, various new parties were legally recognized by the government, along with Acción Democrática and the Partido Comunista de Venezuela. Three of these new parties were prominent: the Copei, the Unión Republicana Democrática (URD), and the Partido Revolucionario Proletario (Comunista). In addition, several much smaller parties were registered, although they had little impact on the political life of the republic.

The Copei (derived from the name Comité Pro Elecciones Independiente) was a party with a Christian Democratic orientation similar to that of many groups that appeared in Europe after World War II. In the 1945 to 1948 period it was the most conservative of the major parties and was the haven of many of the reactionary elements in the country's politics, though its national leadership was in the hands of men of the moderate Left. It was headed by Dr. Rafael Caldera, who for a few weeks after October 18, 1945, had been Attorney General in the revolutionary government, but resigned because of disagreement with Acción Democrática.

The Unión Republicana Democrática was a party of ill-defined ideology. It was established principally by people who had been office holders in and supporters of the Medina Angarita government. Although it claimed to be a "liberal" party, and to be of the moderate Left, it frequently criticized the "socialistic" tendencies of the Acción Democrática regime. It was headed by Jóvito Villalba, one of the leaders of the 1928 student uprising against Gómez, and head of the Students Federation in the years immediately following Gómez' death.

The Partido Revolucionario Proletario was a faction of the Venezuelan Communists. During the Medina Angarita regime they had split over the question of the attitude they should assume toward the administration then in power. Medina had legalized the Communists as the Unión Popular, which worked closely with the government; however, a dissident group withdrew from the Unión

Popular to establish once again the Partido Comunista de Venezuela. During the Acción Democrática government, the latter was legalized, and those still in control of the Unión Popular reorganized it as the Partido Revolucionario Proletario (Comunista).

The Revolutionary Government Junta introduced universal suffrage, extending the franchise to illiterates. To facilitate this, each party was given a color and became known popularly by the color that was assigned to it. Members of Acción Democrática thus became known as Blancos (Whites); the Copeyanos as Verdes (Greens), the URDistas as Pardos (Browns), the members of the PCV as Rojos (Reds), and the members of the Partido Revolucionario Proletario as Negros (Blacks).

Three elections were held during the AD tenure of power. On October 27, 1946, a National Constituent Assembly was chosen; on December 14, 1947, a new President, Congress, state legislatures, and the city council of Caracas were chosen; and on May 9, 1948, all other municipal councils were elected. In all three of these elections, Acción Democrática won handily, capturing from 70 to 78 per cent of the votes. Copei was the second largest party, obtaining from 13.2 per cent to 21.1 per cent in the three elections. The URD and the two Communist parties together each received a little more than 3 per cent in each poll.[20]

In retrospect, the Acción Democrática leaders came to the conclusion that they had called too many elections in too short a time. As a result of having three election campaigns in a little more than eighteen months, the country was kept in a constant state of campaign agitation. This added unnecessary instability to the political situation and undermined the regime itself. This lesson was applied when these same people returned to control of the government a decade later.

The Constituent Assembly wrote an entirely new Constitution. This document, which was in the tradition of the most democratic constitutions of Latin America, followed the pattern of the Mexican Constitution of 1917 in setting forth a considerable body of labor and social legislation that Congress was instructed to pass.

The Acción Democrática government was overthrown after a little more than three years for two reasons: its own successes, and the political inexperience of President Rómulo Gallegos.

The Betancourt and Gallegos governments had made giant strides in building a new kind of society in Venezuela. They had made a beginning in transforming the economy from one dependent on a single product to one in which petroleum exploitation, agriculture, manufacturing, and mining all made important contributions. They had begun an earnest attack on the miserably low standards of living of the Venezuelan people, spending large portions of the government's augmented income in this endeavor. They had helped develop important civilian institutions that would in time have created a solid basis for normal civilian, democratic, and constitutional government. In the process of all of this, they had gained exceedingly wide popularity for their party.

All of this perturbed certain of the top officers of the Army, including several who had been instrumental in putting Acción Democrática in power. These men resented the activity of "upstart" civilians in undermining the dominance of the officer caste over the political life of the nation. Furthermore, at least some of them were personally very ambitious. They wanted to have the way open, as it traditionally had been, to the highest posts in the government (including the presidency), by exercise of the customary military pressure and *coup d'état*.

This group was led by Lieutenant Colonel Marcos Pérez Jiménez. President Betancourt, suspicious of his loyalty to the regime, had sent him abroad on missions which kept him away from the center of power; however, President Gallegos allowed him to return, and made him Chief of the General Staff. From that post he began to organize the coup that overthrew the Gallegos government.

Early in November, 1948, the group of military men headed by Colonel Pérez Jiménez presented an ultimatum to President Gallegos. They insisted on an end of the one party government of Acción Democrática, the incorporation of several Army officers in the cabinet, and various other changes in the policies of the government. Although President Gallegos did not submit to this ultimatum, he did nothing to discipline the insubordinate officers. He relied exclusively on the loyalty of the other members of the officers' corps, and refused to make full use of his position as commander in chief of the armed forces. Nor would he accept the offer of the labor movement and his own party to organize civilian resistance to the insurrectionary officers.

Thus, lack of political experience and astuteness on the part of novelist-President Rómulo Gallegos was the immediate cause for the downfall of the Acción Democrática regime. As a result of it, the conspirators continued to plot. Major Mario Vargas, who had been a key figure in the coup of October, 1945, and was the top Army officer closest politically to Acción Democrática, rushed back from a tuberculosis sanitarium at Lake Placid to try to convince Pérez Jiménez and the others not to oust Gallegos. Colonel Carlos Delgado Chalbaud, Gallegos' Minister of Defense, also tried to prevent a coup. Failing in this attempt, both men finally joined the movement against Gallegos, hoping to deflect it and to prevent the establishment of a naked military dictatorship, an effort in which they also failed.

Finally, on November 24, 1948, the conspirators moved. President Gallegos, and all the other leaders of the government upon whom the insurrectionists could lay their hands, were arrested. Valmore Rodríguez, President of the Senate, and constitutional successor of President Gallegos, attempted to establish a new center of government at Maracay, but failed when, after some hesitation, the local garrison joined the revolt.

With the overthrow of the government of Rómulo Gallegos, the prelude to the Venezuelan Democratic Revolution came to an end.

Chapter Three

The Pérez Jiménez Regime

The nine-year dictatorship from November 24, 1948, to January 23, 1958, preceded the Venezuelan Democratic Revolution. The regime in power during those years, particularly during the period when Marcos Pérez Jiménez served as President of the Republic, was of a brutality equal to or surpassing that of the notorious Juan Vicente Gómez. The Pérez Jiménez dictatorship rivaled that of the Dominican Republic's Rafael Leonidas Trujillo for the record of the most ruthless, corrupt, and tyrannical regime in power in Latin America.

The effect of the dictatorship on the people of Venezuela was profound. It served to convince the overwhelming majority of the citizens that their country had had enough of the traditional type of military dictatorship, and should never go through that experience again. This conviction became well-nigh universal among the workers and peasants, who had had few doubts on that score for two decades, but it also became widespread among the country's leading industrialists and merchants. Even many of those who had profited considerably during the Pérez Jiménez regime became firm opponents of the dictatorial form of government. By the time Pérez Jiménez was overthrown, nearly every important political leader, and all of the parties, were convinced of the need for the kind of program of reform and development that Acción Democrática had attempted to carry out between 1945 and 1948.

With the overthrow of President Rómulo Gallegos, the rebels put power into the hands of a new Junta Militar de Gobierno, composed of three officers, Colonel Carlos Delgado Chalbaud, Lieutenant Colonel Marcos Pérez Jiménez, and Lieutenant Colonel Luis Felipe Llovera Páez. It has been reported that in the first meeting of this Junta, Pérez Jiménez tried to take over leadership of the Junta, but was prevented from doing so by Colonel Delgado Chalbaud, who pointed out that he was the ranking officer in the group. For the next two years, Delgado Chalbaud served as President of the Junta. As is customary after such a *coup d'état*, the Junta Militar assumed not only executive authority but also the power to legislate. It continued to govern the country until December, 1952.

The Junta Militar allowed little opposition. One of its first acts was to outlaw Acción Democrática, and a few months later it also declared the Red Partido Comunista de Venezuela illegal. However, for the rest of its life, the Junta maintained the legality of the Copei, the Unión Republicana Democrática, and the Black Communist Partido Revolucionario Proletario.

The policies of these three parties varied considerably. The Unión Republicana Democrática was clearly favorable to the new regime. Its members accepted posts as state governors and other officials of the regime. The Copei made it clear within a few days, through the person of Dr. Rafael Caldera, that it had had absolutely no participation in the coup against the Acción Democrática regime. Nevertheless, it did not forbid its members to hold office in the Junta Militar regime, and some of its more conservative members did have minor posts during the first couple of years.

The Partido Revolucionario Proletario was frankly favorable to the regime. It gained considerably from it, since after February, 1949, it controlled the only regional labor federation, the Federación de Trabajadores del Distrito Federal, which was permitted to function legally and openly. This federation continued active until shortly before the fall of the Pérez Jiménez regime. Its members served on committees which "investigated" the actions of the fallen AD regime in the states of Anzóategui and Falcón. Its paper continued to be published for some time after the fall of President Gallegos.

During the two years in which Colonel Carlos Delgado Chalbaud remained head of the Junta Militar, the government continued many of the main programs that had been begun by the AD regime. These programs were in no way expanded, however, and as projects already in hand were completed, the programs were allowed to lapse. Thus the irrigation schemes started by the AD government were brought to completion, but new ones were not begun. Schools under construction were completed, but then the school construction program lapsed. Training of new teachers fell off, so that by 1951 only 56 per cent as many students were attending normal schools as in 1948.

Nor did the Junta Militar pursue the Acción Democrática programs in other fields of economic and social development. Thus, the appropriation for the Corporación Venezolana de Fomento declined by approximately 20 per cent between 1948 and 1951. The agricultural and grazing department of the Corporación was eliminated altogether. The agrarian reform program was suspended, except for a handful of very expensive colonization projects on government-owned land. The general redistribution of the land which had been provided for in the 1948 Agrarian Reform Law was abandoned. At the same time, the organizations of agricultural workers and peasants, grouped together in the Peasants Federation, the Federación Campesina, were destroyed.

The process of augmenting wages and salaries came to an end, in part because the trade union movement was all but destroyed. Acción Democrática trade union leaders were jailed in large numbers during the first weeks of the military regime. On February 25, 1949, the government declared illegal the Confederación de Trabajadores de Venezuela and all of its constituent regional and industrial federations. On March 9, 1949, the reorganization of all of the country's local unions was decreed, all executive committees were removed, and members holding office on the date of the decree were expressly banned from re-election. The meetings at which new officers were elected had to be presided over by an official of the Ministry of Labor.

This offensive against the organized labor movement by the Venezuelan government was thoroughly investigated by the International Labour Organisation (ILO). The report of the ILO investigating committee headed by Jef Rens, which was published in 1950 under the title *Freedom of Association and Conditions of Work in Venezuela,* reached the conclusion that "the trade union organizations in Venezuela do not enjoy freedom of action and of organization," and added the following comment: "The labor movement has become in Venezuela an indispensable factor for the normal functioning of labor relations. The disappearance or definitive weakening of the trade union organizations brings about the disappearance or weakening of a regulating element essential for the social life of the country."

The first phase of the military dictatorship came to an end on November 13, 1950, with the assassination of Colonel Carlos Delgado Chalbaud, President of the Junta Militar. In an astoundingly brazen manner, he was kidnaped in full daylight, taken to the outskirts of Caracas, and there murdered. The apparent author of this crime was General Rafael Simón Urbina, an old military politician closely associated with Colonel Marcos Pérez Jiménez; however, when Urbina took refuge in the embassy of Nicaragua, he was turned over to the police, and was soon afterwards murdered in jail. Thus, it was never possible to ascertain for whom Urbina had acted. The only thing certain is that the chief beneficiary of the removal of Delgado Chalbaud was Pérez Jiménez.

Nonetheless, Pérez Jiménez did not seize full control of the military government immediately. The Junta Militar was reorganized, with a civilian, Germán Suárez Flamerich, replacing Colonel Delgado Chalbaud as President of the Junta, which stayed in office for another two years.

During this second phase of the Junta Militar regime, the brutality of the dictatorship was intensified. One secretary-general of the underground Acción Democrática organization, Leonardo Ruiz Pineda, was shot dead in the streets of Caracas. The military government established one of the world's most inhuman concentration camps, Guasina, on an island in the Orinoco River.

The Copei party in an open letter to the Junta on June 20, 1952, said the following about Guasina: "The very nature of Guasina merits public censure and promotes national anguish, because it is an unhealthy, inhospitable, unpopulated place completely out of contact with the rest of the country, converted into a center of exile for political prisoners. Furthermore, it appears without doubt that not only are the climatic and geographical conditions the worst possible, but also sanitary and medical care is virtually nonexistent. The prisoners are provided with bad and insufficient food, and what is worse, the political prisoners are submitted to continuous maltreatment, and to forced labor, under pain of severe and terrible punishment. Finally, the prisoners are kept rigorously incommunicado with their families and the outside world in general." [1]

Four years after it had seized power, the military regime made its greatest mistake: It called elections. Apparently the leaders of the government decided that they had sufficiently intimidated the opposition and the populace at large, and could afford to go through the motions of converting their *de facto* regime into a "constitutional" government.

Acción Democrática, which was outlawed, was not allowed to participate in the poll; however, the Copei and the Unión Republicana Democrática named full slates of candidates for the Constituent Assembly that was to be elected on November 30, 1952. The government organized a party of its own for the occasion, the Frente Electoral Independiente (FEI).

The campaign was intensive. Although outdoor meetings of the two nongovernment parties were not permitted, both the Copei and the URD held large indoor rallies. The author was in Venezuela during part of the campaign and can vouch for the fact that both Copei and URD orators were stringent in their criticisms of the regime.

Acción Democrática decided at first to order its members to abstain from voting, but as the result of brutal activities of the government in suppressing two revolt attempts that occurred during the campaign, popular desire to use the election as a means of demonstrating repudiation of the regime in power became overwhelming. Underground leaders of the AD charged their supporters to vote for the Unión Republicana Democrática.

The results of this situation were awkward for the military government. The election was orderly, and when the returns began to come in, they showed that the URD had won a smashing victory, receiving 54 per cent of the popular vote, with the Copei receiving 15 per cent, and the government party, FEI, getting only 25 per cent of the ballots cast. Faced with this situation, Colonel Marcos Pérez Jiménez did not hesitate. He suspended the counting of the votes, arrested the principal leaders of the URD, whom he deported, and announced that he was assuming office as Provisional President "in the name of the armed forces."

The reaction of the election victors of the Unión Republicana Democrática did not measure up to the circumstances in which they now found themselves. Although Jóvito Villalba and other URD leaders had been warned on numerous occasions by the underground AD chiefs that Pérez Jiménez would not allow them to enjoy the fruits of victory if they won the election, they refused to believe this.

On the night of the election, when the first reports of polling results began to show a URD victory, Alberto Carnevali, then secretary-general of the underground Acción Democrática organization, conferred with URD chiefs, urged them to call their supporters into the streets to defend their victory, and to prevent any attempt by Pérez Jiménez to cancel the results of the election. He promised the URD leaders that the Acción Democrática underground would join the URD supporters. Carnevali insisted that the united forces of the opposition could in all likelihood mobilize public support and organize sufficiently impressive street demonstrations to thwart the efforts of Pérez Jiménez to negate the will of the people.

The URD leaders could not be convinced of the need for such action. A few days after the election, however, they were summoned by Minister of the Interior Laureano Vallenilla Lanz to his office "to confer on the election results." Naïvely, the URD chiefs accepted this invitation, and upon their arrival they were hustled off to the airport and into a plane. A few hours later they found themselves in Panama with not much more than the clothes on their backs. Meanwhile their party was outlawed, and the government rounded up its secondary figures and sent them off to jail or Guasina.

As Provisional President, Colonel Pérez Jiménez ordered a recount of the votes cast on November 30. His recount showed an "overwhelming victory" for the government's Frente Electoral Independiente, which was said to have won fifty-nine of the one hundred and four posts in the Constituent Assembly, the rest of the seats being apportioned to the URD and the Copei.[2]

A little more than a month after the election, the puppet Constituent Assembly met in Caracas. The few URD and Copei deputies who took their seats were promptly expelled from their respective parties. The assembly wrote a new Constitution, cut to the demands of the dictator. As one of its last acts, it named Marcos Pérez Jiménez "Constitutional President."

For the next five years, Pérez Jiménez remained in firm control of the government of Venezuela. His regime was a tragedy for his nation and its people. Not only did he preside over one of the most tyrannical governments that Latin America has known in the present generation, but his administration recklessly wasted the largest income that Venezuela had ever received or was likely to receive in the predictable future.

The principal objective of the dictator and those associated with him was to use their positions of power to enjoy themselves while the regime existed, and to pile up abroad as much wealth as possible, for use when they no longer could exercise their gangster-like control over the nation. Corruption and graft reached heights that had not even been imagined under the dictatorship of Juan Vicente Gómez, and that were unequaled in Latin America except by the bloody tyranny of Trujillo in the Dominican Republic. No one will ever know how much illicit wealth was amassed by those who ran the Pérez Jiménez dictatorship. No one did business with the government during those years without lining the pockets of those in charge. All conceivable means of siphoning off income from the government treasury, and from private firms doing business with the regime, were resorted to. The corruption descended from the highest into the lowest echelons of the regime.

The illicit gains deposited abroad during this period constituted a serious drain on the economy of the country. Moreover, the hundreds of millions of dollars extracted from the country might have been used to develop and diversify the economy, or develop the nation's social capital of schools, hospitals, and similar institutions.

The New York *Times* reported shortly after the departure of Pérez Jiménez that he had carried with him a fortune of $235 million. How much others in the dictatorship were able to take abroad will probably never be known.

The government of Pérez Jiménez reversed the policies of previous regimes with regard to the exploitation of the country's subsoil resources, particularly petroleum. The Acción Democrática government of the 1940's had made it a basic principle that no new concessions should be given to the international oil companies. During the Junta Militar period, this policy was continued, though there were serious pressures to change it. The reversal came about three years after Pérez Jiménez seized the presidency. On February 11, 1956, the Ministry of Mines and Hydrocarbons issued a statement that the government was going to open the country to new oil concessions. This statement cited the reasons for this change of policy to be: (1) to give access to new capital; (2) to equalize, with an upward tendency, production of various regions of the country."

Rómulo Betancourt has expressed what he considers to have been the reasons for the change in oil policy by the Pérez Jiménez government: "(1) the pressure of the 'big seven' of the international cartel, anxious to acquire that part of the petroleum reserves which still remained in the hands of the nation, convinced that this was the last chance . . . ; (2) the bankruptcy of public finances because of the incapable and corrupt administration; (3) the unlimited concern to increase their already large private riches upon the part of the beneficiaries of the regime. . . ."[3]

During the remainder of the Pérez Jiménez regime there took place a scramble for new concessions. Representatives of the major oil companies have maintained that they made no illicit payments to government officials to obtain concessions. Nonetheless, the receipts coming to the government as a result of the granting of new concessions almost doubled the national budget. It thus provided sizable additional resources from which the officials of the regime were able to siphon off money into their own pockets.

No less damaging to the Venezuelan economy than the diversion of public funds into private pockets and foreign banks under the Pérez Jiménez dictatorship was the misdirection of the national income into what can be described best as "pyramid building." The government concentrated its huge expenditures on projects that were spectacular, individually expensive, and easy for the foreign visitor to see. Enormous sums were spent on the complete reconstruction of the capital city of Caracas. Centro Simón Bolívar, a complex of the Rockefeller Center type, was erected in the center of the city, to house most of the ministries. Along broad boulevards built out from the center of the city rose large middle- and upper-class private housing developments, many of them constructed by people closely associated with the dictatorship. Several individual projects of considerable magnitude and exaggerated cost were built as part of this over-all reconstruction of Caracas.

One of the most impressive Caracas projects was the new Officers' Club. In reality, a magnificent residential hotel, it had luxurious apartments, a large swimming pool, gaming rooms, a restaurant, and many other embellishments. Reportedly, this was the world's most expensive officers' club.

A project of even greater expense and even less utility was the funicular railway and the hotel built on Ávila Mountain. This twenty-story hotel, perched an hour's ride above the city, submerged in clouds much of the time, was a prize white elephant; however, it represented a vast expenditure of money, and hence many millions of dollars in commissions to insiders of the Pérez Jiménez regime.

Even more fantastic was the *helicoide,* a many-storied shopping center constructed around the side of one of the hills of Caracas. One of its features was a series of ten movie theatres, each showing the same motion picture, so timed that one could enter one or the other of them at almost any time during the day or night and see the picture from the beginning. On a more patriotic level was the Avenue of the Founding Fathers, a large memorial park and monument to the forgers of the independence of Spanish America.

Even some of the more worth while projects of the Pérez Jiménez government were carried out in an extravagant and ill-conceived fashion. Thus, the huge workers' housing projects constructed in Caracas during the last two years of the Pérez Jiménez government were masterpieces of poor construction and mismanagement. Ranging from ten to thirteen stories high, many of them had faulty elevator service, inadequate sewage disposal, and insufficient water supply. These housing developments tended to create more problems than they solved. Workers who had been living in the huts on the hills around the city were forcibly moved to the government's "super-blocks." There they were charged excessive rents. After the overthrow of Pérez Jiménez, many of the tenants abandoned these projects.

The same comment may be made about the two major industrial projects undertaken by the Pérez Jiménez regime. These were the iron and steel plant in the Orinoco River Valley and the petrochemical plant at Morón, near Puerto Cabello. Both of these enterprises were planned on a grand and expensive scale. The latter was constructed on land purchased from a member of Pérez Jiménez' cabinet. From a technical point of view, both the iron and steel plant and the petrochemical installation were planned backwards. Those parts of the enterprises that were logically the first to enter into production were scheduled last in the construction plan, while those required in the final production processes were scheduled earliest.

The labor movement that had been built up during the Acción

Democrática regime disintegrated during the first year after the fall of President Gallegos. For several years thereafter the only organized labor group that was allowed to function freely and without persecution by the government was the Federación de Trabajadores del Distrito Federal, led by Rodolfo Quintero, top figure in the Black Communists.

The tacit alliance between the dictatorship and the Black Communists was very obvious. Quintero and other leaders of the Federación were allowed to go in and out of the country, to attend congresses of the World Federation of Trade Unions and the Confederación de Trabajadores de América Latina, the Communists' world-wide and hemispheric trade union groups. They held large outdoor public meetings, which were forbidden for any groups opposed to or even critical of the government.

Other labor groups had no such freedom. Although the four other parties, that is, Acción Democrática, the Copei, the URD, and the Red Communists, all maintained small groups of unions under their control, these organizations were constantly persecuted by the police, were forced to change their headquarters frequently, and generally had life made as difficult as possible. During the last years of the Pérez Jiménez regime, these party-controlled labor federations were all driven underground.

Nor was the government satisfied with the Black Communists' organizations. The dictatorship wanted a national labor confederation that would be a completely pliable tool, and in 1952, under the tutelage of the Ministry of the Interior, a First National Convention of Independent Unions was held. The outcome was the organization of the Movimiento Obrero Sindical Independiente de Trabajadores (MOSIT). The government threw its full support behind the MOSIT, which was headed by an ex-Communist, Rafael García. Luxurious Trade Union Houses were built in Caracas and other cities to accommodate the MOSIT national headquarters and its regional organizations. In 1955 the MOSIT was rechristened Confederación Nacional de Trabajadores, and became an affiliate of the Peronista hemispheric labor group, Agrupación de Trabajadores Latino Americanos Sindicalizados (ATLAS).

The suppression of free trade unionism by the dictatorship caused serious embarrassment for the regime on several occasions. In June, 1950, the Thirty-third Conference of the International Labour Organisation rejected the credentials of workers' delegates named by the Junta Militar. The most embarrassing incident of all occurred in April, 1955. A world-wide petroleum conference organized by the International Labour Office met in Caracas at that time. One of those addressing the opening session of the meeting on April 25 was Adrianus Vermeulen, Dutch trade union leader and member of the administrative board of the ILO. His discourse was a strong criticism of the labor policies of the Venezuelan dictatorship. Soon after delivering his speech, Vermeulen was deported to Curaçao by the dreaded secret police, the Seguridad Nacional. The conference thereupon adjourned sine dic, without considering any of the items on its agenda. In reprisal, Pérez Jiménez withdrew Venezuela from the ILO in May, 1955.

The tyranny of the Pérez Jiménez dictatorship was brutal in the extreme. The government's chief instrument of terror was the Seguridad Nacional, headed by the notorious Pedro Estrada. It organized an intricate network of espionage, which operated not only throughout the civilian community but even in the armed forces.

No political parties were allowed to function under the Pérez Jiménez regime. Even the Frente Electoral Independiente, which had been the government's instrument in the 1952 elections, was not heard of subsequently. Acción Democrática had been suppressed at the end of 1948, the Unión Republicana Democrática was suppressed just after the 1952 election.

The regime was particularly ruthless in persecuting the Acción Democrática underground. Two of its secretaries-general were killed, a third died in jail, still another was arrested in 1954 and spent the rest of the dictatorship in prison. Although during the first half of the dictatorial regime, Acción Democrática was able to maintain an underground organization in virtually every part of the country, during the last years the persecution of the government greatly weakened its activities. Nevertheless, the AD Underground, continued to be the strongest element in the illegal opposition.

Although the Copei was never outlawed, it was not able to function openly during the presidency of Pérez Jiménez. It was not allowed to hold public meetings, its press was suppressed, and its leaders were frequently arrested, and though most of them were released in a short time, the party had its quota of long-time political prisoners, deportees, and martyrs. The Copei was particularly important in the Universidad Central de Venezuela in Caracas, where it led the fight against the regime by the professors and the students. The university autonomy established during the Acción Democrática regime was ended by the Junta Militar in October, 1951. In the next year the Universidad Central was closed by the government, and its doors remained shut for more than a year.

Absolutely no freedom of the press was allowed in Venezuela as long as Pérez Jiménez was President. Some of the principal papers were owned by leading figures in the dictatorship, and other papers were thoroughly intimidated and censored by the regime.

Thousands of political prisoners were held by the Seguridad Nacional, with Guasina concentration camp, the San Juan de los Morros Penitentiary, and the Ciudad Bolívar jail being the favorite sites of incarceration. The Seguridad Nacional developed torture to a fine art in these various political prisons.

Torture and imprisonment were by no means the only terror tactics used by Pedro Estrada and his cohorts. Many of the finest figures in Venezuelan public life were killed by the Pérez Jiménez secret police. These included the two secretaries-general of the underground Acción Democrática, Leonardo Ruiz Pineda and Antonio Pinto Salinas. A third top official of AD, Alberto Carnevali, died in a prison hospital from lack of adequate medical care. Another victim was Wilfrido Omaña, a captain in the Army who was disaffected from the regime. Hundreds of less famous people suffered a similar fate at the hands of the dictatorship.

The oppression of the Pérez Jiménez regime aroused the ire of the Venezuelan hierarchy of the Catholic Church. On May 1, 1957, the hierarchy issued a pastoral letter denouncing the government's social policy as well as accusing the regime of suppressing essential liberties. From then on, there was open hostility between the government and the Church authorities, and many priests participated actively in the underground struggle against the dictatorship.

Even the terror methods of the Seguridad Nacional were not sufficient to resolve the problem presented by the expiration of Pérez Jiménez' term as "Constitutional President" early in 1958. If the dictator was to continue in office, it was necessary for him to be "re-elected."

Pérez Jiménez, unwilling to risk a repetition of the fiasco of the election of 1952, could not permit any other candidate to run against him, not even a hand-picked puppet nominee. If he were to do so, the still potent opposition underground would likely instruct its followers to cast their votes for the second man, thus once more presenting Pérez Jiménez with the embarrassing necessity of reversing election results by force.

For many months the question of how the dictator's re-election would be carried out was postponed. Early in 1957 the government issued vague statements to the effect that "free elections" would be held to resolve the question of the presidential succession. Few people took them seriously. Even so, the newly united opposition decided to support the candidacy of Dr. Rafael Caldera, head of the Copei and the only major party chief who was still allowed to live more or less freely in Venezuela. It was almost certain that his candidacy would be largely symbolic, but it was agreed that some kind of open opposition should be made to the efforts of Pérez Jiménez to re-elect himself.

Finally, only a few weeks before the election, scheduled for December, 1957, the government announced that it proposed to hold a plebiscite, instead of an election with a choice of candidates. The voters would be asked to answer the simple question "Should General Marcos Pérez Jiménez continue as President of the Republic during the next constitutional term?" No provision was made as to what would occur in the unlikely case that the voters answered "No." When election time came, each voter was presented with two cards, one inscribed "Sí," the other "No." He put the one he favored in an envelope and deposited it in the voting box. Only a small part of the population voted, knowing full well what the results were to be before the plebiscite was held. Government employees and those working for firms doing business with the government were required to bring to work with them the day after the election their "No" voting cards. This requirement assured the victory of Pérez Jiménez.

Although on the surface the plebiscite seemed to resolve the problem of how the dictator's continuance in office would be assured, it proved to be the final act that broke the hold of the dictatorship on the nation. To the average Venezuelan this kind of election was both so ludicrous and so outrageous that it could not be tolerated. The plebiscite apparently caused the people of Venezuela to lose their fear of the regime. From the day of the vote, the regime was harassed by street demonstrations, plots, and disturbances, ending, only a few weeks after the plebiscite, in the fall of the dictatorship.

In the early morning of January 1, 1958, the Air Force and the Army garrison at Los Teques, capital of the state of Miranda, rose in revolt. Although the uprising was suppressed within a few hours, the situation did not return to normal. Riots, in which students, residents of the huge housing blocks built by the dictatorship, and other people of Caracas participated, filled the streets of the capital city. The leadership of the opposition was in the hands of a Junta Patriótica, composed of representatives of Acción Democrática, the Copei, the URD, and the Communists. The Junta had the tacit support of the Church hierarchy and even of elements in the armed forces.

On January 22, 1958, the Junta Patriótica called for a revolutionary general strike. It was started at noon by the ringing of church bells throughout the country and by the honking of automobile horns (forbidden by the government). The strike was almost universally effective, and was accompanied by the renewal of street rioting, with increasingly violent clashes with police and soldiers. In the early morning of January 23, the leading members of the armed forces waited upon Pérez Jiménez. They told him that a plane had been warmed up, and presented him with a diplomatic passport. An hour or so later he was on his way to exile in the Dominican Republic, and the government power had passed into the hands of a five-man revolutionary Junta de Gobierno.

With the fall of Pérez Jiménez, the more than nine years of ruthless dictatorship came to an end. The road to the Venezuelan Democratic Revolution was open.

Chapter Four

The Provisional Regime

The five-man Junta de Gobierno that came to power after the exile of dicator Pérez Jiménez in 1958 was composed of one representative each of the Army, Navy, and Air Force, and two of the country's leading businessmen, and was headed by Admiral Wolfgang Larrazábal. Through a turbulent year that saw several changes in the personnel of the Junta, a provisional government charted Venezuela's course toward a constitutionally elected, democratic regime. Leaders of the provisional government did much in both a positive and a negative way to prepare tasks of the constitutional regime.

Although some of those in the government were friendly to one or another of the major parties, the parties themselves agreed during the provisional regime that they would not participate in the government, and thus would avoid raising the issue of apportioning jobs to members of the parties. Almost without exception, members of the provisional government did not belong to any of the existing political parties. The cabinet was composed largely of members of the managerial and professional classes without any party affiliation. Most of the chief economic posts in the provisional government were held by members of the business group whose most important leader was Eugenio Mendoza, the country's largest industrialist and a member of the Junta de Gobierno during its first months.

Undoubtedly, the single most important accomplishment of the Junta de Gobierno during 1958 was to prepare for and conduct the elections that were the essential prelude for a democratic regime.

If for nothing else, the provisional government won the appreciation and praise of the vast majority of the citizens of Venezuela.

In order to be able to assure democratic elections, in fulfillment of the first promise made by the regime after the flight of the dictator, the Junta had to overcome the opposition of those who, particularly in the armed forces, were opposed to the establishment of a democratic civilian government. This required not only constant vigilance to thwart attempts at a *coup d'état* but also a thorough purging and reorganization of the nation's armed forces. Most of the top military officers associated with the dictatorship, as well as the principal civilian figures in the Pérez Jiménez regime, left the country soon after the dictator departed. However, there remained in the armed forces many who had profited from the Pérez Jiménez government, or who believed in the right and even the duty of the armed forces to rule the country. Throughout the year 1958 the Junta set about removing such people, cashiering those who openly opposed the new policies, and arranging missions abroad for others whose loyalty to the provisional government was in question.

In spite of these measures, two serious attempts were made to overthrow the new government. On July 22 and 23 and September 7 and 8 sizable portions of the garrisons in and around Caracas were mobilized against the government. Although the majority of the soldiers stayed loyal, as did the Navy and Air Force personnel, these attempted *coups d'état* came within an ace of success. Probably the decisive factor in preventing their success was the solidarity of the civilian population behind the government. This solidarity was expressed not only in meetings in the streets, and particularly in the university, but also by a phenomenon unique in Venezuelan history. Both in July and September the reconstituted Confederación de Trabajadores de Venezuela and the leading employers' organizations declared joint general strikes and general lockouts. Economic life came to a standstill. The people demonstrated their determination to resist all efforts to reimpose a dictatorship.

The suppression of these attempted *coups d'état* was evidence of the rebirth of democratic political activity among the Venezuelan citizenry. With the overthrow of the dictator, the exiles streamed back to their homeland, the jails were emptied of their political prisoners, and the rights to freedom of the press, speech, and assembly were re-established. Agitated political discussions such as had not been heard for almost a decade became common among people of all kinds and conditions.

The political parties revived immediately. Their underground organizations of the dictatorship period emerged to mount big demonstrations in Caracas to welcome back their leaders from exile or imprisonment. Throughout the country, they engaged in intensive activity to rebuild their ranks and to reconstruct their organizations.

The parties that held the center of the stage were the ones that had been prominent in the 1945 to 1948 period. It soon became evident that Acción Democrática was still by far the largest political organization in the country, although it was not as dominant as it had been during the three years it ruled the country. The reports that it had been eliminated by the ruthless persecution of the dictatorship were given the lie by its rapid recovery as soon as the tyrant had fallen. The Unión Republicana Democrática was perhaps closest politically to the provisional government. The Copei party, rechristened Partido Social Cristiano Copei, revived in its old strongholds in the Andean states and established local organizations throughout the country. Finally, there was the Communist party. The split that it had suffered in the early 1940's, which had given rise to the Red and Black parties in the 1945 to 1948 period, had disappeared by 1958, and the Communists emerged as a single group during the provisional government period.

Several attempts were made to organize new parties. The most interesting of these was the group known as Integración Republicana. It aspired to be the spokesman for the businessmen and managerial folk who did not feel adequately represented in any of the older parties. Although it seemed to give promise during the provisional regime of becoming a force of some consequence in the political life of the country, its poor showing in the election at the end of 1958 doomed it to extinction.

During most of the provisional government period there was some confusion in the political scene because of the continued existence of the Junta Patriótica, the group that in the last months of the dictatorship had assumed the leadership in the fight against Pérez Jiménez. Although it was a delegate body, composed of representatives of the four parties—Acción Democrática, the Copei, the URD, and the Communists—there were those who seemed to aspire to convert it into still another party. Once the dictatorship was overthrown, however, it had no particular purpose to serve, and by the end of the provisional regime had all but ceased to exist.

The leaders of the political parties, and particularly the leaders of the Acción Democrática, the Copei, and the URD, were determined that the stability of the new democratic regime that they were helping to establish should not be undermined, as was that of 1945 to 1948, by violent quarrels among them. As a result, at the very beginning the leaders of these groups, together with the Communists, met regularly to try to evolve common approaches to the immediate problems facing the regime and its program of paving the way for a new constitutional government. Although the Communists by common consent were soon dropped from these discussions, the leaders of the other parties continued their consultations throughout the provisional government period.

The political parties were not the only groups to re-emerge. The organized labor and peasant movements were also reborn. The captive labor movement patronized by the dictatorship disappeared with its sponsor. Each of the political parties, however, had maintained small nuclei of unions under its control throughout the dictatorship, and the trade union leaders directed their efforts toward unifying these, and establishing united unions in every field of employment and in every region of the republic.

In the unions, as in the political arena, the watchword in the provisional government period was unity. The unions included the Communists as well as the members of the three democratic parties; and in all union elections, the four groups put up joint slates of candidates, attempting to apportion the nominees roughly in relation to the strength of the parties in the unions. The chief loser by this process was Acción Democrática, which had completely dominated the labor movement during the 1945 to 1948 period, and which was still by far the largest element among the workers. The principal gainers were the Copei and the URD, which had very small followings in organized labor but were given posts in union executive bodies even when they had few rank and file members. The Communists also gained to some extent in terms of representation, and a great deal in terms of influence, by this temporary united front policy in the labor movement.

Along with the reorganization of the unions of urban workers, there was an even more extensive process of rebuilding of peasant unions. These had all but disappeared during the Pérez Jiménez regime because of the persecution of the dictatorship. Now they were revived, and the great majority of the peasants were brought within their ranks. Acción Democrática's influence over these unions was greater than over the urban workers' unions.

Freedom of the press was re-established. Although *El Heraldo*, the newspaper owned by the Minister of the Interior of the dictatorship, Laureano Vallenilla Lanz, disappeared, numerous new weeklies were established by the various political parties, unions, and other organizations. The columns of all of these papers were filled with articles and commentaries by journalists and political leaders of all of the parties and interest groups.

One characteristic of the press during this period was the almost complete immunity from criticism enjoyed by the Communist party. This was due both to the considerable degree to which the Communists had been able to infiltrate the journalistic profession during the dictatorship and to the desire for national civilian unity, which ruled out for the time being bitter polemics of any kind. The only ones who did not seem to feel themselves bound by this agreement to soft-pedal recriminations were the Communists themselves.

The revival of political and civic activity was accompanied by government activities to prepare for the promised elections. The first step was to write a new electoral law. This was completed by July, and the new statute was in most respects similar to that which had been in effect during the 1945 to 1948 period. It provided for universal suffrage, procedures for registering legal political parties, voting by lists of candidates of the various parties, the list of each party being printed on paper of a distinctive color to facilitate voting by illiterates.

The elections for President, Congress, state legislators, and municipal councilmen were called for December 7, 1958. The process of selecting candidates was completed only a few short weeks before this date. The principal problem was that of trying to find a procedure for translating the spirit of national unity into concrete form through a broad coalition that would include all of the country's major parties.

The stumbling block was finding a suitable person to be the joint presidential candidate of all of the parties, since it was early agreed that each party would run its own lists of candidates for the other posts. Throughout the middle months of 1958 the parties engaged in widespread discussion and endless negotiation; however, not only did they fail to reach agreement on who the individual should be, but they found it impossible to decide whether the nominee should be an independent or a member of one or another of the three democratic parties. In a penultimate phase of the negotiations, Acción Democrática even came to the point of suggesting the substitution for President of a multiple government council on which all three parties would have representatives.

Finally, only a few weeks before the election was scheduled, the party leaders agreed to disagree. It was decided that each of them would, if it so desired, name its own candidate. Acción Democrática chose its founder and principal figure, Rómulo Betancourt. The Partido Social Cristiano Copei did likewise, running Rafael Caldera. The position of the URD was more complicated. This party's logical candidate was Jóvito Villalba, its founder and "maestro." On the other hand, it had been closest of all of the parties to Admiral Wolfgang Larrazábal, first head of the Junta de Gobierno, and its leaders saw in him a figure who, if he were to head their ticket, stood a good chance of overcoming the admittedly substantial lead of Acción Democrática. Although Larrazábal had insisted earlier in the discussions that he would run only if he were named by all three of the major parties, he finally agreed to be the nominee of the URD.

The smaller parties did not run presidential candidates of their own, but backed one of the three major nominees. The Communists enthusiastically endorsed Larrazábal, being as eager as the URD to destroy the influence of Acción Democrática, and sure of the fact that if Larrazábal won with their support, they would be able to use government backing to gain control of the trade union and peasant movements. The very small Partido Socialista de Trabajadores and the new Integración Republicana endorsed Rafael Caldera. Only Rómulo Betancourt ran as the nominee of just one party.

The campaign was short but hard fought. Admiral Larrazábal concentrated most of his campaigning in the central part of the country, and relied heavily on radio and television. Betancourt, in contrast, barnstormed throughout the country, continuing the process he had been following since his return from exile of becoming reacquainted with local peasant, labor, and intellectual leaders who had been his party's backers in the past, and coming to know new figures who had risen since the end of the dictatorship. Rafael Caldera also campaigned throughout the country.

The results of the election were a surprise to many observers both in Venezuela and abroad. There were several reasons why many people thought that Admiral Larrazábal was the sure winner. First, there was wide belief that Acción Democrática had emerged from the dictatorship weaker than was actually the case. Second, there was already dissension within AD, and one faction of the party was anything but enthusiastic about the nomination of Betancourt. Third, the popularity of the Admiral in Caracas and some other major cities was patent. Finally, there was a strong campaign by some of the opponents of AD to the effect that if Betancourt were to win, the armed forces would not allow him to take office. It was felt that the almost decade-long campaign of Pérez Jiménez and his associates to picture Betancourt as the sworn enemy of the military men would make the latter unwilling to see him assume the presidency once again. It was also argued that fear of such an eventuality would make many people who might otherwise be sympathetic with AD refrain from voting for Betancourt.

The critics were confounded. Although the popularity of Larrazábal in the major cities was borne out by the election results, the factor upon which his supporters and well-wishers had not counted was the almost complete support for Acción Democrática and Betancourt among the peasants. The dissension within AD proved to be of little importance insofar as the election results were concerned. Furthermore, the fear of the armed forces' reaction to Betancourt's victory did not seriously influence the great bulk of Acción Democrática's peasant and worker supporters. This issue was probably a false one in any case, because there is some evidence that the military would have been considerably less happy with Larrazábal's victory than with Betancourt's.

Rómulo Betancourt won with approximately 49 per cent of the total vote; Admiral Larrazábal ran a strong second, and Rafael Caldera came in a surprisingly poor third. Acción Democrática won a clear majority in both houses of Congress and in most of the state legislatures. The Unión Republicana Democrática rode the wave of Larrazábal's popularity to become the country's second largest party, in popular vote and representation in Congress. It won a majority in several state legislatures, and in the city councils of Caracas, Maracay, and several other cities and towns. The Copei won a majority only in the mountain states of Táchira and Mérida. Like Acción Democrática, it did poorly in Caracas. The Communist party came in fourth, far behind the other three parties, but with enough votes to seat half a dozen members of Congress and to gain representation in several state legislatures and city councils, including that of Caracas, where it was the second largest party.

The electoral process promised by the Junta de Gobierno was completed a little more than two months after the votes were cast, when on February 13, 1959, the newly elected President took office. The members of Congress and the state and municipal legislatures had taken their oaths some days before.

Although the re-establishment of constitutional democracy was the major achievement of the provisional government, it took important actions in a number of other fields. Some of these were of fundamental long-range importance and became integral parts of the democratic social revolution that President Rómulo Betancourt was to make the cornerstone of his constitutional administration. (Other policies of the Junta de Gobierno, particularly in the economic field, were less fortunate.) Of basic importance were the provisional government's policies in the fields of agrarian reform, education, and petroleum policy. The regime's moves in these areas were a prelude to what the constitutional government was to do.

The process of agrarian reform, which had been started by the Acción Democrática regime of 1945 to 1948 and was suspended during the dictatorship, was renewed by the provisional government. The Instituto Agrario Nacional was reorganized, with a leading role being given in it to representatives of the reconstituted Peasants Federation. The Instituto Agrario carried forward throughout the year a program of settling peasants on land confiscated from high officials of the dictatorship, or on other land in the possession of the government. Since no new agrarian reform law was passed during this period, the Instituto Agrario functioned largely on a pragmatic basis.

A serious effort was made by the provisional government to come to grips with the educational problem. During Pérez Jiménez' regime the number of illiterates had risen by leaps and bounds, several of the existing normal schools had been closed, and the increase in school-age population far outran the increase in the number of school buildings and teachers. All of this was reversed during the provisional regime, and a vast program of teacher training, school construction, and expansion of other educational services was launched.

In the realm of petroleum policy, always a key issue in Venezuelan economic and political life, the Junta de Gobierno took strong action with the revision of the income tax law enacted in December, 1958. The most important feature of this law was an increase in the tax on the oil and mining companies, which in the case of the petroleum concerns raised the share of their profits captured by the government from the 50 per cent established during the first Betancourt administration in 1946 to close to 70 per cent. Although there were vehement protests from the oil companies, the provisional government did not back down on its decision.

Less positive were certain other actions of the provisional government. That which has perhaps been most criticized was the Plan de Emergencia. This plan was enacted in response to the urgent pressures of the vast number of unemployed inherited from the dictatorship, particularly in Caracas. Most of those unemployed were construction workers, and the plan provided for paying unemployed workers the same wages they would receive if they were working, but without providing them with employment. This amounted to a huge dole, given on terms that had never been equaled in any other country.

The Plan de Emergencia was disastrous both from an economic and from a social point of view. Not only did it provide a built-in pressure group which demanded a serious drain on the treasury for which the state got little palpable return in an economic sense, but it accustomed large numbers of workers to receiving the going wage without doing any work. It added tremendously to the government's financial burdens at a moment when its finances were in a critical condition. Moreover, it encouraged the drift of people from the interior to the capital city, a movement that had been very marked during the dictatorship and proved economically harmful to the whole country, as well as socially and politically very dangerous for Caracas. The only possible justification for the Plan de Emergencia was political expediency. But even in a political sense it created tremendous long-range problems, though it temporarily resolved a political crisis.

A somewhat similar measure was taken by the provisional government with regard to the huge workers' housing projects that had been constructed in Caracas during the last few years of the dictatorship. Some 13 per cent or more of the population was living in these rabbit-warren-like apartment buildings, and the discontent of their occupants was at a high pitch in the early months of the provisional government regime. The residents of the housing blocks had played a leading part in the street fighting that preceded and followed the overthrow of the Pérez Jiménez government, and there was constant fear that they would be mobilized against the provisional regime if some incendiary issue should arise.

The answer of the provisional government to this problem was simple: Suspend rent payments in the housing blocks. The 130,000 people living in these apartments were suddenly told that they need only pay rent "if they could afford it." Very few found that they were "able" to pay thereafter. This provoked a major crisis in the Banco Obrero, the institution charged with building and maintaining low-cost housing. It found itself stripped of the funds upon which it had hitherto depended for the maintenance of the projects under its control and had to devote all of the revenue it received from the national treasury to this end. Thus it was unable to go forward with new housing developments. This problem of nonpayment of rent continued for several years after the installation of the constitutional regime.

Another much-discussed policy of the provisional government was its handling of the short-term government debt inherited from the Pérez Jiménez regime. In its last years the dictatorship had adopted the policy of failing to pay many of its bills to construction companies, and these firms turned around and sold the government's IOU's to banks in Venezuela and to purchasers abroad, particularly in the New York money market. Furthermore, many firms apparently had not even been able to get the government to acknowledge its indebtedness to them.

With the overthrow of the dictatorship, most of the holders of these unfunded debts of the Venezuelan government demanded payment. The total sum involved was some $1.4 billion.[1] After some hesitation, the provisional government decided to honor all of these obligations, and to try to pay them off as quickly as possible. Its argument for doing so was that if the debts were not paid promptly, Venezuela's credit status would suffer gravely, particularly in view of the fact that large portions of the debt were held abroad. Those opposed to payment said that many of the debts were the results of graft and fraud and that they should all be carefully investigated before payment was made; and that in any case the government could not afford to pay out such vast sums of money in a short period.

The provisional regime has also been seriously criticized for the chaos of public administration during its incumbency. The sudden and basic nature of the change of regime undoubtedly gave rise to some of the difficulties. Furthermore, the Junta de Gobierno set up a commission to study and alter drastically the methods of public administration, and to lay the basis for the establishment of a civil service system for the first time. Nonetheless, among the deficiencies of the administrative apparatus was the great lack of adequate law enforcement personnel, especially in the capital city.

It is difficult to make an objective judgment of the accomplishments of the provisional government; however, it may be observed that the regime left the country with a considerably greater financial mess than had existed when it took over, and that it tended to think in terms of resolving short-term problems, often without considering the long-term effects of its solutions to these problems. On the other hand, these and other serious weaknesses of the regime are of relatively little significance in the light of the fact that it carried out its major promises of turning the country over to those whom the citizenry had elected to direct its affairs. Furthermore, it did so with a dispatch, an orderliness, and a fairness that are rare in Latin America.

Chapter Five

Objectives and Methods of the Revolution

The Betancourt government of 1959 to 1964 was forced to try to do everything at once for Venezuela and its people, to repair the damages of more than a century and a half of neglect and irresponsible leadership. With few exceptions, the military dictatorships that had ruled Venezuela from the time it proclaimed its independence shelved the country's accumulated economic, social, and political problems. Only with the advent of a constitutional democratic regime did the full gravity of these problems become apparent; and only then was it possible for the people to insist that the government attempt to resolve them.

The fundamental task of the democratic regime was to carry out an economic, social, and political revolution, to change the structure of the nation. It had to undertake this task in the face of immediate problems provoked by the short-run economic crisis that resulted from the curtailment of the oil industry, the collapse of the construction business, and the flight of capital.

The Betancourt regime's approach to Venezuela's complex problems was determined both by the ideology and philosophy of the parties and men in control of the government and by the circumstances of the Venezuela of the early 1960's. Both of the political parties that bore major responsibility for Venezuela's Democratic Revolution—the Democratic Socialist Acción Democrática and the

Christian Social Copei—endorsed a mixed economy of public and private enterprise in which the guiding role is taken by the state. Even had their philosophy been different, the great importance that the state possessed in the nation's economy because of its participation in the profits of the oil industry would have made this type of approach to the problems of social reform and economic development inevitable.

A fundamental principle underlying the Venezuela Democratic Revolution is economic and social planning. The key institution set up to supervise the process of transforming Venezuela into a nation with a modern and prosperous economy was the Oficina de Coordinación y Planificación (Office of Coordination and Planning), commonly known as Cordiplan. This body depends directly upon the President of the Republic, and its chief has cabinet status. From its inception, Cordiplan was headed by Dr. Manuel Pérez Guerrero, one of the nation's leading economists, Minister of Finance during the Betancourt regime of the 1940's, and a man with long experience, during the years of exile, as an official of the United Nations Technical Assistance Board.

The tasks allocated to Cordiplan were manifold. Its first job was to coordinate the activities of the many government ministries and independent agencies dealing with economic and social problems. Under previous regimes each of these institutions was a little empire, complete unto itself, following whatever policies and programs were favored by the particular individual serving as its chief. No ministry or independent agency took into account work similar to its own being accomplished by other branches of the government. The result was a great deal of bureaucratic jealousy, duplication of effort, and waste of resources.

This tradition was too deep-seated to be ended quickly; however, Cordiplan was able to make some progress at the outset. It organized a series of committees to deal with specific problems in which more than one governmental agency was concerned. All agencies dealing with a given problem were represented on a committee by high-echelon people, frequently by a minister or agency chief. These committees met regularly, and sought to work out general policies as well as to avoid duplication of effort and expenditure. Industrialization, medical and health problems, and the agrarian reform were three of the fields in which Cordiplan committees were particularly active.

The preparation of the budget offered Cordiplan another opportunity to coordinate the activities of various government agencies. Starting with the preparation of the 1962 budget, a committee composed of representatives of the Ministry of Finance, the Banco Central, and other financial branches of the government, met for several months in Cordiplan's offices to work out details of the budget. As the problems of each ministry or independent agency were dealt with, its representatives were called into these conferences.

In addition to this type of short-range coordination of the government's economic and social efforts, Cordiplan undertook more long-range planning. One project was the elaboration and supervision of a Four-Year Plan. The first Four-Year Plan was submitted to consideration of the President and Congress early in 1960 and was adopted late in that year. It set forth general goals in terms of economic and social development to be achieved during the last four years of President Betancourt's term.

The planning technique adopted for Venezuela by Cordiplan was somewhat different from that which has been popularized in the Soviet Union, India, Ghana, and other developing countries. Instead of providing a specific date at which the first Four-Year Plan would end, and the second one begin, Dr. Pérez Guerrero and his colleagues adopted a system of annual revision of the Plan, through which the accomplishments of the past year would be assessed and new targets would be set, so as to cover one additional year. Thus, as long as the system continued, the Plan would never come to an end, but would be modified progressively, always keeping the targets for a four-year period in view.

The Four-Year Plan proposed government expenditure in the economic and social fields, and also estimated private investment in those areas. Presumably, activities of all relevant government organizations were to conform to the Plan, and were to be designed to elicit the necessary private expenditures.

In another type of long-range planning undertaken by the Cordiplan group, specific programs were elaborated for various sectors of the economy. One of the first such programs to be completed was that for the nation's highway system. Although one of the few important contributions to the country's economic development that had been made by the dictatorship was an extensive road network, there were still important gaps in this network by 1958 and there was need to extend it into areas that had as yet been untouched by it.

During 1960 and 1961 Cordiplan worked out a detailed program for an extension of the nation's highway network. It took into consideration the need to open up important new agricultural areas, the need to improve the communication of older areas with their markets, the development of industry in various parts of the country, and the desirability of tying more closely to the nation very isolated areas that had had little communication except by airplane and mule track with the rest of the country. By the middle of 1961 this road program was ready to be incorporated in an orderly fashion into the Four-Year Plan.

Cordiplan initiated a program of the same type to provide every district capital with requisite public services. (A district is equivalent to a county in the United States.) A thorough study was made of the state of the streets, sewerage systems, water supplies, electric power facilities, schools, and medical services in each of the two hundred major cities and towns. Cost estimates were then prepared, and funds for the first part of a three-year program to remedy the deficiencies were allocated in the 1962 budget.

A survey of the country's irrigation needs was completed early in 1962, and a group of Mexican experts in irrigation was brought in to help Cordiplan draw up a long-range plan for developing the country's water resources for agriculture. This is one of the most acute problems for the nation in the next two or three decades. In his annual message to Congress in March, 1963, President Betancourt announced that henceforward a large part of the considerable funds which had theretofore been spent on road construction would now become available for building irrigation systems as a result of the completion of the trunk highway network.

New hospitals and a national electric power system were among the other projects for which Cordiplan developed long-range plans.

One major drawback to the effectiveness of the initial work of Cordiplan was the lack of adequately trained personnel for carrying out its planning efforts. To overcome this, Cordiplan established, in cooperation with the Universidad Central de Venezuela, a graduate course in economic planning. This course was designed particularly for young officials in various government ministries and independent agencies. The hope of Dr. Pérez Guerrero was that within a few years he could develop a cadre of officials throughout the government who would have both training and experience in the techniques of planning economic growth.

In addition to its basic work of studying and planning for economic development, Cordiplan was given certain special tasks. One of these was the development of a national civil service system. (Traditionally, the dictator and his close associates bestowed government jobs upon those whose loyalty to the incumbent regime had been tested.) This project was begun during the provisional government period by a special government personnel committee. Its purpose was to study the functioning of all government agencies, with an eye to improving their efficiency and to stabilizing administrative and personnel policies. With the advent of the constitutional regime, President Betancourt transferred the operation of this committee to the jurisdiction of Cordiplan, and Alberto López Gallegos, a leading figure in Acción Democrática and former official of the United Nations, was named to head it. It was given the additional duty of drafting a civil service law to provide reasonable conditions of tenure, seniority, and retirement for government employees. Political considerations had prevented the enactment of such a law by the end of Betancourt's term.

Another special operation placed under the supervision and control of Cordiplan was the Oficina de Desarrollo Comunal (Community Development Office), organized early in 1961. Headed by a dynamic social worker, Carola Ravel, the Community Development Office operated with a small staff to seek out natural leaders in local communities who could undertake the work of stimulating their fellow citizens to community action on public works.

Typical of the early work of the Community Development Office was a street repair project in the La Pedrera ward of the town of Crespo in the state of Aragua. In line with its function of helping the people to help themselves, the office coordinated the work of the Ministry of Public Works, the government of the state of Aragua, and the people of the ward. The Ministry donated some of the materials necessary to repair the streets, the state of Aragua provided the rest, and the people of La Pedrera contributed voluntary labor to complete the project. The total cost of this work was 30,000 bolívares.[1]

Although the Community Development Office was operating in only about half of the states by the end of 1963, it had already begun to produce significant results. Its work was of particular importance because of the need to overcome the tendency of most Venezuelans to wait for "the government" to meet all of their problems. The idea that an individual, a small group, or a community can solve its own problems is still a strange one to most Venezuelans. In seeking to convince a significant portion of the population to try to help themselves, the Community Development workers are making a major contribution to the economic and social advance and civic maturity of the Venezuelan people.

The work of the government's Community Development Office was supplemented by the efforts of a private organization known as Acción. Organized in 1960 by a group of graduate students of the University of California at Berkeley, it began operating in Caracas early in 1961. It set about organizing classes, the construction of small social centers, and other related activities among the people of the poor barrios in the hills above Caracas.

Present-day Venezuelan democratic leaders strongly believe in making use of both public and private initiative to promote the economic development of the republic. Although of the opinion that certain basic industries should be in the hands of the state, they wish to leave ample room for and encourage private enterprise.

The government necessarily plays a considerable role in economic growth, since 90 per cent or more of the $2 billion a year in foreign exchange comes in as a result of the operations of the country's petroleum and mining industries. Most of this foreign currency passes through the hands of the government, in the form of income and other taxes and revenue from the sale of the royalties turned over to the government by the oil and mining companies.

The democratic regime has sought to use the inevitably great influence of the state to achieve rapid economic development. For example, the Betancourt government felt it essential to keep state-owned heavy manufacturing plants as levers in the general development of the economy. To this end it continued the construction of the steel plant at Matanzas, in the Orinoco River Valley, and a petrochemical firm at Morón, near Puerto Cabello on the Caribbean coast, which had been begun by the Pérez Jiménez government.

In other fields, too, government influence has assumed major importance. This is obvious in agriculture. There the agrarian reform has already widely changed property patterns, while loans of the Banco Agrícola y Pecuario have helped a large percentage of the peasants and ranchers. The democratic regime likewise sought to use technical assistance as a means of bringing about the most efficient use of the nation's land resources. In each region, efforts are being made to develop the kinds of crops best suited to its climate and soil. Apparent, too, are the benefits of government banking institutions, including not only the Central Bank but also government development banks for industry, agriculture, and housing.

The Betancourt regime also sought to encourage private enterprise, both domestic and foreign, to play a major part in the process of economic development. This attitude was shown by the government's large increase in the resources of the Corporación Venezolana de Fomento for lending to private enterprises in the manufacturing field, and by its adoption of a policy of drastically improved tariff protection for private firms establishing new industries or expanding old ones. An additional indication of the Betancourt government's support for private enterprise was its welcoming of private participation in new industries being established under government leadership.

Venezuelan democratic leaders are clearly determined to use wherever possible persuasion instead of force. This principle was firmly applied in the agrarian reform. Not only was the 1960 Agrarian Reform Law drawn up by a commission representing all interests even remotely involved with the problem, but those losing land under the reform have been adequately compensated. Moreover, whenever agrarian reform settlements involved the transfer of peasants from one part of the country to another, all such transfers were made on a voluntary basis.

The same principle was used in dealing with the problem of locating new industrial plants. Although the government favored the establishment of new manufacturing enterprises in the cities and towns of the interior rather than in Caracas, it did not seek any legal powers to force entrepreneurs to follow this policy. Rather, it used its credit and tariff policies to induce those planning to set up new plants to follow the government's wishes.

The economic policy of the Venezuelan democratic regime after 1959 was fundamentally nationalistic. Although in no sense xenophobic or extreme, the Betancourt policy of nationalism was nonetheless real. It was reflected in the decision of the President and his associates that the country's basic manufacturing industries—iron and steel, petrochemicals and aluminum—should be in the hands of firms in which the Venezuelan government has a majority interest. Following principles laid down in the early 1940's by Acción Democrática, the Betancourt regime constantly reiterated its determination to give no more new concessions to foreign oil companies. It also established a government petroleum firm, which in the beginning was intended to compete in both the national and international markets with the international companies, but was expected in the long run to take over these companies' concessions when they expire in the 1970's and 1980's. The regime also laid plans for the establishment of government firms to participate in the exploitation of the country's mineral resources.

The Betancourt regime made consistent efforts to strengthen political democracy. Although faced with a succession of threats and actual attempts to overthrow it from both extreme Right and extreme Left, it maintained civil liberties intact during most of its first two years in office.

With an attempt by extreme Leftists to overthrow the regime by street rioting, and a call to popular insurrection in October and November, 1960, President Betancourt did ask Congress to suspend certain constitutional guarantees. Although full constitutional normality was restored several times, further revolt attempts and the extreme Leftist campaign of terrorism and would-be guerrilla warfare resulted in further suspensions of constitutional guarantees. Most of the last three years of the Betancourt administration was marked by some limitations on full constitutional freedom.

However, the Betancourt regime used sparingly the special powers given it by Congress. The two extremist parties were virtually untouched by the government until the Carúpano and Puerto Cabello revolts in May and June, 1962, when the President "suspended" their activities, and the police closed their headquarters. Even after the extremists launched campaigns of urban terror and attempted guerrilla war in the rural areas late in 1962, the principal leaders of these parties were left alone, although it was known that the organizers of the campaign were members of Congress. Not until late September, 1963, were the PCV and MIR congressmen arrested, after terrorists blew up a train.

The commitment of the Betancourt regime to political democracy was shown conclusively by the 1963 election campaign. Seven candidates, representing all shades of opinion except the small group of extreme Leftists who were in open revolt, campaigned freely, in the press, in the streets, and over radio and television.

Despite certain obvious weaknesses of the Betancourt regime, which will become clear further on in this book, it was, on balance, successful, and the transformation taking place in Venezuela has significance for the whole hemisphere.

The methods and objectives of the Betancourt regime were those of the Latin American democratic Left. In detail, they were adapted to the history and circumstances of Venezuela. In their totality, however, they represent one of the paths open in the New World to convert the economically underdeveloped nations, many of whose social and economic institutions still reflect their colonial and semi-feudal past, into twentieth century states with diversified economies and modern social systems.

Part Two

The Politics of the Democratic Revolution

Chapter Six

The Government Parties

As a result of the Pact of Punto Fijo, signed by the three presidential candidates a few days before the December, 1958, election, President Rómulo Betancourt formed a coalition government upon taking office. The three major democratic parties—Acción Democrática, the Unión Republicana Democrática and the Copei—had agreed by February 13, 1959, upon the basis for the establishment of the coalition regime, and upon a basic governmental program that it should seek to carry out.

Until the day before President Betancourt took office, however, it was not clear what the exact composition of the coalition would be. On the morning of the inauguration it was publicly announced that Acción Democrática would have two members of the cabinet, and the other parties would each have three, while the rest of the ministers would be independents. Agreement was also reached on the distribution of other key posts, such as the directorates of independent agencies of the national government and the governorships of the states (appointive posts under the Venezuelan Constitution).

The apparently minority position of Acción Democrática, which had won the election in December, 1958, was explainable on two grounds. In the first place, President Betancourt, who presided over cabinet meetings, was officially considered to be the third member of the AD group. Second, most of the independents who were part of this first Betancourt cabinet were in fact friends of Acción Democrática. This fact reflected one of the idiosyncracies of Venezuelan politics, that each of the democratic parties has a number of "fellow travelers" who, though not members of these parties, are sympathetic to them and generally work in collaboration with them. Thus, in the December, 1958, election, each of the three parties had on its list of candidates at least a few people who were not registered members of their organizations.

Although the presence of a number of AD fellow travelers in the cabinet aroused some opposition in the other two parties, particularly in the Unión Republicana Democrática, the coalition as established on February 13, 1959, was accepted for a considerable period by all of the parties involved.

Throughout most of the first two years of the Betancourt administration the President governed with the participation of the three democratic parties. In November, 1960, however, after many crises and threats of crises, the URD finally withdrew from the government. Since its position, even when its members held office under Betancourt, was at best equivocal, we shall deal in the present chapter only with the two parties that were indisputably loyal to the revolutionary democratic regime—Acción Democrática and the Copei—and shall postpone our discussion of the role of the Unión Republicana Democrática to the next chapter, which deals with the opposition parties, one of which URD frankly became after November, 1960.

The main burden of leadership of the Venezuelan Democratic Revolution fell upon the Acción Democrática party. Even though other parties worked with AD in the coalition government of Betancourt, AD was basically responsible for the regime's successes and its failures.

Acción Democrática had primary responsibility for initiating the Venezuelan Democratic Revolution not only because it became the most powerful party in the government after February 13, 1959, but also because the revolutionary program was essentially the program that AD had advocated for the quarter-century of its existence. Although dissidents within Acción Democrática and some outsiders—both Venezuelans and foreigners—have asserted that AD in power after February 13, 1959, was essentially different from AD before that date, the author does not agree with this.

From its inception, Acción Democrática was a party that sought to represent the interests of several groups in Venezuelan society. It aspired to be the political spokesman of the peasants, the urban workers, and more progressive elements of the middle and upper classes. Its program for a fundamental change in the economy, society, and political life of the country underwent some modifications to keep up with the passage of time and the alteration of institutions, but has not varied in its broad lines.

From the beginning, Acción Democrática advocated a thoroughgoing agrarian reform. It urged placing the land in the hands of those who cultivate it, and providing the new owners of the soil with the credit facilities and technical knowledge and implements necessary to cultivate it successfully.

Acción Democrática consistently supported a policy of economic nationalism, particularly with regard to the oil industry, the country's principal source of foreign exchange. It argued that Venezuela must get the largest possible return from this industry, contingent on the maintenance of the competitive position of Venezuelan oil in world markets. It advocated the establishment of a nationally owned oil firm able to compete with the foreign companies operating under concession, and recommended that all further concessions should be given to this national firm, which should be prepared to take over the concessions held by foreign companies when these expire.

The AD also consistently advocated the use of the resources drawn from the oil industry to develop other sectors of the Venezuelan economy and to improve the living conditions of the great majority of the people, who had been untouched by the oil prosperity that the country has experienced for a generation. To this end, Acción Democrática proposed aid for the development of agriculture, help for the growth of manufacturing industries, and the provision of adequate housing, medical care, schooling, and the elementary public services such as paved streets and roads, sewer systems and water supplies to the cities, towns, and villages of the republic.

Finally, the AD consistently advocated the establishment of a democratic regime, in which elections will take the place of *coups d'état* as the method of changing government, and in which all of the citizens will be assured the rights to freedom of speech, press, assembly, and the sanctuary of their homes. It argued that without democracy the social and economic aspects of its program are not only incomplete but will prove to be but a hollow shell insofar as the happiness and well-being of the citizenry are concerned.[1]

In spite of more than nine years of ruthless persecution by the dictatorships in power from November, 1948, until January, 1958, Acción Democrática remained the largest single party in Venezuela. Its support varied among different elements of the population. As the December, 1958, election indicated, AD had overwhelming majority support of the peasantry. It dominated the reborn Peasants Federation. The principal spokesmen for the farm workers, tenants, and squatters were leaders of the Acción Democrática party. The party continued to be the majority group among the peasantry even after some of the Peasants Federation leaders abandoned the AD early in 1962.

Although AD had controlled most of organized labor during the 1945 to 1948 period, its influence on this segment of the population was considerably weaker when its underground organization emerged after the Pérez Jiménez dictatorship. This was attributable to several factors: the unceasing propaganda of the dictatorship against Acción Democrática, the personal popularity of Admiral Larrazábal among the urban population, and the fact that the Black Communists had been able to function openly among the workers almost without interruption through most of the dictatorship period. The AD nevertheless had a slight majority among the organized workers in 1958, and was as strong as it had ever been among the oil workers. During the first three years of the Betancourt regime, AD regained much of the ground that it had lost in organized labor in the years of the dictatorship.

Acción Democrática from its beginning had considerable influence among the professional and intellectual classes. A number of the country's outstanding literary figures, including the novelist Rómulo Gallegos and the poet Andrés Eloy Blanco, were among the founders of the party. Although AD was probably weaker in these groups after 1958 than it had been a decade earlier, its representatives were elected as heads of the principal professional organizations of doctors, lawyers, journalists, teachers, and others.

The party also started out as the dominant element among the university students, both in the Universidad Central de Venezuela in Caracas and in the provincial universities. It emerged from the dictatorship with this leadership still intact; however, the AD student leaders in 1958 were closely allied with and infiltrated by the Young Communists, and when the top leaders of the Acción Democrática students withdrew from the party in April, 1960, to form what became the Movimiento de Izquierda Revolucionaria, the AD was reduced to a small minority in the Universidad Central. The party's situation in the provincial universities was strong even in the latter years of the Betancourt administration, however, and it had more adherents among secondary school students than any other political group.

Acción Democrática was faced with serious internal problems when the dictatorship fell. The machinery of the party's underground organization was in the hands of young people in their twenties, or even younger, who were professional men or student leaders. They tended to resent the returning "older generations" and the assumption by the old leaders of positions of influence and prestige in the country's political life. The older leaders of the party sought to deal with this problem by leaving the young people in control of the party machinery until the AD convention scheduled for August, 1958.

In addition to this conflict of generations, however, a more fundamental problem separated the young leaders from their elders: the attitude that the party should assume toward the Communists. During their underground activities in the university, the young AD leaders had worked closely for several years with the Communists there. Furthermore, many of them had been thoroughly indoctrinated by their Communist friends. Whereas the publications of Acción Democrática were severely controlled by the dictatorship and it was exceedingly difficult for the young members to study the works of Betancourt and other leaders of their party, Communist publications circulated comparatively freely. It was from these that the AD student leaders received most of their political education. It is also possible that the Communists had succeeded in installing some of their own number in the ranks of the student Acción Democrática leaders. In contrast, Betancourt and most other old Acción Democrática leaders returned from exile, jail, or hiding as anti-Communist as they had been in 1948. From the day of his return from abroad, Betancourt made it clear that he wanted nothing to do with the Communists, and his position shocked the younger generation.

There were other sources of conflict. While still in exile, Betancourt and top leaders of the party entered into agreements with leaders of the other two democratic parties, the Copei and the Unión Republicana Democrática, to work closely together for the restoration and maintenance of democratic constitutional government. The young AD members were much opposed to the party's having any relations with the Copei, which they regarded as a conservative, if not reactionary, party. They were even more violently opposed to forming a coalition government with the Copei, as Betancourt agreed to do even before the December, 1958, election was held. They were not so opposed to the participation of the URD in this coalition regime.

The young people of Acción Democrática were also impatient with the "slowness" and "timidity" of the Betancourt regime in dealing with the country's problems. They tended to become disillusioned when the constitutional regime failed to solve all of the country's difficulties immediately. They were particularly unhappy about the nature of the agrarian reform undertaken by the Betancourt regime. They desired a more drastic program for redistributing the country's land, and were highly critical of the methods proposed for determining and paying compensation to the expropriated landholders.

Nor were the young people pleased with the foreign policy of the Betancourt regime, particularly the government's relations with the United States and Cuba. They were violently anti-Yankee and wanted Betancourt to adopt the same position. Betancourt, on the other hand, though determined to assert fully the national sovereignty of Venezuela, felt that the best hope for the political democracy and social progress of Venezuela (and Latin America in general) in which he believed, was to enlist the support of the United States. He had had friendly relations with the liberals and the labor movement in the United States when he was in exile, and he continued to maintain these after his return to Venezuela.

There was sharp disagreement also about the Fidel Castro regime in Cuba. Although AD had helped Castro's struggle against Fulgencio Batista, and applauded the downfall of the Cuban dictatorship, the older leaders were worried by Castro's violent attacks on their old friend and associate, Costa Rican ex-President José Figueres, who likewise had aided Castro's struggle against Batista. They were also somewhat concerned by Fidel's friendliness to the Communists, and his unfriendly attitude toward Betancourt during his visit to Venezuela a few weeks after coming to power in Cuba. As the Castro regime developed into a pro-Communist dictatorship, the older AD leaders became increasingly cool toward it. In contrast, the young AD leaders were enthusiastic about Fidel's regime from the beginning, and their enthusiasm did not wane in spite of the character of the Castro government.

The disagreement within the Acción Democrática party came out in the open only a few months after the overthrow of the Pérez Jiménez dictatorship. The party's convention in August, 1958, was marked by the emergence of an opposition group consisting of much of the young element, and led by Domingo Alberto Rangel, a member of the Chamber of Deputies during the 1945 to 1948 period. They expressed their disagreement with the party leadership by opposing the idea of naming Betancourt as the party's candidate for President.

A number of the dissident leaders were on Acción Democrática's ticket for Congress and state and local offices. These included Rangel and Simón Sáez Mérida, last underground secretary-general of AD. Although both were elected to the Chamber of Deputies, their opposition to the older leaders, who had returned to control of the party in the August, 1958, convention, was not mitigated. Relations became increasingly strained between the two groups.

Matters finally came to a head in April, 1960. The issue over which the split in the party occurred was the signing of a new contract between the oil companies and the Petroleum Workers Federation (Federación de Trabajadores Petroleros, known popularly as Fedepetrol). In the negotiations for this contract, Domingo Alberto Rangel was a technical adviser of the Fedepetrol, and had agreed to the terms that were incorporated in the contract. Once the contract was signed, however, he attacked it violently, arguing that it was disadvantageous to the workers, because it did not provide for "stability" of the companies' employees.

The youth organization of Acción Democrática supported Rangel's position, and announced a public meeting in Maracaibo to make its position clear. Meanwhile, however, the AD leaders among the petroleum workers were infuriated by Rangel's action, and threatened to bring charges against him within Acción Democrática. In the view of this conflict, the national executive committee of AD told the youth organization to cancel its meeting. When it refused, and the meeting was held, charges were brought before the party's disciplinary tribunal against those responsible for the meeting and those who spoke at it, including Rangel.

The split soon spread throughout the country. One of AD's senators and thirteen deputies of the party proclaimed their solidarity with the dissidents. In several states enough AD members of the legislatures deserted the party to deprive it of a majority. Nearly all national leaders of the party's youth organization also joined the splitters, as did the national leaders of the White Collar Workers Association and some state labor leaders belonging to AD.

The split in the party did not become as serious as some feared that it might. The great majority of the party's trade union leaders, and almost all AD members in the Peasants Federation, remained loyal, and the only important pre-1958 middle-class leader of the party who was expelled was Domingo Alberto Rangel. Within a year and a half, AD had more than recovered from the effects of the split. It had recovered most of the trade union positions of the dissidents, and was even regaining ground among the students, particularly outside of the Universidad Central.

Those who were expelled from or quit Acción Democrática at first called themselves Acción Democrática de Izquierda, but at their first convention in July, 1960, rechristened the group Movimiento de Izquierda Revolucionaria (MIR). Within a short time the MIR was virtually indistinguishable ideologically from the Communist party. The MIR members became violent opponents of the Betancourt government, and openly proclaimed their intention of overthrowing it by popular insurrection, or civil war, whenever the opportunity to do so presented itself.

About a year and a half after AD's expulsion of the MIR faction, a more serious split occurred in Acción Democrática. This schism did not occur on ideological grounds, but rather involved a struggle for power and differences of opinion on tactical matters. Unlike the MIR split, old-time party leaders were found on both sides of the new division.

The core of the leadership of the party consisted of the men who had founded it almost a quarter of a century before, and who held key posts in the government after February, 1959. These people, who were generally known as the "Old Guard" of the party, were headed by President Betancourt and included Raúl Leoni, President of Congress, Gonzalo Barrios, leader of the Acción Democrática bloc in Congress, Luis Beltrán Prieto Figueroa, principal spokesman for the party on educational matters, and

Carlos D'Ascoli, main authority of AD in Congress when economic and financial matters were up for discussion.

Associated with these leaders was a group of somewhat younger men, who reached national leadership during and after the Pérez Jiménez dictatorship, among whom Luis Agusto Dubuc, Betancourt's Minister of the Interior, was an outstanding figure. Most of the top Acción Democrática leaders in the labor movement, such as Augusto Malavé Villalba, the secretary-general of the Confederación de Trabajadores de Venezuela, Luis Tovar of the Petroleum Workers Federation, Pedro Bernardo Pérez Salinas, and Senator Francisco Olivo, trade union secretary of the party, were also generally aligned with the Old Guard group.

In frequent opposition to policies and positions taken by the Old Guard after the expulsion of the MIR was an informally organized group of younger leaders known popularly as the Grupo ARS. Their name was given them by the anti-Acción Democrática press of Caracas, and was taken from a public relations firm, Publicidad ARS, the slogan of which was "Let us think for you." The newspapers implied that this was in effect what the Grupo ARS within AD was saying to Betancourt. The principal figure of this wing of the party until December, 1961, was a young senator, Raúl Ramos Giménez.

The ARS group had first appeared during the 1945 to 1948 period, when it criticized the Betancourt and Gallegos administrations for moving "too slowly." Although the ARS discrepancies with the Old Guard were smoothed over during the period when the party was in the political wilderness, they were revived after the overthrow of Pérez Jiménez.

The Grupo ARS differed with the Old Guard more on tactical matters than in principle. They were not ideologically hostile to the leadership of the party, as the members of the MIR had been; indeed they took the lead in seeking the expulsion of the MIR early in 1960. However, they generally felt that the government was not moving fast enough in its reform program, and they blamed this in large part on the presence of the Copei party in the coalition government. They were also somewhat unhappy about the administration's foreign policy, feeling that Venezuela should more closely align with the neutralist group in world politics than President Betancourt was willing to have it do.

The rivalry between the Old Guard and the Grupo ARS came

to a head at the end of 1961. In December the ARS majority on the national executive committee of the party expelled from their ranks and from the party itself the minority associated with the Old Guard, including Raúl Leoni, Gonzalo Barrios, Luis Beltrán Prieto, and others. Leoni, as president of the party, refused to accept this decision and appealed to the party membership.

Finally, on January 13, 1962, two rival conventions, both claiming to represent the "authentic" Acción Democrática, were held in Caracas. The Old Guard convention re-elected Leoni as president of the party, and Dr. Jesús Paz Galaraga as secretary-general. The ARS convention named Senator Raúl Ramos Giménez as president, and the former assistant secretary-general, José Ángel Ciliberto, as secretary-general.

President Betancourt attempted to prevent the open break between the two groups. Although he was known to sympathize more with the Old Guard than with the Grupo ARS, he conferred at length with Senator Ramos Giménez the day before the two conventions met, seeking some way to bridge the gap between the two factions. When his efforts failed, he demonstrated his support of the Old Guard by inviting the delegates to its convention to a public reception.

In the beginning the ARS split threatened to be very serious for Acción Democrática, but it was clear by 1963 that it had not fundamentally weakened the party, even though the ARS took with it a considerable number of state leaders of the party, as well as most of those heading the youth section which had been reconstituted after the desertion of the MIR faction.

Almost without exception the labor leaders of Acción Democrática sided with the Old Guard. For some time after the ARS split, however, the party faced a serious problem in the ranks of its peasant followers. Ramón Quijada, founder and president of the Federación Campesina (Peasants Federation), sided with ARS, as did a majority of his executive committee; however, they were unable to take the rank and file of the peasant organizations with them. Before the ARS split, Ramón Quijada had been losing control of the Peasants Federation. Most of its local groups in the central states of the republic were by 1961 under the leadership of Armando González, peasant leader and AD deputy from the state of Carabobo. In 1961 a split occurred in the federation local group in the state of Anzoátegui during which a majority revolted against Quijada's leadership. Local Acción Democrática peasant leaders in several other states were also opposed to him, and in the states of Táchira and Mérida, the peasants were under Copei control.

When the Old Guard-ARS split occurred, Quijada and most of the other top figures in the Peasants Federation sided with the ARS. In December, 1961, however, the Confederación de Trabajadores de Venezuela officially intervened in the affairs of the federation, ousting its leaders and naming a provisional committee under the leadership of Armando González to reorganize the group.

The González group used the personal influence of Rómulo Betancourt in their efforts to reorganize the peasant movement, for the President rallied elements loyal to the Old Guard during his several trips to the interior during the early months of 1962. The González forces were also aided by the fact that the government transferred a subsidy that Congress had appropriated for the Peasants Federation, from the Quijada group to that of González.

Within six months, the overwhelming majority of the local peasant organizations were aligned with the González faction. Early in June, 1962, that faction held a national congress to formalize the reorganization of the Federación Campesina, which was attended by 3,400 delegates. The new federation, of which Armando González was elected president, was accepted by the Confederación de Trabajadores de Venezuela as a regular affiliate. The ARS influence among the peasants was further reduced during the 1963 election period when Ramón Quijada abandoned the party to support the presidential candidacy of businessman Arturo Uslar Pietri instead of the ARS nominee, Raúl Ramos Giménez. Quijada was elected to the Chamber of Deputies from the city of Caracas on the Uslar Pietri ticket.

The effects of the ARS split were very serious insofar as the position of the administration in Congress was concerned. Over twenty members of the lower house went with the ARS, depriving the Betancourt government of a majority in the Chamber of Deputies. When that body met in March, 1962, it deposed Rafael Caldera as its President, and a member of the ARS was named to the post, with the support of the ARS, the URD, the MIR, and Communist deputies. However, the Old Guard-Copei coalition still enjoyed a majority in the Senate.

Although the ARS leaders at first indicated that they would

continue to support the administration, the dynamics of politics soon took them into the opposition, where together with the URD they came to constitute what was usually referred to as "the democratic opposition," as opposed to the "subversive opposition" of the MIR and the Communist party. Within a year of their split from the Old Guard, they had become as violent in their verbal attacks upon the Betancourt government as any other opposition group.

With the exit of the Unión Republicana Democrática from the government in 1960, the importance of the Copei's participation in the regime grew considerably, since its loyal support of the constitutional government was a key factor in the regime's growing stability.

The Copei had evolved considerably during the dictatorship. When Acción Democrática was in power between 1945 and 1948 Copei adherents were the most violent opponents of the regime. At that time they included many of the conservative elements of Venezuelan political life, and the party had a marked clerical tinge, particularly in the mountain states of Mérida, Táchira, and Trujillo, where there were frequent clashes, some of them bloody, between AD and Copei members. Less than a month after the overthrow of President Rómulo Gallegos, the principal leader of the Copei, Rafael Caldera, came out with a public statement denying all Copei complicity in the military movement that had ousted AD from power. During the succeeding four years, the Copei generally maintained a wait-and-see attitude toward the military regime.

At the time of the 1952 elections, the Copei participated, and came in third, after the URD and the party of the dictatorship, the Frente Electoral Independiente. However, when Pérez Jiménez seized the presidency and altered the results of the election, the national executive committee of the Copei forbade any party member to take a seat in the new Constituent Assembly, which had in effect been hand-picked by the dictator. When several Copei members took their seats anyway, they were immediately expelled from the party.

Although the Copei was never officially outlawed by the dictatorship, it was unable to function openly as long as Pérez Jiménez remained President. Its principal leaders were frequently jailed for short periods of time, while lower-ranking figures in the party were jailed for longer periods or were exiled; a few were even killed by order of the regime.

As a result of this experience, the Copei moved strongly to the Left. Most of the conservatives who had seen it as the principal bulwark against the "radicalism" of Acción Democrática fell by the wayside during the dictatorship. The leaders of the party became firm adherents of a radical interpretation of the social teachings of the Catholic Church, and became much more determined to keep the party free of Church control than they had been in the earlier period.

Hence, the leaders and the bulk of the members of the Copei were fully ready to participate, after the fall of Pérez Jiménez, in a regime that would bring about revolutionary changes in the economic structure, social fabric, and political life of Venezuela. During the provisional regime, the Copei worked alongside Acción Democrática and the URD to assure the return to democratic constitutional government; and once Betancourt was elected, they were willing and anxious to participate in his administration, to aid in carrying out the programs of agrarian reform, industrialization, economic independence, and democratic government to which he was pledged.

The election of 1958 was a disappointment for the Copei. Although they had had no hopes of winning the presidency, they had been confident that they would be able to win more than the 15 per cent of the popular vote that they received. The party had a majority position only in two states, Mérida and Táchira, and lost the principal cities even in these states to AD. Along with AD they did very badly in Caracas, and their support in other parts of the country varied; in some they received a mere handful of votes, in others they achieved the position of second strongest party.

The Copei was weak also in the trade union movement. Although as a result of the coalition policy adopted by all of the major political forces in the labor movement during the first three years after the fall of Pérez Jiménez the Copei received numerous posts in trade unions throughout the country, the incumbents were generally unable to maintain their positions when election contests began early in 1961.

Although the Copei had pockets of strength in unions scattered throughout the country and constituted a small minority in the labor movement as a whole, its importance went far beyond either its general electoral strength or its ability to win posts in the trade unions. Particularly after the expulsion of the MIR from Acción Democrática early in 1960, Copei influence in the organized student movement became of great importance to the coalition government. Whereas Acción Democrática lost nearly all of its following among the students of the Universidad Central in Caracas, and found its strength considerably depleted in the student bodies of other universities, the influence of the Copei grew dramatically. In the student elections in the Central University early in 1961, the Copei emerged as the single strongest party, although outnumbered by the three-party coalition of PCV-MIR-URD. In the following two years it further increased its following, although still unable to achieve a majority. In one or two of the provincial universities, the Copei was the majority group, and in the University of Carabobo, AD and the Copei were able in alliance to defeat the coalition of the extremists.

The Copei was also important to the coalition because of its real though intangible influence among important interest groups. It was certainly the party preferred by the Church hierarchy, although the hierarchy did not try directly to interfere in its internal affairs. It was probably the party that was regarded as the least noxious by important elements in the officer caste of the armed forces. And in spite of its turn to the Left after 1958, the Copei still had the sympathy of important elements among the industrial and commercial classes. The Copei's continued presence in the coalition regime certainly tended to engender more confidence in the government among those groups than they would have had, had Copei not been in the Betancourt regime. This confidence made them less ready to participate in conspiracies against the regime than they otherwise might have been.

Finally, Copei cooperation with the Betancourt government was important because it assured the administration a majority in Congress until the second split in AD at the end of 1961. Although after the MIR split, Acción Democrática still had a clear majority in the Senate, it was only the largest minority in the Chamber of Deputies, and needed the support of the small though crucial group of Copei legislators to assure a majority for the government on controversial issues.

The growing strength of the Copei was reflected in the election of December, 1963. Not only did the party's presidential nominee, Rafael Caldera, come in second among seven candidates, but the party was able to elect at least one member of the Chamber of Deputies from every state but two, whereas five years earlier its electoral strength had been largely confined to the mountain states and a handful of other areas.

In contrast to the Unión Republicana Democrática while it was in the government, the Copei was loyal in word and in deed to the administration of which it was a part. The author has heard Copei ministers defend the policies of the regime with a fervor and sincerity that would have done credit to President Betancourt himself. Only rarely did Copei periodicals attack their coalition partners, though individual Copei politicians, particularly in the lower echelons, tended to do so rather frequently.

The AD-Copei coalition was never altogether free of differences of opinion. There was some bickering over the apportionment of jobs among members of the two parties, and on occasion the leaders of the two parties had different points of view on the tactics that the administration should follow. Generally, the Copei leaders acted as responsible members of the administration of which they were a part, speaking as members of the government coalition, and displaying willingness to bear part of the blame for its failures or share credit for its successes. They insisted on the absolute necessity for the constitutional regime to last out its term of office and to carry out its program. They argued that they continued in the government, not to support President Betancourt or his party, but rather to achieve those objectives that were to the advantage of all Venezuela.

The attitude of the Copei toward the coalition regime was demonstrated by a resolution proposed by the party's delegates to a world congress of Christian Democrats held in Santiago, Chile, in August, 1961. This resolution, passed by the congress, advocated as a general policy for Latin America an alliance of Christian Democratic parties with Democratic Socialist parties for the purpose of stabilizing political democracy and carrying forward programs of basic reform on which the two groups, in spite of the philosophical differences of the two types of parties, were in agreement.

The most severe test of Copei loyalty to the regime came during the 1963 election campaign. Although the Copei favored a joint

AD-Copei candidate for President, this proved impossible when Acción Democrática named Raúl Leoni, whom Copei leaders felt they could not back, as AD candidate. The Copei then chose Rafael Caldera as its nominee, but the coalition continued on a governmental level, Copei leaders remaining in President Betancourt's cabinet and other key posts.

Chapter Seven

The Opposition Parties

From its inception, the Betancourt government was faced with bitter opposition from both Left and Right. Whereas the Right-wing opposition was expressed not so much through political parties as through conspiratorial activities, that of the Left found its main expression through the Partido Comunista de Venezuela, the Movimiento de Izquierda Revolucionaria, the Unión Republicana Democrática (after November, 1960), and the AD-ARS (after January, 1962).

Neither the Left-wing nor the Right-wing antagonists of the Betancourt administration acted as what one might call a "loyal" opposition. Indeed, this has been one of the greatest difficulties of the Venezuelan Democratic Revolution. Its leaders have not been faced with opponents who were willing to confine their opposition to competition for the electoral support of the citizenry. Rather, nearly all opposition groups, although willing to enjoy the democratic freedoms provided them by the regime, were resolved to use *coup d'état,* insurrection, and even guerrilla warfare against the government, given a favorable opportunity.

The Communist party was in opposition to the Betancourt regime from the day that government took office. Although some of the good feeling among all parties that had characterized the early days of the provisional government persisted in the early weeks and months of the Betancourt regime, and hence limited at first the bitterness of the antagonism between the Communists and the government, this phase soon passed.

A conflict between the revolutionary democratic regime and the Communists was inevitable. The Communists understood very clearly that if the Betancourt government was successful in carrying out thoroughgoing reforms in the social and economic structure of Venezuela in a democratic way, there would be little chance that the Communists would develop into anything more than a minority party with nuisance value but no real prospect of achieving power. Furthermore, the Communists were not part of the Betancourt government, and they had little opportunity to infiltrate it or influence it from within. Finally, the foreign policy of the democratic government, to seek an independent position for Venezuela while cooperating where possible with the United States, could only engender the bitterest opposition of the Communists.

From the very beginning, Betancourt made it clear that although he desired the fullest degree of consultation and cooperation among Acción Democrática, the Copei and the Unión Republicana Democrática, he had no intention of consulting with or otherwise including the Communists in his coalition regime. He said exactly this in his inaugural address on February 13, 1959.

This position of Betancourt's was in no way inconsistent with his past history. He had once been in the Communist movement, but had broken with it in 1935 and from then on had been a consistent and conscientious opponent of the Communists. During the 1958 election campaign he was the only candidate who dared to criticize them. He made it clear that although he favored giving them the same democratic rights as were enjoyed by all other political groups, he had no intention of forming any sort of popular front with them.

The Communist party enjoyed an advantageous position at the beginning of the Betancourt regime. Although some of the Communists had collaborated with the dictatorship during most of its existence, they joined the opposition during the last period of the struggle against Pérez Jiménez, and were able to capitalize upon that fact throughout the provisional government, and even in the first months of the Betancourt regime.

Because the Communists had been less persecuted by the dictatorship than had members of other political groups, they emerged from the Pérez Jiménez regime with key positions in the journalistic and legal professions, in the universities, and in the trade union movement. Their members and sympathizers were able to use these key positions in order to put forward Communist ideas and the party's political position under the cover of great respectability. For instance, until about a year after Betancourt took office, Communist journalists held the most important editorial and reportorial positions in the important Capriles chain of newspapers.

Furthermore, the Communists profited from the truce on political controversy among those who had participated in the overthrow of the dictatorship. Although they did not hesitate to question the sincerity and good faith of those who argued for positions different from their own, the Communists themselves were seldom challenged during the provisional regime.

With the inauguration of Betancourt, this situation began to alter. Leaders of the government political parties, columnists and other writers in the press, became increasingly free in their criticism of the Communists. In early August, 1959, a riot occurred in downtown Caracas as the result of the news that President Betancourt was removing Celso Fourtoul, a left-wing member of AD, as engineer in charge of the Plan de Emergencia, and was replacing him with someone else. Several people were killed and wounded during this rioting. Both President Betancourt and Minister of the Interior Luis Dubuc accused the Communists of organizing and directing the disturbances, and a considerable discussion of these charges developed in the press.

By the end of 1959 the Communists had adopted a position of frank opposition to the Betancourt government. Thus a resolution of the Plenum of the Central Committee of the Communist party, published in the December, 1959, issue of the party's monthly magazine *Principios*, stated the PCV assessment of the government as follows: "The Government is active to please the demands of the large bankers, financiers, industrialists, and merchants; vacillates in the face of the monopolists and foreign investors, resents the action and combativeness of the masses, does nothing in the face of the situation in which thousands are unemployed, are without homes, peasants starve. . . .

"The disoriented policy of the government can be summed up thus: all for the rich and nothing for the poor, which is leading to a breach which is every day greater between the people and the government."

Thereafter, as the divergence of the Communist party and the government became increasingly clear, members of the government parties engaged more and more often in polemics, and their reluctance to break off relations with the Communists disappeared as a result of the riots of October and November, 1960. These riots were begun by university students in Caracas and one or two other cities, and they were followed by a revolutionary general strike called by Communist and MIR trade union leaders, as well as a call by the same leaders for a popular insurrection against the Betancourt government. These actions of the Left opposition finally cracked the united front in the labor movement. Open warfare between the Left-wing alliance led by the Communists, on the one hand, and the parties of the government, on the other, broke out in nearly every union in the country. The same kind of conflict took place in the student movement, and in the country's professional organizations.

Although the Communists thus became alienated from Acción Democrática and the Copei, their isolation was by no means complete. From the end of the dictatorship, the Communists had had exceedingly friendly relations with the Left wing of Acción Democrática, and this close association continued after the split in AD and the establishment of the Movimiento de Izquierda Revolucionaria. In addition, the Communists maintained very friendly relations with some groups and individuals in the Unión Republicana Democrática, particularly after the URD quit the Betancourt government.

In the election of December, 1958, the Communists emerged over the nation as the fourth of the four major parties participating, but they were the second largest party in the Distrito Federal. The strength of the Communists, however, came not from their ability to obtain votes, but from their discipline, sense of organization, and influence as holders of key positions in important social institutions.

The members of the Partido Comunista de Venezuela constituted in 1958 the second largest political group in the Venezuelan trade union movement. They had been considerably strengthened by a reunification of the two groups into which they had been divided during the 1940's and 1950's. The Black Communists, who in the 1945 to 1948 period had formed the Partido Revolucionario Proletario, and had been violent opponents of the Acción Democrática regime, were formally dissolved by their own decision in 1953; however, they continued to function as a group in the labor movement, and were permitted by the Pérez Jiménez dictatorship a degree of legal operation that was not allowed to labor groups under the control of the other parties.

With the overthrow of the dictatorship, the long-standing split in the Communist ranks was quietly forgotten. Leading figures of the Black Communists (Partido Revolucionario Proletario [Comunista]), including Cruz Villegas and Rodolfo Quintero, joined the Red Communist party, the Partido Comunista de Venezuela. Quintero had been the principal leader of the Blacks and became one of the principal spokesmen for the PCV in the united labor movement after January, 1958. One of the surprising aspects of this reunification of the Communist party was the fact that the former Black Communists were never brought to task for their collaboration with the Pérez Jiménez dictatorship, even by their bitterest enemies.

The Communist's influence in the labor movement was widespread. They were of considerable importance among the petroleum workers, and constituted the majority group in key manufacturing industries, such as the automobile, rubber, and chemical workers unions. They were also the leading element among the textile workers.

The Communists also continued to have considerable importance in certain professional groups, including the journalists' and teachers' organizations. They were strongest in the organized student movement, where after 1961 they were closely allied to the MIR, and had considerable strength of their own. Among the largest single element of the Venezuelan population, the peasantry, they were unable to make any appreciable advances.

Whereas it is doubtful whether the Venezuelan Communists have entertained any serious hope of coming to power through the votes of their fellow citizens, they have certainly speculated on the possibility of achieving power by one of two other methods.

Through their support of Admiral Larrazábal in the December, 1958, campaign, the Communists hoped that they might be able to weld together an extreme Left-wing coalition of sufficient power to defeat Acción Democrática. Undoubtedly the Communists felt that any Left-wing government in which Acción Democrática did not participate would depend very heavily on the Communists. This could have been true not only because of the ability of the Communist leaders, and the exceedingly compact and efficient organization that the PCV possessed, but also because any such government would depend upon the Communists' influence in the labor movement and other mass organizations for rallying and maintaining popular support.

The alternative open to the Communists after Larrazábal's defeat was the organization of an uprising against the Betancourt regime or its successor. They miscalculated in November, 1960, when they called upon the workers to launch a popular insurrection against the government. For many months after that failure, the Communists appeared to be quiescent.

The XXVth Plenum of the Communist party, held in the spring of 1961, made clear its willingness to use insurrectionary techniques against the Betancourt regime. It called for the "defeat of the policy of the present government and for the formation of a patriotic and democratic government. . . ." Guillermo García Ponce, one of the party's principal leaders, in speaking to a party meeting in Caracas shortly after the XXV Plenum, commented as follows on this slogan of the PCV: ". . . We cannot tell our people to postpone this slogan, that it is a remote possibility, that it is a slogan for use when the peasants are Communists. No, because this slogan, comrades, because of the peculiarities of our country, could become converted in a matter of hours from a slogan of agitation and propaganda into a slogan of action. . . . Then the party must be educated to the effect that this slogan is today a slogan for preparation of forces, of propaganda and agitation, which could be converted in a matter of hours into a slogan of action."[1]

The author can testify that the Communists had not by 1961 lost their hope of launching a violent movement against the regime. The outbreak of a guerrilla war against the Betancourt government was confidently predicted by several Communist leaders in the summer of 1961, with the added assurance that when it occurred, the Communists would "naturally" be part of such a movement.

Guerrilla war and urban terrorism were actually started by Communists and MIR supporters in 1962, with results for the country and the general political situation which we shall note further along. The impact of this violence on the Communist party itself was disastrous. It greatly reduced the popular support of the party, and fomented bitter internal dissension within the Communist party itself.

The Communists lost virtually all of the positions of prestige and power that they had gained in journalism, professional organizations and other important institutions during the provisional government. This was perhaps best reflected in the labor movement. At the end of March, 1963, the Communists and other opposition groups launched a new central labor group in opposition to the Confederación de Trabajadores de Venezuela. One of the principal Communist leaders of the new groups told the author early in April, 1963, that it contained "over 400" unions. It is fair to presume that at least half of these were organizations under Communist control. However, control over 200 or more unions, of the country's total of more than 3,400, was a far cry from the 15 to 20 per cent of the labor movement that the Communists controlled early in the Betancourt administration.

Even more disastrous for the Communists was the fact that the campaign of violence and terrorism provoked violent dissension within their party. In January, 1963, a national conference of the PCV debated a motion introduced by some of the older leaders of the party to cancel the violence campaign; however, the debate was so violent that the meeting broke up in fist fights and the issue was tabled. Some of the more moderate Communist leaders were reported to be fearful that if they were to push the issue to a decision, some of their more violent comrades might actually attempt to assassinate them.

This controversy within Communist ranks threatened to become involved in the wider split taking shape within the international Communist movement between elements favorable to the Soviet Union and those favorable to China. It was also intimately connected with the PCV's relations with the Castro regime in Cuba. Many of the younger party activists were inclined to be favorably disposed toward the Chinese advocacy of violence as the only acceptable Communist road to power, although older leaders were by habit and conviction more friendly disposed to the Soviet Communists and their general position. Furthermore, many of these same youngsters, who had gone to Cuba for training, returned home more loyal to Fidel Castro than to the leaders of the PCV.

The closest party to the Communists throughout most of the Betancourt regime was the Movimiento de Izquierda Revolucionaria, formed by the people who were expelled or withdrew from Acción Democrática in April, 1960. The nature of the MIR became clear soon after it was formed. Its members proudly proclaimed themselves to be Marxists-Leninists. In conversations with the author in

1961 various MIR leaders found it exceedingly difficult to explain the differences between themselves and the Partido Comunista de Venezuela, the country's official Communist party. Usually, this difference was said to be a "matter of tactics," but the author was unable to get any MIR member to define adequately the tactical differences separating the MIR from the PCV.

The MIR adherents were quite frank about their disdain for the procedures of democratic government, although they also had no hesitation about condemning the Betancourt government when it seemed to be violating these procedures. Elections with competing parties, and the democratic rights to freedom of the press, speech, and assembly were referred to as "formal" democracy by the MIR members, and the Castro regime was cited as an example of "real" democracy.

Soon after the street rioting in Caracas and other cities in November, 1960, the party organ of the MIR referred to these events as a "revolutionary movement," led by a "Junta de Liberación," which failed temporarily because of government repression.[2]

Certain leaders of the MIR also made no secret in conversations with the author in 1961 of their intention of following Ernesto Guevara's advice "to turn the Andes into a Sierra Maestra," that is, to launch a guerrilla war against the government, whenever the opportunity to do so should present itself. Meanwhile, from the party's inception, the MIR allied itself with the Communists in the trade union movement, in the student movement, and in Congress and other legislative bodies.

The Movimiento de Izquierda Revolucionaria has not become a major factor in the country's political life. Indeed, the influence of the members of the MIR was probably greater when they were a dissident element within Acción Democrática than after they had broken away to form their own party. They had little independent strength in the labor movement; and even among the students, where their principal support lay, they tended to follow the leadership of the Communists, although they were considerably more influential among the rank and file in the universities than were the members of the PCV.

It is unlikely that the MIR was able to rally many people to its banners who had not formerly been members of Acción Democrática. In a few states there were indications by 1961 that it had drawn off some of the hot-headed members of the Communist party, and they might have recruited a small group from the ranks of the Unión Republicana Democrática. It was also true that appreciable numbers of those who followed the MIR leaders out of Acción Democrática soon left their ranks and either became independents or rejoined AD.

The MIR was not without its internal factional difficulties. In mid-1961 there were indications that a more or less bitter discussion was raging within the MIR concerning the advisability of merging with the Partido Comunista de Venezuela. For their part, it was doubtful whether the Communists would have been anxious to accept in their well-knit and highly disciplined organization many of the hotheads who found their political home in the MIR.

In 1962 the MIR seemed to be falling apart. Early in that year Jorge Dager, the party's second most important leader, withdrew in protest against the MIR's insurrectionary line and formed a rival group, the Frente Democrático Popular. In July of the same year, most of the party members in the Maracaibo area withdrew.

Unlike the Acción Democrática, the Copei, the Communist party, and even the MIR, the Unión Republicana Democrática is a party without any fixed doctrine or program. It has no well-defined position to occupy in the highly ideological pattern of Venezulan political parties. It has become a catchall for those who do not fit in any of the other political groups. After November, 1960, the Unión Republicana Democrática joined the ranks of the opposition to the Betancourt regime. Perhaps this was inevitable in view of the history and the conflicting factions within the URD. Let us recall the URD's beginnings.

Jóvito Villalba, the founder of the URD, was a member of the "generation of 1928," the group of students who revolted against the dictatorship of Juan Vicente Goméz. When the Goméz regime ended in December, 1935, Villalba emerged as president of the Federación de Estudiantes (Students Federation), and formed a part of the first opposition political organization, Organización Revolucionaria Venezolana (ORVE). Most of the founders of both Acción Democrática and the Partido Comunista de Venezuela were also members of ORVE.

When ORVE broke up into the Partido Democrático Nacional, led by Rómulo Betancourt, and the Partido Comunisto de Venezuela, Villalba did not become part of either group. He was not a Communist, and he would not accept Betancourt's leadership in the

PDN (which in 1941 became Acción Democrática). During the administration of Medina Angarita (1941 to 1945), Villalba was a member of the government party, Partido Democrático Venezolano, and was elected a senator with the support of the President.

The Unión Republicana Democrática was first established under Jóvito Villalba's leadership in 1946 during the provisional government regime headed by Rómulo Betancourt. It was composed largely of people who had been associated with the Medina Angarita regime, which Betancourt and his friends had overthrown. The URD was bitterly opposed to Acción Democrática, and leading figures of the URD were accused of plotting with dissident military elements to overthrow its government.

The Unión Republicana Democrática gave at least tacit support to the military revolt that ousted President Rómulo Gallegos in November, 1948. Leading URD figures held public office with the party's blessing as state governors and in other posts until 1952.

When the ruling Junta Militar de Gobierno called elections for November, 1952, the URD presented a full list of candidates. Shortly before polling day, the underground organization of Acción Democrática decided to throw its support behind the URD. At least partly as a result of this backing, the Unión Republicana Democrática won the election overwhelmingly; however, its leaders were all rounded up by Pérez Jiménez and were shipped off into exile, where they remained until the overthrow of the dictatorship early in 1958.

The Unión Republicana Democrática as it emerged after the fall of the Pérez Jiménez regime contained several new elements. As it had been the favorite political organization of the people of the Medina Angarita regime in the 1945 to 1948 period, it became the refuge of small-fry officeholders of the Pérez Jiménez regime after January, 1958. Many former jobholders of the dictatorship who held important positions in the URD were noted by the press. Another new group in the URD after January, 1958, consisted of an element of the old Black Communist party. Led by Luis Miquilena, who became secretary of organization of the URD, this group played a leading role in the councils of the party in the post-dictatorship period.

Finally, a sizable group of young people who had become politically active during and after the dictatorship years played an important part in the Unión Republicana Democrática during the provisional and Betancourt governments. Like the youngest generation in Acción Democrática, the URD young people had worked closely with the Communists during the latter part of the dictatorship, and were much influenced by the ideas and policies of the PCV. They had the Communists' enthusiasm for Fidel Castro and his regime and their hatred for the United States, attitudes which were not shared by most of the older leaders of the URD.

The various elements making up the Unión Republicana Democrática were not held together by a common philosophy or ideology. Some of the URD members characterized themselves as "liberals," others were quite frankly "Marxists," and still others were confused about just what they were. Personal differences with leaders and members of other parties, and the desire for public office were more important factors in keeping the URD together than was ideological consistency. Thus, in some states where the Acción Democrática party was in overwhelming majority, virtually all politically active anti-AD citizens, whatever their ideological convictions, were members of the URD, as the only effective vehicle through which to oppose AD.

For twenty-one months the Unión Republicana Democrática was a partner in the coalition regime of Rómulo Betancourt. Its role was an important one because it had emerged as the second largest party in the country. During this early phase of the coalition, political posts in the administration were equally distributed among the three parties. The URD was given the governorships of those states in which it had won a majority in the election. URD leaders had the posts of Foreign Minister, Labor Minister, and Minister of Communications in President Betancourt's cabinet.

The URD provoked frequent cabinet crises during this period, not all of which were brought to public notice. More often than not the question at issue was the distribution of jobs, the URD being exceedingly insistent upon receiving its "just" share. There were also some differences of opinion between the URD and its coalition partners on issues of policy, and subsequently URD leaders asserted that they had not been consulted concerning many of the major decisions of the government while they were still part of it.

The Unión Republicana Democrática presented two faces to the public during the period it was in the government. Most of its top leaders reiterated the party's support of the administration. At the same time, the party's weekly periodicals were attacking the government and the URD's two partners in the regime, while having little unpleasant to say about the opposition parties. Thus as early as its issue of August 15, 1959, *U.R.D.*, the party's official organ in the Caracas regional area, carried articles accusing Acción Democrática of monopolizing teaching posts in various parts of the country and of using the police to party ends. The same issue, in discussing the riot that had occurred ten days earlier over the suspension of the so-called Plan de Emergencia, accused the government of having continued the Plan in order to provide good jobs for AD members, but did not mention the role the Communists had had in fomenting the riot, a role denounced by leaders of all of the coalition parties.

In the latter part of 1960, relations of the URD with the Betancourt government were strained to the breaking point. The most serious crisis to date arose over the Inter-American Conference in San José, Costa Rica, in August. At that meeting, Foreign Minister Ignacio Luis Arcaya, of the URD, refused to accept the decision of President Betancourt to support a resolution that by implication mildly criticized the regime of Fidel Castro in Cuba. Rather than sign the final document of the conference, Arcaya resigned and went back home.

Although President Betancourt accepted Foreign Minister Arcaya's resignation and appointed independent Marcos Falcón Briceño to replace him, he hoped to avoid this becoming the cause of a general break between the URD and the government. The situation dragged on into November, when the remaining URD officeholders quit the government ranks.

Once it went into the opposition, the URD did so enthusiastically. The URD's members of Congress became pertinacious and unremitting critics of nearly every act of the administration. In almost all of the state legislatures the URD members joined the PCV and the MIR in consistently opposing the policies of the regional executives. In some places the parties combined to refuse approval of the budgets submitted by the governors.

Outside of the legislative branch of government, too, the URD conducted widespread opposition activities against the administration after November, 1960. In the trade union and student movements, the URD in most cases joined the Communist party and the MIR to present a united front against AD and other pro-government forces.

The URD used its official press to issue violent attacks upon the government. It accused the Betancourt administration of being dictatorial, incompetent, insincere, in its efforts to achieve the objectives that it professed. The URD further charged that the administration was servile in its relations with the United States, and intimated that it was corrupt. By implication at least, the URD periodicals justified the use of violent means to overthrow the Betancourt government, until the party broke definitively with the Communists and the MIR in September, 1963.

In August, 1962, the unofficial URD daily *La Hora* went so far as to run a series of articles about General Castro León, who had rebelled against the government in April, 1960. The general was featured as a sterling patriot being persecuted by a despotic regime. These articles hinted at a possible alliance between the Left- and Right-wing opponents of the administration.

Although this exceedingly hostile attitude prevailed for long in the URD, it was not shared by all members and leaders of the party. In one or two states, the URD members of the legislature continued to cooperate more or less cordially with the state administration. In some trade union situations, too, URD labor people refused to go along with the general line of alliance with the Communists, and collaborated with the AD members.

After the Unión Republicana Democrática left the government, there were very serious differences of opinion within the party. These centered around three main issues. First, was the question of what relations the URD should have with the Communists. Some of the principal leaders of the party insisted that their party had absolutely no general alliance with the Communists and the MIR; however, the action of many of the other leaders of the party belied these assertions.

Another issue upon which there was obviously much difference of opinion was the attitude that the URD should adopt with regard to the Fidel Castro regime. Although all factions of the party opposed intervention by any other nation against Castro, many did not want to take a stand in favor of Castro. On the other hand, one of the important leaders of the party, Fabricio Ojeda (who had been head of the Junta Patriótica in the last weeks of the fight against the Pérez Jiménez regime), went so far as to accept a commission in the Cuban Army, and some URD leaders felt that the URD should become in effect the Fidelista party in Venezuela.

Finally, there was profound difference of opinion concerning the attitude that the party should take toward the Betancourt government. Some of the leaders felt that it was essenial that Betancourt complete his term of office, because if he failed to do so, there would be no hope for a democratic regime in Venezuela. Others were less concerned about the issue of democracy, and even joined the MIR in referring to elections and civil liberties as "formal" democracy. They felt that Venezuela could not achieve necessary social and economic changes through the use of democratic procedures. In Venezuela such a position put these URD spokesmen on the other side of the barricades from the government and the parties supporting it. Early in 1962 Fabricio Ojeda, leader of the more fanatical anti-government URD elements, organized a guerrilla band, as a result of which he was expelled from the URD. In August, 1962, he was captured and his band was broken up. Although he escaped from jail a year later, he was soon recaptured.

The democratic opposition found it hard to learn how to conduct a "loyal" opposition. In the case of both the URD and the ARS, once these parties passed over to the opposition, they tended to go to extremes. Instead of criticizing those aspects of the government's policies and program which were weak or misguided, they alleged that the government was "doing nothing," that in effect it had no policies and no program. The upshot of this was to weaken the opposition parties themselves. The peasants to whom they said this knew very well that there was an agrarian reform program, that the government was bringing to the villages schools, sewerage and water supply systems, and electricity, and although they had criticisms of the way these things were being done, they would not accept the opposition charges that they were not being done at all.

In spite of the vehemence of their verbal attacks on the Betancout government, the URD and the ARS did not pass over to violent physical attacks on the regime. In contrast, both the Movimiento de Izquierda Revolucionaria and the Partido Comunista de Venezuela did engage in insurrectional attempts against the Betancourt administration. Starting in 1960, they began a campaign of terror in the major cities, which included intermittent rioting, attacks on individual policemen, soldiers, and members of the government parties, and assaults on banks. In May and June, 1962, Communists and MIR adherents participated in revolts by marines at the naval bases of Carúpano and Puerto Cabello; the second revolt was exceedingly bloody.

Beginning early in 1962, they attempted to organize guerrilla warfare against the regime. However, although they were able to organize a number of small and isolated bands, consisting principally of high school and university students, they ran into strong opposition from the peasants, who reported guerrilla activities to the authorities, and sometimes broke up the guerrilla camps themselves.

Although the administration was very loathe to react to the extreme Left opposition's violence by outlawing the MIR and the PCV, President Betancourt took the first step in this direction in May, 1962, after the Carúpano revolt, when he suspended the activities of the two parties indefinitely. After a new outbreak of terrorism in Caracas early in November, 1962, the government officially requested the Supreme Court to cancel the legal recognition of the two parties on the grounds that they had violated the conditions established by law for the functioning of political parties.

The violence continued throughout 1963. The extreme Left opposition blew up a Sears, Roebuck warehouse and other United States-owned enterprises, and also dynamited oil pipelines on several occasions. They set off a bomb in the United States Embassy, and raided the United States military mission. They intensified attacks on policemen and members of the National Guard, killing many members of both groups.

Although during the first months of the increased terrorism, the acts of the extreme Leftists tended to rally public opinion to support of the government, by September, 1963, there were evidences of growing discontent by rank and file citizens over the government's refusal to arrest Communist and MIR members of Congress who were widely regarded as being the organizers of the terrorist campaign, operating behind the protection of their congressional immunity.

The Betancourt government finally cracked down fully on the top PCV and MIR leaders over the last week end of September, 1963. Orders were issued for the arrest of all Communist and MIR members of Congress, and almost all of them were rounded up within a few days. This action of the government won at least tacit support from the democratic opposition groups, who had become convinced that the extreme Leftists were seeking to overthrow not only the Betancourt government but the whole democratic regime.

The violent nature of the opposition of the Left extremists to the Betancourt administration was a serious handicap to the success of the regime. It not only made it necessary for the government to spend essential time and resources to assure the security of the regime, but also induced actions by the government that limited the ability of President Betancourt and his associates to maintain a regime in which the full democratic rights of all citizens were guaranteed.

Chapter Eight

The Military and the Right-Wing Opposition

Throughout most of the country's life as an independent nation, Venezuela has been ruled by military regimes, and most of the Right-wing opposition to the Democratic Revolution was closely associated with disaffected elements of the armed forces. The tradition of government change by armed force is deeply ingrained, and both civilian and military opponents on the Right remained convinced that the way to change governments in Venezuela is by *coup d'état*. Instead of organizing openly in the political arena and vying for public support with other parties, they tended to resort to conspiracies and insurrections.

This seditious Right-wing opposition consisted of various kinds of people. Besides elements of the armed forces who resented the establishment of a civilian and constitutional regime, it included business people who were beneficiaries of the Pérez Jiménez dictatorship, and resented the ending of graft and illicit get-rich-quick schemes by the subsequent administrations. It also included ideologically conservative businessmen and others who were not able to distinguish between Communism and the means to social change advocated by the Betancourt regime.

The most significant thing about the campaign of conspiracy against the government of the Venezuelan Democratic Revolution is that it failed. This is surprising in view of the violent and consistent campaign that the dictatorial regime carried on against both Rómulo Betancourt and the Acción Democrática party between November, 1948, and January, 1958. Both Betancourt and his party were pictured as violent enemies of the country's armed forces. They were alleged to want to destroy the military. They were accused of having tried to organize a civilian militia to supplant the regular armed forces when they were in power from 1945 to 1948. Worse, they were pictured as being antipatriotic, members of an "international conspiracy," and foes of law and order. Furthermore, wild accusations were made concerning the alleged corruption of the Acción Democrática regime of 1945 to 1948.

As a result of this continuous campaign, hostility to AD and Betancourt was widespread within the armed forces by the time the Pérez Jiménez regime was overthrown. The great majority of the officers were highly suspicious of the nature and intentions of Acción Democrática and its leader even after their victory in the December, 1958, election.

If the constitutional regime was to stay in power, it was essential that the loyalty of the armed forces to the new government be assured. Much of the attention of President Betancourt and his associates thus had to be concentrated on dealing with this problem during the early months of the regime.

One of the first moves of Betancourt as President-elect was to announce his absolute conviction that the armed forces would be loyal to their promises to support the winner of the election. He rejected the idea that there would be any move in the barracks to prevent the new government from taking office.

Subsequent to assuming the presidency, Betancourt made it a point to establish as close contact as possible with the officers and men of the armed forces. He visited all of the important barracks of the country, and engaged in frank discussions with soldiers, sailors, and airmen. He expounded on the program of his government, on the need for establishing a tradition of rule by the will of the majority of the electorate instead of by armed revolt, and he expressed his concern for the professional competence and personal welfare of the members of the armed forces.

These extended conversations with the officers and men of the military went far to change the atmosphere in the barracks. The author heard from several military men of the favorable impression that the frankness, apparent honesty, and sincerity of the President made upon people who had previously regarded him as the incarnation of evil. Although these discussions were obviously not sufficient to assure the loyalty of the soldiers to the regime, they did establish an atmosphere in which the military men were willing to be convinced of the need to support the constituted government.

The Betancourt government took special interest in the personal well-being of the members of the armed forces. Living conditions in the barracks had been primitive during the nine years of the dictatorship. As a result of his visits to the military installations, Betancourt became aware of these conditions and, in his capacity as commander in chief of the armed forces, gave orders to clean up and generally improve the quarters of the common soldiers.

Attention was also paid to the living conditions of the professional soldiers, both officers and noncoms. President Betancourt in his message to Congress on March 11, 1961, described one of the major aspects of this part of the government's activities: "A handicap of the officer and noncom, as of any other person in the middle class, is the lack of a house of his own and the payment of rent which weighs heavily on the family budget. Conscious of this, the government, through the Social Security Institute of the Ministry of Defense, has broadened the policy of individual loans to officers and noncoms for the acquisition of their own houses. The increase of this work can be judged by the fact that whereas in 1959 loans to the amount of 8 million bolívares were given, in 1960 some 673 loans for a total of 61 million bolívares were extended. This is a dynamic program which will not be decreased, and it is worth noting that this is in no sense a donation, since amortization and interest are taken out monthly from the pay of the officers and noncoms who benefit. Nor is there any favoritism in the granting of these credits. . . . Priorities are established in accordance with the number of children and other persons who are dependents of the loan applicant." [1]

Betancourt also won the confidence of the armed forces leaders by his interest in and concern for their ability to carry out their military duties. He was always willing to listen to their problems, but having no pretensions to knowledge of things military, he left them free to manage the technical aspects of their jobs.

In spite of being a military-dominated regime, the dictatorship of 1948 to 1958 had not paid great attention to maintaining high technical standards for the armed forces. This the Betancourt regime did, however. General Antonio Briceño Linares, while Commander of the Air Force, explained the government's policy during the first year of the constitutional government: "In order to improve the means of air defense and achieve the objective of self-sufficiency in reconditioning and repairing aeronautical equipment, the national government, within the budgetary limits available, gave us what was prudently calculated as essential to achieve the two objectives mentioned. . . . I wish to use this opportunity to thank the National Executive and the Congress for their interest and willingness to satisfy our needs without grave detriment to economic and social development of the country. . . ."[2]

The appropriations for the military increased somewhat under Betancourt during the first two years of his regime, though less than the combined appropriations for other items in the budget. For the first time in the country's history, military expenditures were smaller than government appropriations for education in the 1960 to 1961 fiscal year. When the budget was generally trimmed in accordance with the stabilization program adopted by the government in the middle of 1961, the Ministry of Defense took its cut along with other parts of the government, and the military men had their salaries cut along with those of civil servants. On July 18, 1961, the Caracas newspaper *La Esfera* carried news of projected cuts of personnel and costs in various of the country's military units as well as in the training schools of the armed forces.

Betancourt won the confidence of the military chiefs by keeping them out of political controversy. On the one hand, he issued strict orders that the officers of the armed forces make no speeches and issue no statements concerning political matters, either for or against attitudes adopted by the government. On the other hand, Betancourt defended his military subordinates whenever they were attacked for political reasons. At the same time, the President kept the armed forces leaders informed of all important government decisions and policies. Although he did not consult them and ask for advice on matters constitutionally outside of their sphere of competence, he did call together the top military leaders periodically to tell them fully about all aspects of the administration's activities.

From the beginning of the provisional government the chiefs of the armed forces promised to assure the holding of a general election for a new constitutional administration, and to support the right of that regime to govern once it was installed. Throughout the year of provisional government, the majority of the military leaders remained loyal to their promises, although there were exceptions. Two serious mutinies occurred during 1958, in July and September.

With the inauguration of Betancourt, the military chiefs again made clear their intention of maintaining the constitutional government in power. General Josué López Henríquez, when interviewed by the daily newspaper *El Nacional* on June 25, 1959, commented as follows on this subject:

"Anyone who attempts a coup against the government is lost. He will not be able to count on the support of the people or the collaboration of the armed forces. Rather he or the adventurers who try something of this sort will encounter the firm decision of the people, as well as the armed forces, to defend liberty and democratic institutions.

"The feeling of the armed forces is this: to defend at all cost democratic institutions. . . . The people and the army stand together in vigilant defense of democracy."

General Antonio Briceño Linares, speaking in December, 1959, discussed the same subject:

"As can be seen, the false redeemers were mistaken again, for when we accepted in a disciplined way the general decision of the government, we did so with the conviction that we were contributing to overcoming the economic lunacies of the previous regime. But, there is more. We men of the High Command are well informed of the magnitude of the calamities inherited from the dictatorship and of the infinity of economic and social problems that this government has to resolve. . . .

"Beware of him who attempts to take from the Venezuelans the invaluable right to govern themselves according to the results of the free elections of the 7th of December of last year, or who attempts to dirty the soil of the fatherland with regressive aspirations. The well-trained armed forces, together with the civilian organizations, will quickly undertake to thwart these dangerous and unhealthy aspirations." [3]

Admiral Carlos Larrazábal, Commander in Chief of the Navy, and brother of the 1958 URD presidential candidate, issued general orders to the men under his command early in January, 1960. These read in part:

"It is stupid, criminal, and unpatriotic to attempt subversive actions against a free regime elected by the people.

"At present we are at a crossroads of history. The nation has a constitutional government elected by the majority of the Venezuelans. That same government, wrestling with all kinds of problems inherited from the previous regime, confronts the personal ambitions of displaced groups, some of them disaffected, others incapable, the rest disqualified for the work of government, and set on acts of violence to bring us to a politico-military emergency of incalculable proportions. Faced with this situation, and bearing in mind the tremendous responsibility resting upon the armed forces, the General Command of the Navy does not vacillate in choosing the road indicated by the traditional oaths of loyalty to the Constitution. . . ."[4]

The loyalty of the armed forces to the government was put to a serious test during the attempts of the extreme Left to organize a popular insurrection against the Betancourt regime in October and November, 1960. Caracas passed through three or four days of rioting and confusion, and in such circumstances the Venezuelan military, traditionally, would have intervened on its own "to save the nation."

On this occasion, however, the military adhered strictly to the standards of discipline demanded by the Constitution and the country's military regulations. They stayed in the barracks until they were called out by the constitutional President, and then they acted strictly in conformity with his orders.

In spite of the loyalty of the great mass of the armed forces, there continued to be some elements among them who were disaffected with the constitutional government. During the first two and a half years of the Betancourt regime there were two serious insurrections, besides many conspiracies that were aborted before they reached the stage of armed mutiny.

The first of these insurrectionary movements occurred early in April, 1960, in the city of San Cristóbal, capital of the mountain state of Táchira. This uprising was led by General Jesús María Castro León, who had been retired from the Air Force during the provisional government because of suspicions concerning his loyalty. From London, Castro León sent a public letter to President Betancourt, accusing him of being a tyrant and of subverting the country. Shortly afterwards Castro León went to the Dominican Republic, where he and his associates were supplied by Generalissimo Trujillo with false Colombian passports. They entered Colombia on these, and from there smuggled themselves across the border to Táchira. Arriving in San Cristóbal, Castro León succeeded in getting the garrison there to join his revolt.

Castro León expected that once he had seized control of the capital of Táchira, the state from which a large part of the officer corps comes, other garrisons and units would rally to his support. His plans were completely frustrated, however, and after holding out for two days, he and the leaders of his insurrection fled. Most of them were captured before they could get across the frontier to Colombia. Castro León was sentenced by a military court to a long period in prison.

The second full-fledged military insurrection occurred in the city of Barcelona, capital of the state of Anzoátegui, in the eastern part of the country, in June, 1961. This movement affected only a part of the garrison, with the majority of the troops remaining loyal. Some civilians, including some local leaders of the Unión Republicana Democrática, collaborated with the insurgents, but the uprising was suppressed in a few hours by the Barcelona garrison itself.

In 1962 there were two attempted insurrections by naval elements. In May, marine corps and naval personnel in the base of Carúpano in eastern Venezuela revolted, but were suppressed when army units were rushed to the scene. A month later a similar uprising occurred at the country's largest naval base at Puerto Cabello. Several days' fighting between naval elements on the one hand, and army units and armed civilians supporting the government on the other, were necessary before this insurrection was suppressed. Casualties amounted to several thousand.

These two naval mutinies differed from previous military insurrections in their liaison with the extreme Left instead of Right-wing civilian groups. Communist party deputy Eloy Torres was captured while seeking to escape in a boat with rebel naval personnel after the collapse of the Carúpano revolt. MIR deputy Simon Sáez Mérida was implicated in the Puerto Cabello insurrection. The PCV and the MIR openly supported both of these revolts.

It is highly significant that in none of these cases was there a movement among the members of the garrisons of Caracas and Maracay, the two largest military installations in the country, to join the rebels. In recent decades all successful uprisings of the armed forces have had their inception in these two groups.

Numerous plots hatched by dissident Right-wing elements failed before they reached the stage of violent action. Moreover, their instigators had little influence on the mass of the armed forces, and the officers who did participate in them were severely punished.

The most serious of all the attempts against the Betancourt regime was the plot to assassinate the President on June 24, 1960. This was mainly a civilian undertaking with the backing of the Trujillo dictatorship in the Dominican Republic; only a handful of retired Venezuelan military men were involved. The President barely escaped from this incident with his life. His military aide, Colonel Ramón Armas Pérez, was killed instantly by the bomb, and the Minister of Defense, General Josué López Henríquez, was severely wounded. Betancourt himself suffered very painful burns on his hands and his face. It was more than six months before he had recovered from these wounds.

There is no doubt that the behavior of Betancourt at the time of this assassination attempt won him wide respect among the military as well as the general population. He displayed great physical courage and a devotion to duty that even his enemies had to admire. Although he was seriously burned himself, his first concern was with the condition of the other people who had been hurt. He took personal charge of the efforts to trace down those who had perpetrated the attempt to murder him.

President Betancourt made a radio address to the nation only twenty-four hours after the attempt on his life. In this simple speech one can gather much of the quality of the man in this crucial moment. In part, he said:

"I am speaking to you from my sick bed. I must be brief. Among the light wounds that I received yesterday was a burn on the lower lip which makes it difficult for me to enunciate my words.

"I wish to say to the people of Venezuela that they must have full confidence in the stability of their government and in the decision of the President that they elected to complete his mandate, as he has been saying, and today says again, until the 19th of April 1964. . . .

"Fellow Citizens: I am going to end; but before I do so, a few reflections. First, that the country must return to its normal activities. The government has control of the situation. The loyalty of the armed forces to the constitutional regime has been reaffirmed on this occasion. Eight hours after the assassination attempt, with my hands bandaged, I came to Miraflores [the presidential palace], because the captain must be with his ship. It is from Miraflores that I am speaking to you, and here, in spite of my temporary ill health, I continue in direct contact with all sectors of the government, both in the city of Caracas and in the rest of the country. . . ."[5]

If the great majority of the armed forces had not been loyal, this would have been the perfect moment for them to overthrow the constitutional regime. As Betancourt himself emphasized, they did not. Speaking a month after the attempt upon his life, President Betancourt said this with regard to the role of the armed forces on June 24: "On the evening of June 24, when I arrived at Miraflores, I met with the military High Command. It was a meeting of a routine nature. There I merely confirmed what I already knew: that this attempt had connections with one or another junior officer, but that the control of the armed forces was in the hands of the Minister of Defense, of the commanders of the four forces, and of the commander in chief of the armed forces, who is the President of the Republic. I cannot deny that there are still ill-adapted, discontented, or murmuring officers; but there is one thing that is very clear in Venezuela: He who conspires in Venezuela against the constitutional regime will not be treated with leniency or with cruelty. But he will be treated in accordance with the Law. . . . I want to guarantee the country that I have confidence in the armed forces and that the control of the armed forces is firmly in the hands of the government."[6]

The reasons for the loyalty of the armed forces to the existing constitutional, democratic, and civilian government are undoubtedly complex. Even the nature of this loyalty on the part of individual officers and soldiers has varied a good deal, from person to person.

By the middle of President Betancourt's term, the officers of the armed forces could roughly be divided into three groups according to loyalty. A sizable element was by that time enthusiastically behind the constitutional regime, for a variety of reasons. A second group, though it did not like President Betancourt and his party, was nonetheless resolved to support the regime, either because it was constitutional and popularly elected, or because the nature of an alternative to the Betancourt administration was to be feared. A third, infinitesimally small group was still hostile to the government and was actively or passively seeking to overthrow it.

Certainly a major factor in influencing the great majority of the military leaders to be loyal to the Betancourt government was the attitude of the general civilian population. After January 23, 1958, there was almost unanimous aversion among civilians to a return to military dictatorial rule. There was general agreement that the principle of democratically elected constitutional government should be firmly established. These attitudes were shared by the majority of people in all classes and social groups. It was inevitable that the military leaders, who by no means live in a vacuum in Venezuela, should be influenced by the widespread consensus among the civilians, whose brothers, offspring, or parents they were. Although popular backing for the constitutional regime became something less than unanimous as President Betancourt's term progressed, it remained clear to the military leaders that it continued to have the support of a great majority of the populace. They were well aware that a new military regime would be violently opposed by most civilians, including many of those opposed to Betancourt.

The traditional attitudes of the military toward civilian regimes were also greatly affected by the widespread disillusionment of the soldiers, sailors, and airmen in the results of the nine-year-long dictatorship of 1948 to 1958. Admiral Carlos Larrazábal has well expressed this feeling:

"The military men and civilians who rebelled, sincerely or maliciously following the mirage of the *coup d'état,* have left a disconcerting heritage, and they await the implacable judgment of posterity. In such wise they destroyed the framework established by human culture and education, in an illusory attempt to create new molds, without listening to the voice of historical experience and forgetting that he who breaks the rules cannot depend upon them. Thus despotism supplanted public debate; the assembly was asphyxiated by selfishness; the economy of all was frustrated by the profits of a few; liberty was destroyed by persecution." [7]

There was widespread recognition that the group around Pérez Jiménez had used power to enrich themselves at the expense not only of the mass of the citizenry but of much of the military personnel as well. Furthermore, the constant change of government by military insurrection resulted in great instability among members of the armed forces. Each new coup resulted in the removal of those in the military who opposed it. Those who sincerely wanted to make their careers in the armed forces came to the conclusion that their only security was to maintain in power a constitutional and elected regime that would honor the ordinary rules governing military service.

Another major element in the support by the armed forces of the Betancourt government was undoubtedly their growing confidence in the President and in those associated with him in running the regime. Many officers were repelled by the demagoguery that Admiral Wolfgang Larrazábal had employed while in the Junta de Gobierno and during his election campaign, and particularly by his flirtation with the Communists. Many of them started out preferring Betancourt as a lesser evil even in December, 1958, and as time went on became convinced that their dislike of him and his party was largely unjustified, and the result of interested propaganda by the Pérez Jiménez people.

One high officer with whom the author talked summed up this change in the attitude of his colleagues toward the President. He said that he had not known Betancourt before he became President, and had had serious doubts about him, but that after two years' close association with him, he challenged anyone to cite instances in which Betancourt had carried out policies or actions contrary to the interests of the armed forces or of Venezuela.

Numerous military leaders positively supported many of the objectives of the government of the Democratic Revolution. There was sympathy for the nationalist aspects of the regime's petroleum policy and for the government's efforts to industrialize the country. Among some there was even understanding of the need for the agrarian reform, the educational program, and other activities of the regime designed to overcome the conditions that bred social unrest and institutional instability.

This attitude was reflected in the cooperation extended by the armed forces on some of these policies. The Armed Forces of Cooperation (Fuerzas Armadas de Cooperación) was particularly involved in aiding the educational program, and especially the campaign against adult illiteracy. In many isolated areas in which the FAC detachment was the only representative of the national government on the scene, the officers and men spent considerable amounts of time in organizing and conducting literacy classes. Throughout the armed forces, the effort to teach draftees to read and write before they left the service was intensified.

The armed forces also established in 1962 the first of several proposed military agricultural schools, to which draftees could go during the last six months of their training. The purpose of these schools was to teach them to be good farmers once they were out of the armed forces. They were to be taught techniques of sowing, ploughing, and reaping, how to operate tractors, and how to care for pigs, chickens, cattle, and bees.

The military also began a program for cooperating with the government's economic development program. Before the Betancourt administration, there had existed only one engineering battalion in the Venezuelan Army, used mainly for training purposes and to build installations for the military themselves. In 1961 a second engineering battalion was organized. It was used for constructing highways, particularly in the Orinoco River Valley. It was planned in time to establish other such units.

There is no doubt, also, that the Cuban Revolution did much to convince the Venezuelan military of the need to support the constitutional regime. The action of the Castro regime in disbanding the traditional Army, then disbanding most of his own Rebel Army, and entrusting military functions largely to a party-controlled militia, had a profound effect on the thinking of the Venezuelan officer group. Whereas the military leaders were aware that with brute force they could overthrow the Betancourt regime at will, the Cuban struggle demonstrated to them that in all likelihood the installation of a new military tyranny would be followed by a guerrilla struggle and civil war, in which the leadership would be assumed by someone more like Fidel Castro than like Rómulo Betancourt. Should such a conflict begin, the guerrillas almost certainly would receive help from Cuba on a sizable scale, and this the Venezuelan Army would be unable to prevent, given the country's long and unprotected coast line.

Hence, many military men felt that they were faced with a situation in which the real alternative to a democratic social revolution such as that being led by Betancourt was not a good old-fashioned military dictatorship but a Fidelista regime. Convinced that such was the case, many officers not otherwise friendly disposed toward the democratic government, chose the "lesser evil" of Betancourt's regime.

This attitude of the military men was of particular importance after the parties of the extreme Left began a campaign of attempted guerrilla warfare and urban terrorism in 1962. Armed forces leaders were perfectly aware of the fact that the extreme Leftists were trying to prevent the successful conduct of the 1963 elections, and to provoke the military into the overthrow of the Betancourt regime. Awareness of these objectives went far to convince the officers that it was to their own and the nation's advantage to allow President Betancourt to handle the situation, and to confine their role to one of backing up his efforts to restore civil peace and to carry out the election and inauguration of his constitutionally and democratically chosen successor.

Finally, the loyalty of the armed forces was reinforced by a thorough purge of disaffected elements. Betancourt was constantly vigilant for the slightest sign of disloyalty, but without creating an espionage system that would itself engender discontent. The numerous plots and insurrection attempts served to expose publicly those who were disaffected with the regime. These were cashiered from the armed forces and were incarcerated. Other officers whose loyalty was doubtful, but against whom there was no concrete evidence of conspiracy, were provided with decorative but harmless posts as military attachés in Venezuelan embassies abroad.

The traditional insistence of the Venezuelan armed forces on dominating the nation's political affairs has changed since the advent of the democratic regime of Rómulo Betancourt. Although some officers were bitterly enough opposed to the regime to conspire against it or even to attempt insurrection, the great majority were at least passively loyal, while a considerable number actually became enthusiastic about the regime.

By contrast, the Right-wing opponents of the Venezuelan Democratic Revolution had not as yet become convinced that the traditional method of opposing and overthrowing a government by *coup d'état* should be abandoned. They continued to seek insurrectionary elements in the armed forces. Hence, constant vigilance was necessary to prevent a small minority of disaffected officers from plotting against the democratic government in favor of another military tyranny of the traditional type.

Chapter Nine

Democracy and Civil Liberties under Betancourt

One of the basic tasks of the Betancourt regime was to try to bring about the fullest possible understanding and observance of the principles of democracy in Venezuela. In its national existence of a century and a half, Venezuela has had little experience with democracy. Since the *coup d'état* and armed insurrection have been the normal methods of changing from one government to another, tradition is on the side of rule by the will and caprice of the incumbent dictator rather than by the law. Until recently, there has been very little in their background that would help the Venezuelan people to comprehend the democratic form of government. Many citizens are still prone to turn to the use of conspiracy with members of the armed forces, and to terrorism, to combat the democratically elected government, just as they did to oppose dictators such as Cipriano Castro, Juan Vicente Gómez, and Marcos Pérez Jiménez. This has been true of both the conservative or Right-wing opponents of the regime, and those on the extreme Left.

Furthermore, a perturbing event of international concern occurred simultaneously with the installation of the democratic constitutional regime in Venezuela: the success of Fidel Castro's rebel forces in Cuba. His example (and advice) inspired many of those who were combating the Betancourt administration from the extreme Left to resort to violent street demonstrations, rioting, vandalism, and other forms of popular insurrection, while plotting guerrilla warfare against the elected government.

Effective democracy implies not only that the government in power will confine its methods of administration to those for which it can be held accountable by the courts and the voters but also that the opposition will limit itself to constitutional methods of criticizing and attacking the regime. Since many of those opposed to the Betancourt administration did not confine their activities to those of a "loyal" opposition willing to operate within the democratic framework, the government was not able to maintain as broad a guarantee of civil liberties at all times as its leaders would have wished.

The surprising fact, on balance, is not that the regime limited certain civil liberties from time to time, but rather that a high degree of individual freedom was maintained in spite of the preference of much of the opposition for conspiracy, terror, and insurrection. Such limitations as were imposed on individual liberty resulted from serious attempts to oust the regime by force, and not from any conviction on the part of President Betancourt and his associates that they were omniscient and therefore entitled to impose their points of view on the people. Quite to the contrary, they felt that their fundamental task was to keep intact the system whereby the people may periodically choose their rulers, and under which those opposed to the group in power may use every peaceful and constitutional means to question the policies and persons in control of the nation.

The leaders of the principal democratic parties saw in 1958 the dangers to political democracy that might result from relentless enmity between the government and parties of the opposition. Even before returning from exile, Rómulo Betancourt of Acción Democrática, Rafael Caldera of the Copei, and Jóvito Villalba of the Unión Republicana Democrática agreed to cooperate; and for this reason they sought for several months in 1958 to reach agreement on a joint candidate for the presidency, and when this failed, backed the establishment of a coalition regime in 1959. Some of the discord that they had feared began to become evident late in 1960 during and after the serious rioting in Caracas, and when the URD withdrew from the government.

It is worth noting that the first pressure on the Betancourt government to curtail democratic freedoms came from the Communists and from those within his own party who later withdrew to form the Movimiento de Izquierda Revolucionaria. Taking their tip from Cuban events, they publicly demanded that Right-wing opponents of the regime who had been caught in conspiratorial movements against the government should be lined up before a firing squad. "Al paredón" (to the wall) became the favorite slogan of these elements, in spite of the fact that even the Pérez Jiménez Constitution forbade capital punishment, and that this ban was kept in the new basic document put into force in 1961.

The writer was witness to this propaganda by the MIR and the Communist party. At the opening meeting of the second conference of the Inter-American Association for Democracy and Freedom, which took place in the Great Hall of the Central University in Caracas, Communists and MIR members had decorated the hall with the "Al paredón" slogan and attempted to shout down various orators by chanting the phrase. The meeting was held a few days after the San Cristóbal uprising of April, 1960.

After the overthrow of Pérez Jiménez it was universally agreed among the leaders and members of the democratic parties that the Constitution drafted under Pérez Jiménez' supervision in 1953 was not a suitable organic law for the establishment of a solid democratic regime. Nevertheless, it was felt that first priority should be given to elections and re-establishment of a popularly chosen regime, after which the Constitution could be revised to suit the changed circumstances.

One of the accomplishments of the Betancourt regime was the elaboration of a new democratic Constitution for Venezuela. The Constitution inherited from the Pérez Jiménez dictatorship concentrated most of the power of the state in the hands of the President of the Republic, who, according to Rómulo Betancourt, had "powers comparable to those of absolute monarchs."[1] It was also characterized by other limitations of political liberty. Of course, in fact, even the democratic provisions of this Constitution were not observed by the dictator.

The Congress elected in December, 1958, was given constituent assembly powers, and through 1959 and 1960 it worked on a new Constitution. This document, unanimously approved by Congress, was promulgated on February 13, 1961, the second anniversary of the inauguration of the democratic regime. The new Constitution limited the powers of the Chief Executive to those commonly prescribed in a presidential form of government. It also provided that no President could be re-elected until ten years (two presidential periods) after the expiration of his previous term. This provision was adopted in spite of the opposition of some of the important figures in the Betancourt government, and the lack of enthusiasm for it upon the part of the President himself.

The document set forth in some detail the political rights of the citizen, as well as individual, social, and economic rights. This section specified the arrangements to be used for elections, to prohibit the packing of electoral tribunals, and to assure voting secrecy.

Like most modern Latin American constitutions, the Venezuelan one of 1961 set forth extensive economic and social programs, for which Congress was instructed to enact appropriate laws. In many cases the programs already existed, but an innovation was Article 105, which provided that: "The existence of latifundia is contrary to the interest of society. The law will provide for their elimination and will establish the mode of giving land to peasants and agricultural laborers who do not possess it, as well as provide for means to make the land productive." The Venezuelan Constitution thus followed the model of the Mexican Constitution of 1917 in incorporating the agrarian reform in the country's basic document.

One issue that had been bitterly discussed during the 1946 to 1947 constitutional convention received relatively little attention during the discussion of 1959 and 1960. This was the question of federalism. The leaders of all of the parties had come to the conclusion that genuine state autonomy within the Venezuelan federal union was both impracticable and undesirable. Thus, the provision of previous Constitutions whereby the governors of the various states were appointed by the President of the Republic was retained virtually without discussion, and it was provided that "the Executive of the State is the agent of the National Executive in its particular jurisdiction." Significantly, too, the change in name of the country from United States of Venezuela to Republic of Venezuela, which Pérez Jiménez had introduced, was retained. The taxing powers of the states were kept very vague.

Finally, the traditional provision of Latin American constitutions for the temporary suspension of certain individual guarantees was retained, though in restricted form. "In case of emergency, of commotion that might perturb the peace of the Republic or of grave circumstances that affect economic or social life," the President and the cabinet are empowered to suspend certain of the constitutional guarantees, but must submit this decision to Congress within ten days of such action. Congress has the right to pass on the validity of their suspension.

Twenty-one and a half months passed before the Betancourt government took steps to suspend certain constitutional guarantees, in spite of the fact that the administration was subject to most violent abuse from opposition papers, particularly from the Communists' *Tribuna Popular,* the MIR's *Izquierda,* and the periodicals of the URD. Street meetings, public demonstrations, and radio and television were likewise used for this purpose. Even the San Cristóbal insurrection in April, 1960, and the attempt on President Betancourt's life on June 24 of the same year, did not provoke the government to interfere with civil liberties. Nor did it take action during the rioting organized in Caracas by the extreme Left in August, 1959, and October, 1960.

In November, 1960, however, the extreme Leftists of the Partido Comunista de Venezuela and the Movimiento de Izquierda Revolucionaria made an all-out attempt to bring about a popular insurrection. Their occasion was a strike of telephone workers and a threatened walkout of bank clerks. The former was submitted to compulsory arbitration in conformity with provisions of the Labor Law dealing with strikes in public utilities. Ostensibly in support of these two walkouts, groups of students, first in the Fermín Toro High School, and later in the Universidad Central in Caracas, began to riot. They burned buses and automobiles, they attacked stores with brickbats and other lethal weapons. Next, the university students under Communist and MIR leadership barricaded themselves within the precincts of their Alma Mater and began to fire on police and soldiers outside. The latter were not permitted by President Betancourt to enter the university grounds, because the law removed that institution from jurisdiction of the ordinary police and the military.

Meanwhile, the leaders of the PCV and the MIR sought to turn the rioting into a full-scale revolt against the government. After MIR leaders of the bank clerks had declared a national general strike of that group, the MIR and PCV members of the executive committee of the Confederación de Trabajadores de Venezuela issued a call for a revolutionary general strike against the government. Domingo Alberto Rangel and other extreme Leftist leaders published proclamations calling for a popular insurrection.

It is not clear whether the extreme Leftist leaders thought that they had sufficient support from the masses of the workers and peasants of Venezuela to induce these to go into the streets to overthrow the regime. More likely, the Communists and the MIR hoped that they could cause such disorder, confusion, and chaos in the capital city that the leaders of the armed forces would turn against the Betancourt government as "weak" and "incompetent to maintain public order," and would then establish a new military regime. The theory of the extreme Leftists would seem to have been that the setting up of such a regime would be advantageous to them, since it would make it possible for them to gain support among peasants and workers who backed the regime as long as Betancourt remained in power. Whatever their thinking, the extreme Leftists made a serious miscalculation which subsequently cost them dearly.

President Betancourt remained firm but cautious. For four days he allowed the insurrectionary events to run their course. The bank strike frittered out after one day, and there was virtually no response to the call for a revolutionary general walkout; however, the rioting continued, particularly in the vicinity of the university and some of the principal high schools. The casualties in this rioting were considerable, both among the rioters and among the police and National Guardsmen who were attempting to deal with the disorder. Finally, Betancourt ordered units of the regular Army into the streets of Caracas, and within a few hours the uprising had been suppressed. At the same time, the cabinet officially proclaimed a state of emergency and suspended several constitutional guarantees, including freedom of the press, freedom of assembly, and freedom from seizure.

This first suspension of guarantees continued in effect for almost a year and a half. This occasioned a good deal of soul-searching among members and leaders of the two government parties, Acción Democrática and the Copei, and gave the opposition a chance to challenge the sincerity of the democratic pretensions of the regime. The issue of suspension was discussed continuously by the opposition, and the Unión Republicana Democrática weekly paper *U.R.D.* published in large type in each issue the number of days the suspension had lasted. The issue came up for particularly bitter discussion at the end of January, 1961, when Congress debated the matter and upheld the suspension on a strictly party vote, with Acción Democrática and the Copei supporting the measure, and the URD, the PCV and the MIR voting against it.

The opposition used every conceivable occasion to criticize the government on this score. The Minister of the Interior, Luis Dubuc, was summoned before Congress upon several occasions to explain and defend his use of the powers given to the government as a result of the suspension of guarantees. Typical of the attacks is the following comment from a speech by MIR deputy Jorge Dáger, published in the July, 1961, issue of the magazine *Pensamiento Revolucionario,* organ of the National Propaganda Commission of the MIR, which was freely circulating at the time: "Logically, the opposition knows perfectly well that a blow against one party of the opposition is a blow against all the parties of the opposition. Furthermore, we know that a blow against a party of the opposition is a blow against democracy, against free institutions, is a blow against the people. It is, simply and clearly, the continuation of the repressive policy that has been launched by the government, from which it will be impossible for it to free itself until such time as it decides to carry out an authentically popular program, an authentically democratic program respectful of the institutions that this same regime says it is defending and says it wants to make respected. . . .

". . . If we have said it once, we have said it a thousand times, that the indefinite suspension of guarantees, the total limitation of rights for the sectors of the opposition, the arbitrary strangulation of the rights that we Venezuelans have acquired through struggle, dedication, and effort, can lead to nothing other than the conversion of this government into a despotic and dictatorial government. . . . The only difference that we who have a permanent and consistent revolutionary and democratic line can see between the repression carried out by Pérez Jiménez' dictatorship and the repression carried out by the present government is that the Pérez Jiménez repression was carried out by a dictator who admitted that he was a dictator . . . and that the repression of the present time is carried out by a regime which says that it is defending democracy but suspends constitutional guarantees indefinitely, thus submerging and extinguishing democracy. . . ."

The Communists attempted to dramatize their opposition by filing a petition with the Supreme Court. As secretary-general of the Communist party, Gustavo Machado accused the National Guard of illegally seizing the building and equipment of the Communist newspapers *Tribuna Popular* and *Dominguito*. He further demanded that President Betancourt and Minister of the Interior Luis Dubuc be deposed on the grounds that they had violated the constitution. The Supreme Court unanimously rejected the petition of Machado.[2]

Perhaps the government's best defense of its position was a statement made by President Betancourt in his 1961 New Year's Message:

"For less significant and dangerous attempts to overthrow the government than those confronted by Venezuela, those responsible have suffered the ultimate penalty of the firing squad in some other countries of America. In Venezuela, we have not proceeded in this way, nor shall we do so, because we have laws, judges, and tribunals in whose efficacy to adjudicate any kind of delinquency we have full faith.

"Similar kinds of antigovernmental violence have occurred in other countries of Latin America. . . . It is well known by all Venezuelans and Americans that particularly in those countries which have in recent years been freed of dictatorships, the new regimes resulting from popular election have been under constant and coincident fire of a pincer movement coming from those displaced from dictatorial power and those who have exploited and continue to exploit the difficulties and economic and social maladjustments inherited from the regimes of force to discredit the representative regime before the workers, peasants, and students, so as to permit the totalitarian minorities to seize power and impose governments subservient to the world-wide political strategy of the Soviet Union.

"Understanding these generally known facts, the government over which I preside has not sought to elude its responsibilities. . . . Various constitutional guarantees are restricted and will remain restricted until a climate of peace and cooperation among the citizenry has been achieved. . . ."[3]

As a result of government investigation of the causes and development of the 1960 rioting, the police and prosecutors brought charges against the leader of the Movimiento de Izquierda Revolucionaria, Deputy Domingo Alberto Rangel, and Communist Deputy Teodoro Petkoff. The lower courts decided that there was sufficient basis for bringing the two men to trial; however, since they enjoyed congressional immunity from prosecution, the data concerning them had to be passed to the Supreme Court. Once it had upheld the decision of the lower tribunal, the Supreme Court, in conformity with the new Constitution, requested Congress to lift the immunity of the two deputies and permit them to be brought to trial.

The Chamber of Deputies debated the matter for several weeks until its regular session came to an end late in July, 1961. Subsequently, it was taken up by the Permanent Commission of Congress, a body in which both houses were represented and which was empowered by the Constitution to deal with such problems when the two houses were not in session. A Chamber of Deputies committee which first studied the problem recommended that the Chamber refuse to lift the immunity of Rangel, but lift it in the case of Petkoff. The argument of the committee was that the crimes with which Rangel was charged amounted merely to the expression of opinion (he was accused of having called for a revolt against the government), whereas the allegations against Petkoff were that he had actually participated in and led attacks on stores and had helped to burn vehicles. The opinion of the committee of the Chamber was upheld by the Permanent Commission of Congress, and during the last week of August, 1961, this commission decided to lift the immunity of Petkoff. He was subsequently jailed.

Most constitutional guarantees were restored in December, 1961. The government had announced its intention to restore full constitutional rights a month earlier, but the extreme Left organized riots in the streets of Caracas just before this was due to occur, and as a result the President postponed the move. Left-wing opposition papers began to appear regularly as soon as constitutional rights were restored.

Full guarantees were restored on April 1, 1962, but when the Carúpano naval mutiny occurred early in May, they were suspended again. After considerable agitation, guarantees were again fully restored on August 1, 1962. The pattern was repeated early in November, when the extreme Left again launched a campaign of personal terrorism and attacks on banks and other institutions. President Betancourt and the cabinet again partially suspended constitutional guarantees, and these remained suspended during the intensified extreme Leftist terrorism campaign during the following year. Meanwhile, the government began a move before the Supreme Court to have the Movimiento de Izquierda Revolucionaria and the Partido Comunista de Venezuela declared illegal. The court had not rendered a final decision by the end of the Betancourt administration.

Although the enemies of the Betancourt regime sought to draw a picture of complete destruction of civil liberties in Venezuela during the periods in which constitutional guarantees were suspended, this is great exaggeration. The basic elements of Venezuela's democratic structure remained intact, in spite of the repeated partial restriction of civil liberties.

Even under the Pérez Jiménez Constitution, Betancourt characterized his use of the extensive powers it provided as being such "that only the perturbers of public order and the enemies of the democratic regime could have been affected. A prime example of this is the fact that those involved in the [assassination] attempt of June 24 [1960] were turned over to the ordinary courts, and there has been the extraordinary case in Venezuelan history that four judges proclaimed themselves incompetent to sit on this case."[4]

The principal limitations of democratic rights were four in number. First, outdoor political meetings were forbidden without government permission. Second, the freedom of the press was limited. Third, the government was free to raid homes and offices without warrant. Finally, the government was able to arrest people without being obliged to bring them before the courts in a given period of time. Each of these is worth some discussion.

The limitation on outdoor meetings was generally enforced during the periods of suspension of guarantees. Exceptions were made only on May Day, and a few other occasions. Until the beginning of the 1963 presidential election campaign, the ban applied to meetings of both opposition and government parties, and upon occasion unauthorized gatherings sponsored by one or another of the government parties were banned or broken up by the police. However, when the campaign began, the government allowed the supporters of all seven presidential candidates to hold meetings, both indoors and in the streets, although government authorization was still required for the latter.

The suspension of guarantees interfered little if at all with indoor meetings held by any of the country's political groups. Even party conventions were held by opposition parties, including the Communists, without any difficulties being put in their way by the government, during the first suspension of guarantees. At least until the Carúpano revolt, the normal internal life of the parties was little influenced by the suspension. At that time the PCV and the MIR were declared "suspended" by the government, and all of their headquarters were closed. The suspension of these two parties continued even during periods in which constitutional guarantees were restored.

Interference with the freedom of press affected the Communist daily paper *Tribuna Popular* and the MIR weekly *Izquierda,* which were closed down during the first suspension period, and regular radio and television programs of these opposition parties, which were banned. This by no means meant that the Left-wing opposition parties ceased to communicate with the general public. The Communists and the MIR were able to publish newspapers through the device of naming members of Congress as their editors and publishers. Since they enjoyed parliamentary immunity, the government could not touch them. Such newspapers appeared under various names. For instance, the PCV issued the weekly *Gaceta* as the "organ of the parliamentary faction" of the party. Also, there was little or no government interference at this time with mimeographed internal bulletins of these two parties. They also published numerous pamphlets as well as regular editions of the PCV's *Principios* and the MIR's *Pensamiento Revolucionario.* Other extreme Left opposition periodicals appeared in the interior.

Even more important were other outlets not officially associated with the extreme Left. The periodicals of the Unión Republicana Democrática were not suppressed. They continued to publish violent attacks on the government, including guest articles by members of the two extreme Left opposition parties, and articles written by URD members but presenting extreme Leftist views. Furthermore, the daily newspaper *El Nacional* continued to publish regular articles by MIR and Communist leaders, including Domingo Alberto Rangel, Rodolfo Quintero, and Salvador de la Plaza. Members of various opposition groups appeared as guest speakers on radio and television programs.

The Right-wing opposition to the Betancourt government also continued to criticize the government vigorously through the press. Characteristic of this criticism was an editorial in the very conservative paper *La Esfera,* on August 13, 1961, which commented as follows on the first half of President Betancourt's term of office: "*La Esfera,* dedicated to telling the truth whatever it is, cannot be misled by the satisfaction over the maintenance of constitutional government, to hide what has occurred in economic and fiscal affairs and in the public administration—which could not be worse. Thus, although it is certain that our words will not please the government, since it is not the line of this periodical to say things to please or displease, but to call bread bread and wine wine, we must say what is thought and said by people throughout the Republic.

"It is a shame that in making an inventory of these thirty months we must recognize that these have been two and a half years of blind beating about, of making theories and conducting sterile discussions, instead of carrying out the work that Venezuela was hoping for and still hopes for. We don't think that it will be said that we are conspirators because we use the right of saying the truth to declare that the maneuverings of the parties, some responsible for the government and others trying to take advantage of the tumult, have been terrible both for the economy of the country and for the good administration of the state. . . .

". . . Measures and countermeasures have multiplied like insects: vacillation, inefficiency in the carrying out of accords and decisions, always undertaken a year too late, personal feuds over a job for one individual or another, continuous disavowals, and in all of this confusion, a flood of public expenditures spent on useless and even unofficial things. . . ."

The government's ability to raid homes and offices without warrant had more serious results. Communists and MIR adherents protested on several occasions during the first suspension of guarantees about raids on their party headquarters in various parts of the country and on the homes of some of their leaders. The government claimed to have found arms on such occasions, but at least once Minister of the Interior Dubuc had to defend these raids on interrogation by Congress.

Finally, arbitrary arrest was used. One Communist leader told the writer that some 30,000 people had been jailed by the government between February, 1959, and July, 1961. This was without doubt a gross exaggeration, but certainly several hundred people were jailed by the government in suppressing street demonstrations and in making occasional raids on PCV and MIR headquarters.

During virtually all of the Betancourt administration, Congress continued to function normally. It was used as a favorite platform by both Left- and Right-wing opposition to lambaste the government, to vilify ministers, and to criticize acts of the Executive. Until the end of September, 1963, no congressman was arrested, except the Communists' Teodoro Petkoff and Eloy Torres and the MIR leader Simón Sáez Mérida, who were directly incriminated in insurrectional activities. The first two were only jailed after the Chamber of Deputies had lifted their parliamentary immunity; Sáez Mérida was left alone when the Chamber refused to do so.

However, the intensified terrorism campaign of the extreme Left in August and September, 1963, finally convinced the government of the necessity for arresting all Communist and MIR members of Congress, and such a move was undertaken at the end of September. By that time the last session of the Congress elected in December, 1958, had been completed, and the election campaign was fully under way. The government's action aroused virtually no opposition among the democratic opposition parties.

These democratic opponents of the Betancourt regime, as well as most other nongovernmental institutions, felt relatively little impact from the suspension of guarantees. The trade unions, peasant unions, professional associations, and similar bodies held their meetings and conventions, held elections, negotiated collective agreements, and conducted other normal business without impediment. Opposition party members were active in all of these. There was no attempt to use the suspension of constitutional guarantees to conduct a purge of these institutions, or otherwise to influence their decisions or activities.

The limitations imposed upon civil liberties by the Betancourt regime were necessitated by the unwillingness of the opposition groups of both extreme Left and extreme Right to apply constitutional and democratic methods in their struggle against the regime, and do not reflect any lack of belief in democracy on the part of government leaders. Even though the government several times suspended some provisions of the Constitution, it did not use all the power such suspension automatically gave it. It tried to avoid interfering with individual liberties more than necessary to assure the regime's security.

The democratic nature of the Betancourt regime was demonstrated by its conduct of the December, 1963, election. One of the most important political objectives of the regime was successfully to carry through the election for President, Congress, the state legislatures and municipal councils, and to turn over the administration to the victor. Never in the country's history had a democratically elected government served out its full term and given up power to a duly elected successor.

The extreme Left understood very well the importance for the Betancourt government of the 1963 election, if the administration was to maintain its bona fides as a democratic regime. The Leftists therefore brought their terrorist campaign to a peak in the last days of November. They announced a "curfew" of their own, threatening that anyone on the streets after dark on the two nights before the election would be murdered, and provoked severe shooting incidents in various parts of Caracas. The people of Caracas, and of all Venezuela, however, indicated their repudiation of the extremists by totally ignoring the "curfew," and turning out in unprecedented numbers on election day.

The election campaign lasted throughout most of the year 1963. Its first phase consisted of long and detailed maneuvers among various parties and prospective candidates of both the government and opposition camps. It did not become clear until the second half of the year who the candidates would be.

Important elements in Acción Democrática and the Copei were anxious to see nomination of a joint candidate for President by the two parties. President Rómulo Betancourt particularly favored thus continuing into the electoral field the government coalition which had continued throughout his administration.

As early as August, 1962, the Copei officially suggested that the two parties agree upon a nominee who did not belong to either; however, Acción Democrática quickly rejected this idea, arguing that this would be a step backwards for Venezuelan democracy. (Acción Democrática leaders had been willing to accept a nonpartisan candidate in 1958 as a compromise among all the democratic parties, when their relative strength was by no means clear.) The AD chiefs argued that the firm establishment of democracy in Venezuela required the growth of a tradition of party government with full freedom for the voters to alternate the parties in control of the government. Thus, to follow a party-controlled administration by one which did not rest firmly on the support of a party would be retrocession, not progress toward democracy. Furthermore, they argued that as the majority party, AD had the right to have the coalition nominee chosen from its ranks.

During almost a year negotiations between Acción Democrática and the Copei continued. They resulted in several postponements of the national conventions of the two parties. That of Acción Democrática was first scheduled for January, 1963, but was not held until the end of July.

Four candidates were most widely discussed for the AD nomination. One of these was Raúl Leoni, national president of the party and former President of Congress. The second was Gonzalo Barrios, like Leoni a founder of Acción Democrática, and leader of the party in the Chamber of Deputies. The third was Juan Pablo Pérez Alfonso, Minister of Mines and Petroleum. Shortly before the party convention, the candidacy of Carlos Andrés Pérez, Minister of the Interior, a member of the younger generation of party leaders, also gained considerable support.

President Betancourt suggested that the party convention should not make a final decision on the candidate, but rather should authorize the national committee of the party to choose any from half a dozen possible nominees to be authorized by the Convention. It was widely reported that he felt that Leoni, the leading possibility as AD nominee, would not be appropriate because of strong Copei opposition to his candidacy. However, when the Acción Democrática convention was held, the delegates rejected President Betancourt's advice, and nominated Raúl Leoni as their candidate for President. His victory was due largely to the influence of the party's trade union and peasant leaders, who strongly supported him.

The nomination of Leoni, whom the Copei leaders had clearly indicated that they could not support, assured that there would be no electoral coalition between Acción Democrática and the Copei. Shortly after the AD convention, the Copei held its own, and named its veteran leader Rafael Caldera for the presidency for the third time.

Nevertheless, failure of the two parties to unite in the election did not bring an end to the coalition. Copei ministers continued in the cabinet of President Betancourt, and party leaders continued in governorships and other key positions. Furthermore, candidate Leoni hastened to say that if he won the presidency, he would invite the Copei to continue in the administration.

If the electoral position of the coalition was a strange one, with two rival candidates seeking the presidency, that of the opposition was even more confused. Five declared candidates sought election as avowed opponents of the Betancourt regime.

The first candidate of all was Jóvito Villalba. He announced as early as July, 1962, that he was to be his party's nominee for President. It was almost a year before the Unión Republicana Democrática got around formally to nominating him. However, throughout the year and a half preceding the election, Villalba actively campaigned throughout the country.

Villalba's nomination was not without opposition in URD ranks. There was an element in the party which toyed with the idea of supporting Admiral Wolfgang Larrazábal once again, and organizing around him a united campaign of all opposition forces. Villalba stole a march on this faction by the early announcement of his candidacy. Throughout the campaign, Villalba gave considerable evidence that he thought that he had a very good chance of winning the election.

Admiral Larrazábal hesitated considerably before announcing his candidacy, as he had done in 1958; however, his proponents were very active on his behalf as early as July, 1962, when the small Movimiento Electoral Nacional Independiente (MENI), headed by Admiral (ret.) Carlos Larrazábal, Wolfgang's brother, and Jorge Dáger's equally small Frente Democrático Popular, both announced that they would nominate him. It was almost a year before Larrazábal formally announced his candidacy.

The principal conservative opposition to the AD-Copei coalition came from the forces that gathered around Arturo Uslar Pietri. He was an important literary figure as well as the head of the ARS advertising firm and a successful businessman. He had been a leading official of the Medina Angarita regime in the early 1940's, and had been elected senator on the Unión Republicana Democrática ticket in 1958.

For some time, Uslar Pietri had been advocating a return to the policy of granting new concessions to foreign oil companies. He was also highly critical of other aspects of the Betancourt government's economic policy. His objections reflected a considerable body of opinion among the country's businessmen. During the 1963 presidential campaign much of his support came from that group.

The AD-ARS (which had split from the main body of Acción Democrática in part at least over the ambitions of its leader Senator

Raúl Ramos Giménez to be the party's presidential nominee) named Ramos Giménez as the ARS candidate; however, his party split during the campaign. Peasant leader Ramón Quijada, who had to a very large degree been responsible for the split in AD, broke with ARS and announced his support for Arturo Uslar Pietri.

Finally, there was the candidate of the extreme Right-wing opposition to the Betancourt administration. This was Germán Borregales, nominee of the Movimiento de Acción Nacional. This small party had been carrying on an intense campaign against the Betancourt regime on the grounds of its suspected "Communism."

The campaign was extremely active, if not violent. The various candidates scoured the country from one end to the other. The walls of buildings throughout the republic were plastered with posters supporting one or another of the nominees. Radio and television were widely used by all of the candidates. Various programs of the "meet the press" type featured the office-seekers of the various parties for months before the election. Although before the arrest of the principal Communist and MIR leaders at the end of September members of those parties tried to break up campaign meetings, including those of the Unión Republicana Democrática, such activities were less in evidence thereafter.

The administration of the electoral machinery was in the hands of the Junta Electoral Nacional, provided for in the Constitution and chosen by Congress. It included representatives of Acción Democrática, the Copei, the Unión Republicana Democrática, ARS, and the Communists, and supporters of the government were in a minority in the Junta. In spite of this, the Betancourt government did not interfere with the functioning of the group. Only once was there any indication of possible government interference with the functioning of the Junta Electoral Nacional. Late in August Alipio Ugarte Pelayo, a URD member of the Junta, was arrested, under accusation of plotting against the regime. However, other members of the body refused to function until Ugarte Pelayo had been released. He was quickly cleared by the courts of suspicion of conspiracy, and returned to his post on the Junta.

The election was held on December 1, 1963. Ninety per cent of the voters went to the polls. As many observers had foreseen, the victor was Raúl Leoni, candidate of Acción Democrática, who received a total of 957,699 votes, or 32.8 per cent of the total. Rafael Caldera, of the Copei, came in second, with 589,372 votes, or 20.2

per cent of the total. Jóvito Villalba of the Unión Republicana Democrática, came in third, with 551,120 votes, or 18.9 per cent of the total. The other nominees received the following votes and percentages: Uslar Pietri, 469,240 votes, or 16 per cent; Admiral Wolfgang Larrazábal, 275,304 votes, or 9.4 per cent; Raúl Ramos Giménez, of ARS, 66,837 votes, or 2.3 per cent; and Germán Borregales, candidate of the Movimiento de Acción Nacional, came in last with 9,324 votes, or .3 per cent of the total.

The results of the election of members of Congress assured the AD-Copei coalition control of that body. The number of members of each body elected by the various parties was as follows:

	Senate	*Chamber of Deputies*
Acción Democrática	23	65
Copei	9	40
Unión Republicana Democrática	7	29
Uslar Pietri supporters	5	22
ARS	1	6
MENI and FDP	4	16
Partido Socialista Venezolano	—	1

The importance of the results of the December 1 election could hardly be exaggerated. They demonstrated the faith of the Betancourt government in the democratic process. They showed that the voters still supported the Democratic Revolution. They indicated that the process of social change and economic development was to have another chance to continue under the aegis of the democratic political system.

Chapter Ten

Foreign Policy of the Revolution

The foreign policy of the Betancourt government was consistent with its general outlook and its internal policy; however, this part of the Betancourt government's program was very heavily criticized by the opposition, particularly by the extreme Left.

Rómulo Betancourt was the chief architect of his government's foreign policy. According both to the Constitution of 1961 and to its predecessor document, the conduct of foreign relations is the prerogative of the President of the Republic, and President Betancourt made full use of his constitutional powers in this respect. This was particularly the case after the resignation in August, 1960, of Dr. Ignacio Luis Arcaya, the Unión Republicana Democrática leader who was the first Foreign Minister of the constitutional government.

The fundamental objectives of the foreign policy of the Betancourt regime were clear. First, the President sought to promote the country's independence, particularly in the economic field. Second, he sought to use Venezuela's influence to aid the cause of political democracy and national independence throughout America and the world. Third, he sought to strengthen Latin American solidarity.

An analysis of the conduct of foreign relations by the Betancourt government must take account of the posture of Venezuela in the world and of Venezuela's relations with the United States, with the

Soviet Union and its satellites and allies, with the rest of Latin America, and with the underdeveloped countries outside of the Western Hemisphere.

The Betancourt regime made no secret of its general position in world affairs. Acting on the conviction that it had an important role to play among the countries currently attempting to achieve rapid economic development and industrialization, it sought to form a united front with several of these nations on certain economic issues and sought to establish a degree of political solidarity with others. Nevertheless, the government of the Venezuelan Democratic Revolution refused to join any "third camp" in the general world line-up. Its sympathies clearly were with the West in its struggle with the Communist bloc.

The Betancourt regime's objective in forming a united front with the Arab countries was to maintain the price of the product that they all export, petroleum. Venezuelan initiative was largely responsible for the formation of the Organization of Petroleum Exporting Countries (OPEC) in 1960. The Betancourt administration also negotiated with iron-exporting nations to establish a similar organization among them. Venezuela's action was thus not that of a government subservient to the United States.

The Venezuelan democratic regime also indicated its support for the aspirations for independence of territories still under colonial rule. This attitude was most palpable in the Betancourt government's support for the independence of the British colonies of the Caribbean area, but in the United Nations and elsewhere, the Betancourt regime made clear its backing of independence movements in colonies in other parts of the world as well.

Although it fostered the most friendly possible relations with the developing countries, unlike most of them, the Betancourt regime refused to assume a neutralist position in world affairs. The President and other leaders of the regime reiterated over and over again their belief in democracy and their desire to work as closely as possible with the United States and other Western powers. Thus, in addressing the National Chamber of Industrialists on January 31, 1961, President Betancourt commented: "In Venezuela we have a regime which constitutionally respects the right to private property, which is moving toward social justice through an evolutionary revolution (and the terms are neither mutually exclusive nor contradictory), and a government which is frankly and decidedly part of the Western World."[1]

There was some disagreement concerning the extent to which this policy should go. There was a certain sympathy, particularly in the Acción Democrática party, for establishing closer political relations between Venezuela and the neutral states. This difference of opinion within the government ranks emerged over the question of whether or not Venezuela should attend the two conferences of "uncommitted" states, organized under Jugoslav sponsorship and held in Cairo and Belgrade during 1961. Venezuela was invited, and for some weeks it was reported that the republic would send an observer to the Cairo session; however, President Betancourt decided to the contrary, and no Venezuelan representative attended the session.

President Betancourt's decision on the Cairo conference was openly challenged by his own party. The national executive committee of Acción Democrática formally announced that it favored Venezuela's being represented in Cairo, but added that it recognized the constitutional right of the President to determine the nation's foreign policy, and that in any case Betancourt was not considered to be under party discipline with regard to this matter.

The economic position, political influence, and military power of the United States in the Western Hemisphere are so great that the relations of each of the other twenty republics with the outside world are perforce predicated in large part on its attitude toward the nation to the north. The increasing commitment of the United States as a world power during the last quarter of a century, and its interest in having the support of the Latin American nations, first against the Nazi-Japanese combination and then against the Soviet Union and its satellites and allies, have made this problem acute for all of the Latin American countries.

This is particularly the case with regard to Venezuela, whose economic relations with the United States have been especially close. United States-owned oil companies dominate the petroleum industry, which provides 90 per cent of the country's foreign exchange; and United States firms control the iron mining industry, which provides most of the rest. The bulk of Venezuela's trade is conducted with its powerful northern neighbor. Furthermore, the United States has long supplied most of the matériel for the Venezuelan armed forces, and has trained these forces as well. Traditionally, Venezuela has tended to align itself with the United States, regardless of what kind of government was in power in either republic.

Rómulo Betancourt and his associates were fully cognizant of the importance of the close relationship that had existed over long decades between Venezuela and the United States; however, they sought to evolve a different kind of policy from that which had traditionally governed their country's relations with the powerful English-speaking neighbor. They followed a course of behavior that was generally friendly, but not subservient to the United States.

The orientation of the Betancourt government in its relations with the United States was consistent with the policy laid down by the first convention of Acción Democrática after the fall of Pérez Jiménez, in August, 1958. The general statement of party principles adopted at that meeting included the following paragraph concerning Venezuelan-United States relations:

"AD considers that Venezuela, and Latin America in general, has an economic and geopolitical community of interest with the country of greatest power in the hemisphere: the United States. This community of interest determines the system of relations in which the United States needs Latin America and Latin America needs the United States. That system of relations should be maintained on a defined and clear basis which does not involve colonial-type submission or permanent conflict. AD, yesterday and today, has criticized the negative aspects of the foreign policy of the United States in its relations with Venezuela and with the rest of America, and has recognized the favorable aspects of that policy, when they have been manifested. But it has done so and will continue to do so in its own language and style . . . because if we deny that Venezuela can be a satellite of the United States, we equally reject the idea that a Venezuelan political party could become an ideological satellite of the Soviet Union, and that it could function as a chessboard pawn in the international strategy of the so-called Eastern Bloc." [2]

The Betancourt government endeavored to maintain a position of dignity with regard to the United States. The leaders of the regime reiterated upon various occasions that they had no intention of engaging in "blackmail" with the United States. Their position with regard to world affairs was taken on the basis of principle and ideological conviction; and they would not base their attitude on any question on what the United States was or was not willing to extend to Venezuela in terms of economic aid.

Although maintaining a generally friendly attitude towards the United States, the government of Betancourt did not hesitate to disagree publicly with the North Americans when its policies were opposed to theirs. This occurred on several occasions with regard to the problem of the Trujillo regime in the Dominican Republic. Before the San José Conference of American Foreign Ministers in the summer of 1960 the Venezuelan government made clear its unhappiness over the hesitancy of the United States to back sanctions against the Trujillo regime. Later, when the United States increased the Dominican quota in the United States sugar market in spite of the partial blockade voted in San José, the Betancourt regime was strong in its denunciation of this act.

In 1962, when the governments of Arturo Frondizi in Argentina and Manuel Prado in Peru were overthrown by military coups, the Betancourt administration again followed policies that diverged from that of the United States. Although the United States recognized both new regimes, Betancourt refused to maintain diplomatic relations with either of these countries until constitutionally elected governments were established in Peru on July 28, 1963, and in Argentina on October 12, 1963. Nor did Betancourt recognize the regimes in Ecuador and Guatemala which took over by force early in 1963, although the United States hastened to grant them recognition.

On the problem of the commercial treaty between the two nations the Venezuelan regime also showed its independence of the United States. When Betancourt was inaugurated, his intention was to seek a revision of the existing treaty, which had been signed by Pérez Jiménez and was held by many Venezuelans to limit the possibility of Venezuelan industrialization. When this proved to be too long a process, the Venezuelan government proceeded to put into effect a policy of exceedingly liberal interpretation of the treaty, a policy that after some hesitation was accepted by the United States Embassy and the Department of State in Washington.

The Betancourt regime took the lead among Latin American governments in welcoming the Alliance for Progress program of President John F. Kennedy. This program suggested a joint effort of the Latin American countries and the United States to foster social change and rapid economic development in the Latin American republics. It was agreed that countries wishing to qualify for aid under the program should plan their economic growth, and enact agrarian and tax reforms if such were not already under way.

The author heard Minister of Commerce Lorenzo Fernández, who headed the Venezuelan delegation to the special meeting of the Economic and Social Council of the Organization of American States held in August, 1961, at Punta del Este, Uruguay, explain that the Venezuelan government regarded the Alliance for Progress as developed at that conference to represent a fundamental change in United States policy toward Latin America. It was a basic commitment, Fernández argued, to give long-needed aid to the economic development of the area. Since the Latin Americans had been asking for such a change for over a decade, he concluded that they could not possibly do anything but welcome it.

The Venezuelan delegation to Punta del Este took a prominent part in organizing the details of the Alliance for Progress. It cooperated closely with the United States delegation in assuring that agrarian reform and equitable tax systems were incorporated in the over-all structure of the program agreed upon at this inter-American conference.

At the time of the adoption of the Alliance for Progress at Punta del Este, Venezuela already fulfilled one qualification for receiving aid under the program, because of the agrarian reform law on the books. In 1962 a new tax law was passed, and early in 1963 Venezuela submitted its development plan. During the Betancourt administration, the country received aid for rural housing, sewerage and water supply systems, and other projects under the Alliance.

Two basic factors influenced the Betancourt regime's policy toward the U.S.S.R.: first, the general orientation of the Venezuelan government in world affairs, a position basically opposed to the ambitions and policies of the Soviet Union regime; second, the relationship between the two nations as leading world producers of petroleum.

Although the Betancourt regime maintained frequent informal contact with the Soviet Union, it did not re-establish diplomatic relations with the U.S.S.R., which had been broken off after World War II. The President by no means ruled out the possibility of re-establishing relations, however, and such a move was officially supported by Acción Democrática, although the Copei did not favor it.

More important than the issue of recognition was the problem presented to Venezuela by the Soviet Union's petroleum production. By the early 1960's the U.S.S.R. was beginning to export oil in considerable quantities, particularly to Western Europe. The Venezuelan government feared that these Soviet Union sales, which were on terms more favorable to the customers than those under which Venezuelan oil was sold, would begin seriously to undermine the position of Venezuelan petroleum in West European markets.

The answer of the Venezuelan regime was to enter into negotiations with the Soviet Union on the matter. Informal contacts were made, and in the middle of 1961 Minister of Mines and Petroleum Juan Pablo Pérez Alfonso visited Moscow. He sought assurances that the Soviet Union would not engage in a dumping policy, and also sounded out the possibility of the U.S.S.R.'s joining the Organization of Petroleum Exporting Countries. Although he received no assurances on the latter score, Pérez Alfonso returned from Moscow with optimistic comments on the Soviet Union's willingness to limit its exports to Venezuela's established customers. Subsequently, the Soviet Union did cooperate informally with OPEC.

Conscious of their role as leaders of the democratic Left in Latin America, the leaders of the Venezuelan Democratic Revolution endeavored to cultivate their relations with individuals, parties, and governments that they considered to be their counterparts in other Latin American countries. They also put themselves and their government in firm opposition to subversion by dictatorships, of either the Right or the Left, of the movement toward social change and political democracy.

Thus, the parties in the government served as hosts to the second conference of the Inter-American Association for Democracy and Freedom, an organization of which Rómulo Betancourt was a founder in its first conference in Havana in 1950. The second conference met in Caracas and Maracay, Venezuela, in April, 1960. It brought together leaders of national revolutionary, Christian Democratic, and related parties from all over the hemisphere, including a group of liberal political leaders and intellectuals from the United States and the colonial West Indies.[3] President Betancourt spoke at the opening session of the conference, and Rafael Caldera, chief of the Copei, was the principal speaker at its closing meeting.

While in exile during the nine years of dictatorship, leaders of Acción Democrática had established close relations with leaders of their counterpart parties in other Latin American countries. They continued to maintain these contacts once their party was in control of the government of Venezuela. Thus Acción Democrática participated in a Congress of National Revolutionary Parties held in Lima, Peru, in February, 1961. At that meeting a loose federation was founded among these parties, which included, besides AD, the Partido Aprista Peruano; the Bolivian government party, Movimiento Nacionalista Revolucionario; the Febrerista party of Paraguay, the Liberación Nacional party of ex-President José Figueres of Costa Rica, and Governor Luis Muñoz Marín's Popular Democratic party of Puerto Rico.

The Copei also maintained close contacts with its brother Christian Democratic parties. A large Venezuelan delegation attended the world congress of Christian Democratic parties held in Santiago, Chile, in August, 1961, and there sponsored a resolution calling for a general policy in Latin America of alliance between Christian Democratic and National Revolutionary parties, such as existed in Venezuela.

Various democratic political leaders of Latin America visited Venezuela as guests of the Venezuelan government. These included ex-President Pedro Aramburu and President Arturo Frondizi of Argentina, President-elect Jânio Quadros of Brazil. The relationship between the Mexican and Venezuelan revolutions was underscored during the visit of President Adolfo López Mateos of Mexico. During his trip abroad in February, 1963, President Rómulo Betancourt returned López Mateos' visit, and also attended the inauguration of President Juan Bosch of the Dominican Republic.

Even though the revolutionary democratic regime of President Betancourt sought to establish close political connections with its political counterparts and friendly regimes elsewhere in the hemisphere, it did not immediately decide to join the movement for economic unity of Latin America. The leaders of the government announced their intention ultimately to join the Latin American Free Trade Area (LAFTA), the attempt of several Latin American countries to abolish trade barriers among themselves. However, the Venezuelans made no haste to do so, since they wanted to have Venezuela's industrialization program further advanced, so as to be in a favorable bargaining position when they began to negotiate for mutual tariff concessions with members of the LAFTA.

One of the major foreign relations problems facing the Venezuelan constitutional government was that of the Dominican Republic.

During the period of the Pérez Jiménez dictatorship there had existed close cooperation between that regime and the even more tyrannical regime of Rafael Leonidas Trujillo. Subsequently, Trujillo expended much energy and money in attempting to upset the democratic government in Venezuela.

Various of the Right-wing military attempts against the Betancourt regime were directly aided by the Trujillo government. This was the case in the abortive rebellion led by General Jesús María Castro León in April, 1960. Even more direct was the connection of Trujillo and his regime with the attempt to assassinate President Rómulo Betancourt in June, 1960. After this attempt the Venezuelan police uncovered information indicating that Trujillo himself had participated in planning it, and that the bomb and timing device used had been supplied by him.

On the basis of this information, Venezuela presented official charges to the Organization of American States against the Dominican government, and demanded that the OAS take immediate action against the Trujillo regime. As a result of this demand, a Conference of American Foreign Ministers convened in San José, Costa Rica, in August. For the first time in the history of the OAS, a member state was condemned by the OAS, and it was agreed that economic sanctions would be levied against it.

At the same time that it was pressing its case against the Trujillo regime in the OAS, the Betancourt government was aiding the opposition forces within the Dominican Republic. Moral and other backing was extended to various Dominican opposition groups, particularly to the Partido Revolucionario Dominicano, headed by Juan Bosch, which had close relations with Acción Democrática. After the assassination of Trujillo in May, 1961, the Venezuelan government broadened this policy to help several other democratic opposition elements that developed within the Dominican Republic.

The Betancourt regime showed its moral backing for the regime of Juan Bosch, inaugurated as President on February 27, 1963. It provided some technical help to Bosch's efforts to reorganize and develop the Dominican economy. When the Bosch government was overthrown by a military coup in September, 1963, the Venezuelans broke off diplomatic relations with the Dominican Republic.

Equally as important as its relations with the Dominican Republic were the Betancourt regime's attitudes and policies with regard to the Castro regime in Cuba. The Betancourt and Castro governments came to power within a few weeks of one another, and their importance as alternative roads to revolution in Latin America were apparent from the beginning.

During the year 1958, after the fall of the Pérez Jiménez dictatorship, Castro's guerrilla fighters received substantial support in arms and ammunition from the Venezuelan provisional government. Leading Venezuelans also played an important part in the political struggle against Fulgencio Batista. Rómulo Betancourt was instrumental in bringing together in Caracas representatives of virtually all of the groups that were fighting Batista, including Castro's 26th of July movement, to sign the "Pact of Caracas." This document pledged close cooperation among all of the signatory groups in the struggle to overthrow the Cuban dictator, and promised the establishment of a democratic government once victory had been achieved.

With the victory of Castro in January, 1959, there was vast enthusiasm in Venezuela for the new revolutionary Cuban regime. This support extended to all but the most reactionary elements of the Venezuelan political spectrum. Zeal for the Cuban Revolution reached a frenzy when, within a month after he reached Havana, Fidel Castro himself went to Venezuela to express his gratitude for the help his forces had received during the Cuban civil war.

In Venezuela generally, enthusiasm for the Castro regime continued until the middle of 1960, though with waning strength. During this period there were many reciprocal visits of Cuban and Venezuelan government and political leaders; the Venezuelan and Cuban labor movements signed a "unity pact" and agreed to work together to establish a new Latin American labor confederation.

Even in this period, however, there were signs of disillusionment with the Castro regime in Venezuelan democratic circles. As early as February, 1959, during Castro's visit to Venezuela, there was consternation in Acción Democrática circles about the snide remarks that Castro was reported to have made about the Venezuelan President. When Raúl Castro, Fidel's brother, passed through Venezuela six months later, he was not received by President Betancourt. Democratic elements in the Venezuelan labor movement were disillusioned when the Castro regime in May, 1960, jailed the leader of the Confederación de Trabajadores de Cuba, David Salvador, with whom they had cooperated closely since the triumph of the Cuban Revolution. All Venezuelan democrats were shocked by the words of

Major Ernesto Guevara, who, in addressing a group of visiting Venezuelan students shortly afterwards, urged them "to convert the Andes into a Sierra Maestra," that is, to organize a guerrilla war against the Betancourt government.

Relations became even cooler in August, 1960, when President Betancourt instructed the Venezuelan delegation to the San José Conference of American Foreign Ministers to sign the mildly chastising resolution against Cuba that was adopted there. This decision by Betancourt provoked the resignation of the Foreign Minister, Ignacio Luis Arcaya, of the URD.

The final ideological break between the Venezuelan Democratic Revolution and the Castro Revolution in Cuba came at the end of 1960. When the elements in Venezuela pledging loyalty to Fidel, that is, the Communists, the Movimiento de Izquierda Revolucionaria, and some elements of the Unión Republicana Democrática, attempted to organize a popular insurrection against the Betancourt regime, the Venezuelan democratic leaders denounced Fidelista intrusion into Venezuelan politics.

As the tyranny of the Castro regime became more intense, an increasing number of its victims sought refuge in foreign embassies in Havana. Many of them, including the man Castro made President of Cuba in January, 1959, Dr. Manuel Urrutia, went to the Venezuelan Embassy. By August, 1961, there were nearly three hundred people in the crowded quarters of the Venezuelan diplomatic mission, and the Castro government refused to let any of them leave the country. It went further, and declared the Venezuelan chargé d'affaires to be *persona non grata,* to show distaste at the willingness of Betancourt's embassy to give asylum to so many of its opponents. By the middle of September, however, most of these refugees had been given safe-conducts out of Cuba—though Dr. Urrutia was not among these.

The Betancourt regime finally broke relations with Castro's Cuba on November 11, 1961. At the Punta del Este Conference of American Foreign Ministers in January, 1962, it supported the move to suspend the Castro government from the Organization of American States. In October, 1962, during the crisis over the Soviet government's attempt to convert Cuba into a missile base, the Betancourt regime strongly supported the Kennedy administration's insistence that Soviet missiles be removed from all Cuban bases.

The Venezuelan democratic revolutionary government thus

sought to develop an independent foreign policy, in general alignment with the West in world affairs. Within this general framework, it sought to strengthen the economic bargaining power of the underdeveloped countries, and to convince the democratic industrial nations of the need to help the economic growth of the developing peoples. The Venezuelan government also sought to strengthen the democratic current that has been running in Latin America since the middle of the 1950's. In doing so, it opposed dictatorships of both Right and Left, and made clear its belief that democracy is not secure in the Western Hemisphere unless it is accompanied by changes in the economic and social structure of the Latin American countries which are long overdue.

Part Three
The Program of the Democratic Revolution

Chapter Eleven

The Economic-Financial Problem

The economic crisis that hampered the efforts of the Venezuelan government to transform the national economy and public services during part of the Betancourt regime was provoked partly because the desired reforms implied a fundamental change in the nature of the economy. For some years prior to 1959, the Venezuelan economy had been primarily dependent on the petroleum industry and the construction trades. With the advent of the Betancourt administration, multiple programs were initiated to diversify the economy through the development of manufacturing and agriculture.

During the Pérez Jiménez administration the extraordinary boom in the economy was financed largely by the tremendous expansion of the oil industry. This was the result in part of fortuitous circumstances, such as the Korean War, the crisis in the Iranian oil industry, and the struggle over the Suez Canal, but was also stimulated by the policy of the Pérez Jiménez regime from June, 1956, until its fall of granting new concessions to the oil companies; the consequent heavy investment in a search for new sources of oil reached unprecedented proportions.

The other cornerstone of the economy of the period of the dictatorship was the gigantic expenditure by the government on public works, particularly in the Caracas area. Incredible sums were expended on transforming the capital from a relatively small city of colonial design into a metropolis boasting the most striking modern architecture; on the building of a vast road system; on the construction of huge government buildings, of the world's most expensive officers' club, of a funicular railway overlooking the city, and of the Humboldt Hotel on the top of one of the highest hills.

The wasteful luxury public works program of the Pérez Jiménez regime was riddled with graft and corruption. Huge fortunes were made overnight, at the expense of the government. Money flowed in all directions, and for a portion of the population at least, life seemed very easy indeed.

New capital entered the country during and just after the Suez crisis (1956 and 1957), when international capital was shifted in large quantities from Europe and the Middle East to the Western Hemisphere, particularly to the United States and Venezuela.

The policy of concentrating economic activity in the oil industry and public works in Caracas and a handful of other cities aggravated the problem of unemployment, for it drew hundreds of thousands of people from the country, where, though their standard of living was very low, they at least were self-sufficient. Countless numbers were unable to find work, though in the euphoria of the time, and under the repression of the dictatorship, this fact hardly became public knowledge before the fall of Pérez Jiménez. Index numbers of the relative increase of total employment and unemployment indicate that the problem of unemployment grew increasingly serious each year (see Table I).

TABLE I

Index of Employment and Unemployment in Venezuela, 1950 to 1959

Year	*Total Employment*	*Unemployment*
1950	100	100
1951	103.18	119.73
1952	108.38	111.59
1953	109.73	126.72
1954	117.08	130.00
1955	120.27	161.48
1956	126.27	153.90
1957	131.74	168.03
1958	133.94	214.60
1959	137.77	237.28

Source: Guillermo Muñoz: *La economía nacional y las medidas de urgencia,* Acción Democrática, Secretaría Nacional de Propaganda, Caracas, June, 1961, p. 15.

The highly artificial economic structure had begun to collapse even before the end of the dictatorship. In spite of its huge resources, the government was falling increasingly behind in its payments to contractors. Instead of paying them in cash, it gave them short-term notes. They in turn went to the Hotel Tamanaco, where they sold these at a 20 per cent discount to American middlemen who were more or less permanently resident there. These brokers promptly sold the Venezuelan government paper to leading New York banks.

The false euphoria of the Pérez Jiménez regime continued into the provisional regime period of 1958 and 1959. It was nourished by the ill-conceived Plan de Emergencia, whereby unemployed construction workers were paid without working. The economic situation became extremely wobbly during this intermediate period, however, for the provisional regime made a serious error in agreeing to pay off immediately the short-term debts of the dictatorship, instead of seeking to fund them into a medium-range bond issue.

The constitutional regime fundamentally changed the orientation of the government's economic policy. It abandoned the construction of pyramid-like public works in the capital city, and cut down drastically on the graft. It turned the burden of its expenditures to the interior of the country. It gave large credits for the expansion of industries in Valencia, Maracay, and other cities to the west of Caracas. It spent large amounts on the agrarian reform, and even larger amounts on building schools, training teachers, constructing rural water supplies and sewerage systems, and establishing medical centers in the interior towns and villages.

As government expenditures were no longer concentrated in Caracas, the city began to suffer. The construction industry, which, aside from the government bureaucracy, had been the principal source of income in the capital, was sharply curtailed, and to the consternation of entrepreneurs, large fortunes could no longer be made overnight. The collapse of the construction trade led to crisis in those industries serving it. Cement production fell to half of the industry's capacity; metallurgical output fell, as did glass production. Unemployment in Caracas mounted. The real estate and stock market booms collapsed.

An added element in the growing crisis was the fact that capital began to leave the country again. During the provisional government and the first year of the constitutional regime, many of those who received payment of debts owed from the Pérez Jiménez regime took these funds out of the country. Businessmen who had little faith in the future of the nation sought to provide for all eventualities by building up their bank accounts in the United States and Europe. Moreover, international funds deposited in Venezuela during the Suez crisis were moved out of the country. Add to this the flight of some $500 million a year, mainly in ill-gotten gains, during the latter part of the Pérez Jiménez dictatorship.

The sizable government deficit during both the provisional regime and the first years of the constitutional administration also stimulated the outward flow of capital. By providing additional purchasing power that could easily be converted into foreign exchange, the deficit increased the flow of funds abroad.

At the same time, the oil policy of both the provisional and constitutional regimes hastened the trend toward an economic letdown. After January 23, 1958, no new concessions were given, and the declared policy of the government was that no more would be given. As a result, exploration for new sources of oil came to a near-halt, and foreign capital for oil ventures no longer flowed freely into the country. Since Venezuela had long had a deficit on its visible balance of payments, the cessation of capital imports for oil exploration and the continuation of the flight of capital caused a heavy drain on the country's foreign exchange reserves down to the latter part of 1960. This drain intensified the feeling of uncertainty of many businessmen, particularly in the area of Caracas, and was to a considerable degree responsible for their "lack of confidence."

The situation in Cuba, with its reverberations in Venezuela, cannot be overlooked as another disturbing factor in the economy. The example of the Castro regime's ruthless wholesale confiscation of private wealth in the island, and its support of extreme Left-wing political circles in Venezuela, increased the uneasiness of many businessmen, particularly those operating in the Caracas region.

Finally, the Betancourt administration was subject not only to repeated attempts at *coup d'état* by Right-wing extremists but also to persistent efforts to stir up popular rebellion by the Communists and their allies. Hence fear for the stability of the constitutional regime in Venezuela itself undoubtedly was a major factor in the economic crisis.

Reports of the economic crisis, widely publicized both in Venezuela and abroad, presented a distorted picture of the situation of the country as a whole; the contrast between the situation of the capital and the oil fields area, on the one hand, and that of the rest of the country, on the other, was intensified.

Whereas there was economic crisis or decline in the Caracas and petroleum regions, there was rapid economic growth and development in many other parts of the country as a result of government policies of stimulating industry and agriculture. Production reached new heights in most crops during 1960, 1961, and 1962, and output in many manufacturing industries, including textiles and food-processing, grew rapidly and substantially. Progress in Valencia, Maracay, Cagua, Barquisimeto, and several other cities of the interior created optimism there. Maracaibo was moderately optimistic, and even the poverty-stricken mountain states of Táchira, Mérida, and Trujillo had great hope that through self-help and government aid administered by the new Corporación de los Andes, the economy of that area would begin to develop and diversify.

The constitutional regime attempted to deal with the economic crisis in several ways. Betancourt's first Minister of Finance, José Antonio Mayobre, negotiated a loan of $200 million from private United States banks as a stop-gap measure to halt the flow of capital abroad. He also sought to pare the government budget by reducing both the size of the bureaucracy and its pay. Although he brought about a 10 per cent reduction of government salaries, he was unsuccessful in reducing the number of employees because of the political problems involved.

In November, 1960, Mayobre made a suggestion that brought a crisis in the government. He urged that the Venezuelan monetary unit, the bolívar, be devalued. Two of the parties of the coalition, the Copei and the URD, threatened to leave the government if this measure was adopted. Although the URD left the cabinet shortly afterwards for other reasons, Betancourt could not afford to have the Copei go into the opposition. He therefore accepted Mayobre's resignation.

The President's choice as Mayobre's successor was Tomás Enrique Carrillo Batalla, a well-to-do businessman and banker, with a well-earned reputation as an expert economist. As part of his extensive program for the recuperation of the economy, he urged a revitalizing of the construction industry and a simultaneous reduction in excess government personnel. His suggestion was that the Ministry of Public Works undertake immediately several needed construction projects in Caracas and elsewhere, to be executed by private contractors. The firms receiving the contracts would be required to adsorb a certain number of workers released by the government. Furthermore, Carrillo Batalla suggested that the government seek sizable funds, totaling some $900 million, from the United States government and international lending institutions for its program of economic development and reform.

Carrillo Batalla also advocated the establishment of exchange control. This part of his program was carried out promptly. Certain goods were permitted to enter the country at what had been the exchange rate of 3.35 bolívares to the dollar, but for other products, the bolívar was allowed to find its own level, which by the middle of 1961 had been established at approximately 4.5 bolívares to the dollar. In March, 1961, the list of products favored by the official rate was reduced. The establishment of exchange controls had the effect of considerably reducing the outward flow of capital, and within a few months ended this flow altogether. As a result, the deficit of $27 million in Venezuela's balance of payments of 1961 was converted into a surplus of $5 million in 1962.[1]

Carrillo Batalla stayed in office only four months. When the Ministry of Public Works procrastinated about carrying out the program that he had outlined, the Minister of Finance resigned. He was succeeded by another leading businessman, Andrés Germán Otero, who was closely associated with the powerful economic group headed by Eugenio Mendoza.

Later in 1961 the government took other measures designed to overcome the crisis. In May it pushed through Congress a program for bringing the budget more nearly into balance. Salaries, including those of the military, were again cut 10 per cent, and the appropriations for nearly all ministries and independent agencies were sharply reduced. The government budget in 1962 for the first time in several years showed a surplus of some 665 million bolívares.[2]

The government also negotiated sizable loans from various international lending agencies, to be spent on various development programs. By the end of July, 1961, the administration had been authorized by Congress to accept some $100 million from the Export-Import Bank of the United States; $70 million from the International Bank for Reconstruction and Development; and $10 million from the Inter-American Development Bank. These funds were to be utilized principally to stimulate the activities of the Banco

Obrero and the Corporación Venezolana de Fomento.[3] In 1962 further loans of $90 million for the Banco Obrero and of $27 million for the Instituto Nacional de Obras Sanitarias were received under the Alliance for Progress.[4]

Until the middle of 1961 the Betancourt government's program to deal with the economic and financial crisis was largely deflationary. However, in August, 1961, emphasis was shifted to another, more expansionist program. It included the expenditure of 200 million bolívares on construction projects of various kinds, financed partly by a loan from the oil companies and partly by loans from international lending agencies. The program also called for the relaxation of rent control on new housing built as part of the program and the encouragement of municipal governments to relieve builders of local taxes for a five-year period. Finally, the government undertook a program of reinsuring private mortgages, somewhat like that of the Federal Housing Authority in the United States.

The Creole Petroleum Corporation endorsed the government's efforts by establishing a subsidiary to invest funds in joint enterprises with Venezuelan businessmen in fields unconnected with the oil industry. The new firm's initial investment was $10 million, but it was indicated that if the program succeeded, this amount might be very considerably increased.

Although there was some improvement in the economic picture by the end of 1961, the situation remained critical. The 1962 budget provided for reductions in vital economic development programs, as well as in housing and the agrarian reform measures. The crisis thus continued to endanger the fundamental objectives of the Betancourt regime at that time.

To an outside observer, the economic crisis of 1960 and 1961 appeared to be attributable in large part to the timidity of important elements of the Venezuelan business community. Because businessmen felt unsure about the political future of their country, they refused to invest their available funds in productive enterprises, and at the same time tried to ship these funds abroad. Caught in this vicious circle, largely, though not completely, of their own making, they imperiled the political situation still further, and made the fate of their existing investments that much more dubious. Furthermore, many of these same businessmen showed a selfishness that was self-defeating. Not only did they insist on immediate repayment of the debts owed them by the Pérez Jiménez regime, but they continued to resist strongly all government attempts to increase or even to collect taxes.

The government itself lacked consistency in its attempts to handle the crisis. Although adopting deflationary methods early in 1961, it turned to projects that would have the reverse effect a few months later. There seemed to be a good deal of confusion on the part of the government's economic advisers as to the best method of handling the crisis, and perhaps as to the exact nature of the crisis itself.

With the definite adoption of an expansionist instead of a deflationary policy, however, the Betancourt administration began to make definite headway against the economic recession. During 1962 the government launched a series of construction projects in the Caracas region, principally designed to relieve bottlenecks in the city's overcrowded street and highway system. This program, carried out by the autonomous government agency Centro Simón Bolívar, headed by a former businessman, Henrique Velutini, set high standards in efficiency and economy such as had seldom been seen in Venezuelan public works before. The projects of the Centro Simón Bolívar and the expenditure of some 200 million bolívares on help to private construction helped to restore the rhythm of economic activity in Caracas.

The economic recovery during the latter half of the Betancourt regime was reflected in the growth of the country's Gross National Product. Whereas the GNP had risen only 1.4 per cent in 1960 and 1.7 per cent in 1961, it jumped up 6 per cent in 1962. In the last year, the product per inhabitant of Venezuela increased appreciably. The foreign exchange position of the country also improved markedly. By October 15, 1963, Venezuelan gold and foreign exchange reserves stood at $734 million, the highest position since August 1950.[5]

Chapter Twelve

The Agrarian Reform: General Outlines

The agrarian reform is the most fundamental economic and social change being brought about by the Venezuelan Democratic Revolution. As in most of Latin America, it is essential to the emergence of a modern, diversified economy and a society with greater social mobility; and without such reform political democracy cannot be firmly established.

Traditionally, the oligarchy in Latin American countries has been composed of the large landholders. They have dominated the workers and tenants on their estates, and they have had a monopoly on education, have controlled local law enforcement, and have shared direction of political affairs with the military. With certain exceptions, Venezuela conforms to this pattern.

The key aspect of agrarian reform in Venezuela is the redistribution of land. Although a successful agrarian reform will involve other factors, such as credit for the new landowners and technical assistance and training for them, the indispensable measure is transfer of land ownership.

Usually transfers are carried out regardless of the wishes of the old proprietors. To North Americans the seizure of privately owned land by the government in order to transfer it to someone else may seem arbitrary, if not unjust. Yet, the expropriation of property for reasons of public utility is common in the United States and other highly industrialized democratic countries. If the government decides to build roads or create parks on private lands, it can acquire them by eminent domain, compensation being made to the owners. The Venezuelans and other Latin Americans regard land redistribution as a measure of public utility, as necessary for the well-being of the community at large.

One argument made by advocates of agrarian reform is that it is socially just. They reason that it is not proper for a small group of large landowners to control the lives of a multitude of tenants and agricultural laborers. Nor is it right that a powerful few receive sizable income as the result of the labor of others, while themselves making a very small contribution to the productive process.

Economically, too, there are important arguments favoring agrarian reform. As long as the cultivated land remains in the hands of a few people, the average agricultural tenant and laborer is "outside of the market," that is, he receives so little money income that he has almost no purchasing power. This limits the possibility of building manufacturing industries, since the market is much smaller than would be indicated by the size of the population.

A large landholding system also limits the possibility of economic growth in another way. This system, based as it is on very cheap labor, provides little incentive for the introduction of modern techniques or equipment in agriculture or for increasing output. As a result, agriculture remains backward, and productivity is low. The prices of foodstuffs and raw materials stay up, and frequently the farmer is unable to meet the national requirements for many products that could quite easily be produced in the country.

Venezuela has other reasons for agrarian reform. Migration of landless peasants to the urban centers not only threatened to undermine agriculture but also created pressing social problems in Caracas, Maracaibo, Barcelona, Cumuná, and some other cities. It was essential to develop a national policy that would help to keep the peasants on the soil. Such a policy could be effective only if life in the rural areas was made attractive. The prospect of owning land could be a powerful incentive for the peasant to stay in the country. Hence, the agrarian reform is basic to the program of keeping the rural population from invading the cities.

The conuqueros present additional problems, for these migratory squatters retreat to the mountainsides, live in flimsy huts, and scratch only a miserable living out of poor soil. About every three years the conuquero has to move to another spot because the topsoil has washed away. There are parts of the country, particularly in the mountain states of Mérida and Táchira, where large mountain areas have been denuded of forest cover. As the population of the country increases, the squatters can be expected to destroy larger and larger parts of the nation's soil resources.

Dr. Raúl Cabrita Perilli, a leading forestry engineer, speaking to a meeting of the Venezuelan Society of Natural Science in August, 1961, noted the damage being brought about by the conuquero system. He pointed out that in addition to causing widespread deforestation and erosion of the soil, the conuquero made almost no contribution to the national income, since he produced barely enough for his own family's subsistence. His insecure economic situation fostered instability in family relations, with consequent high rates of illegitimacy and loose marital ties. The isolation of the conuquero from his neighbors made it virtually impossible to provide him with medical care, educational facilities, electricity or any other amenity of modern civilization.[1]

Venezuelan agriculture suffers not only from a high degree of concentration of land ownership but also from the fact that a large proportion of the cultivated units are either very large or very small —the twins evils of latifundia and minifundia. Furthermore, many of those working the land have little or no title to the areas that they cultivate.

The agricultural and livestock census of 1950 showed that of the 234,730 agricultural units then in use, only 43.8 per cent were cultivated by their owners or part-owners. Some 15.5 per cent were farmed by renters, 6.5 per cent by sharecroppers, and 34.3 per cent by squatters with no legal right to use the land they were occupying. By the time the census of 1956 was taken, only 25.1 per cent of the cultivated land units of Venezuela were being farmed by their owners, and there had been a great increase in the number of parcels planted by squatters.

The degree to which concentration in ownership and cultivation existed was demonstrated by the 1950 figures, which showed that the 43.8 per cent of the total number of farms being cultivated by their owners or part-owners accounted for 81 per cent of all of the land in use. Rented farms amounted to only 3.1 per cent of the total area, and sharecropped farms had 1.9 per cent of the area.

VEN

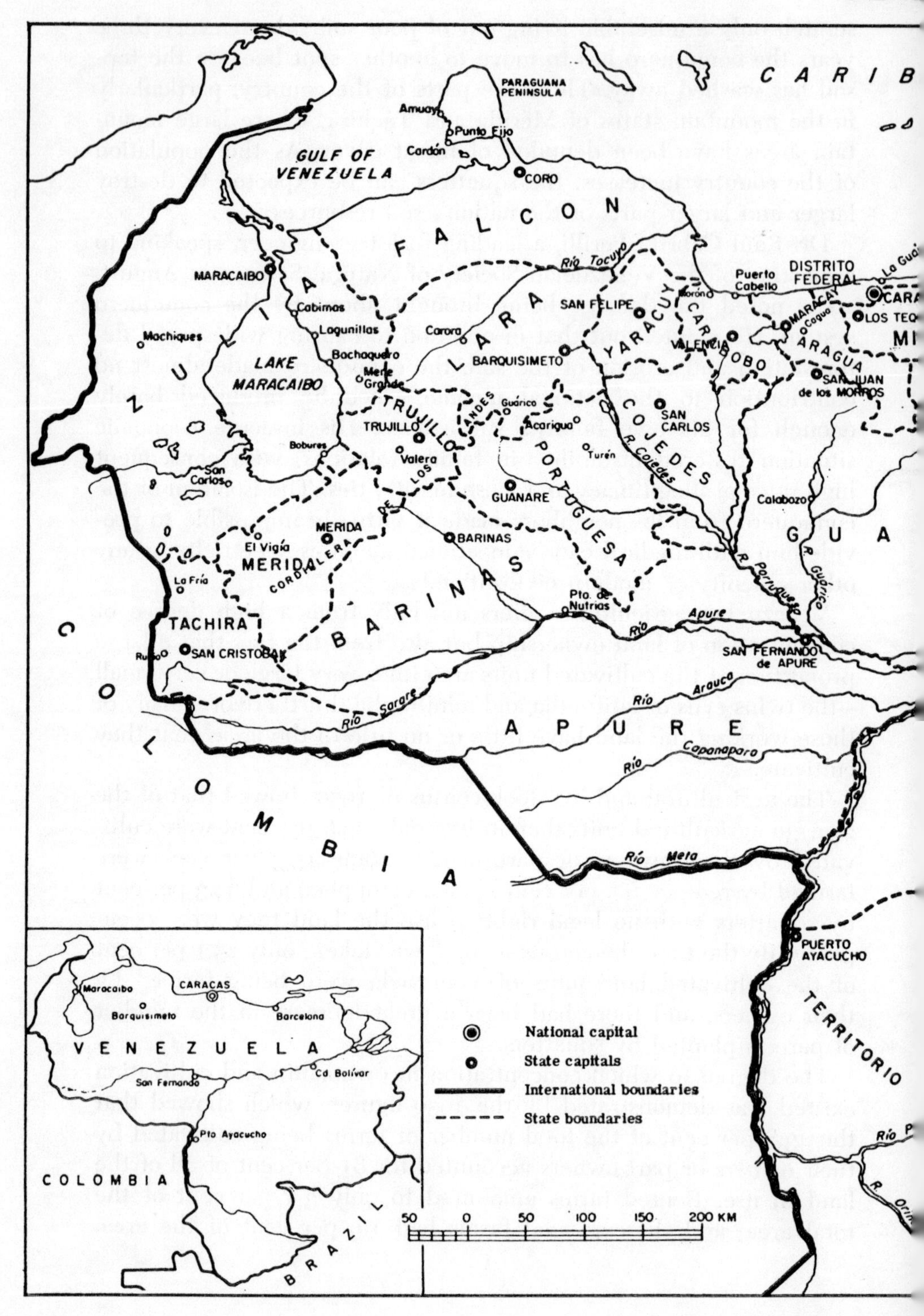

PARAGUANA PENINSULA
Amuay
Punto Fijo
Cardón
GULF OF VENEZUELA
CORO
FALCON
MARACAIBO
Cabimas
Lagunillas
Machiques
LAKE MARACAIBO
Bachaquero
Mene Grande
ZULIA
Bobures
San Carlos
Río Tocuyo
Carora
LARA
BARQUISIMETO
SAN FELIPE
YARACUY
Morón
Puerto Cabello
CARABOBO
VALENCIA
DISTRITO FEDERAL
MARACAY
Coquo
ARAGUA
SAN JUAN de los MORROS
TRUJILLO
Valera
ANDES
LOS
DE
Guárico
Acarigua
Turén
SAN CARLOS
COJEDES
R. Cojedes
GUANARE
PORTUGUESA
Calabozo
GUA
R. Guárico
R. Portuguesa
MERIDA
El Vigía
CORDILLERA
BARINAS
La Fría
TACHIRA
SAN CRISTOBAL
Rubio
Pto. de Nutrias
Río Apure
SAN FERNANDO de APURE
Río Arauca
Río Sarare
APURE
Río Capanaparo
COLOMBIA
Río Meta
PUERTO AYACUCHO
TERRITORIO
Maracaibo
CARACAS
Barquisimeto
Barcelona
VENEZUELA
Cd. Bolívar
San Fernando
Pto Ayacucho
COLOMBIA
BRAZIL
National capital
State capitals
International boundaries
State boundaries
50 0 50 100 150 200 KM

JELA

AN SEA
NUEVA ESPARTA
LA ASUNCION
Carúpano
CUMANA
SUCRE
GULF OF PARIA
TRINIDAD
Pto. la Cruz
BARCELONA
Caripito
MATURIN
ANZOATEGUI
Aragua de Barcelona
R. Guanipa
MONAGAS
TUCUPITA
alle de Pascua
El Tigre
Barrancas
CO
Pto. Ordaz
San Felix
TERRITORIO FEDERAL
DELTA AMACURO
CIUDAD BOLIVAR
Upata
Río
ORINOCO
Río Caroní
Cerro Bolivar
Río Caura
BRITISH GUIANA
OLIVAR
LA GRAN SABANA
Río Paragua
AMAZONAS
BRAZIL

The 34.3 per cent of the farms cultivated by squatters accounted only for 10.9 per cent of the total area used for agriculture and grazing.

Furthermore, farms of over 500 hectares (approximately 1,250 acres) represented 64.2 per cent of the total land in use, although they accounted for only 2.4 per cent of the total number of farms. At the other extreme, 53.7 per cent of all agricultural and livestock units had less than 5 hectares (12.5 acres) apiece.[2]

Commenting on these figures, the economic subcommission of the Agrarian Reform Commission noted: "These characteristics show the extreme degree of concentration of land resources in a few large units and the existence of an extremely large number of very small farms, with the majority of agricultural families working as part-time wage earners on neighboring large haciendas. The bad economic and social repercussions of such an agrarian structure, both for agriculture and for the national economy as a whole, are evident and do not need to be summarized here. It is natural that such a structure would result in uneconomic use of resources, low productivity, and mere subsistence income for the great mass of the rural population, as well as great inelasticity of production and other highly defective conditions which presently characterize Venezuelan agriculture."[3]

The subcommission added the following comment on the problem of government owned land: "the state is in Venezuela a relatively large landowner. Unfortunately, there exists very little information concerning the total land held by it, and a special survey would be necessary in order to determine the magnitude and location of the lands belonging to the national, state, and municipal governments. It should be noted that most of the land cultivated by renters and squatters falls in this category."[4]

The Acción Democrática regime of 1945 to 1948 had started an agrarian reform program, first dividing land that had been taken from "malefactors" of the Medina Angarita government, and then in 1948 passing a basic law for general land redistribution. However, President Rómulo Gallegos was overthrown before the program had been able to alter fundamentally the pattern of Venezuelan landownership. Much of the land granted to peasants between 1945 and 1948 was returned to its previous owners by the dictatorship.

With the overthrow of the Pérez Jiménez dictatorship, all three major democratic parties were agreed that an agrarian reform program was necessary, and this belief was shared by most elements of the community, even including many agricultural landlords. The provisional government reactivated the Instituto Agrario Nacional (IAN), and it undertook immediately to parcel out among landless peasants numerous estates seized from members of the Pérez Jiménez regime. Between the fall of the dictatorship and the promulgation of the new Agrarian Reform Law in March, 1960, the IAN settled some 3,623 peasant families on over 675,000 hectares (1.5 million acres).[5]

During the 1958 election campaign, Rómulo Betancourt made land reform the most important plank in his platform, and he won the support of the overwhelming majority of the peasants on the basis of his past performance and his promises for the future. Even before he was inaugurated, the provisional government set up an Agrarian Reform Commission to study the problem of agrarian reform, and to draw up a bill on the subject to be presented to the new Congress that was to come into office simultaneously with the establishment of the constitutional regime.

Meanwhile, another prerequisite of a successful agrarian reform had been fulfilled. This was the organization of a network of peasant unions, which could cooperate with the land reform program that the government proposed to undertake. The Peasants Federation, established during the 1945 to 1948 Acción Democrática government and composed of more than two hundred local unions, had been suppressed during the more than nine years of dictatorship. As soon as the dictator was overthrown, however, the process of organizing the peasants got under way once again. A provisional organizing committee was established, consisting of members of the four principal parties—Acción Democrática, the Copei, the URD, and the Partido Comunista—although Acción Democrática had a strong majority in the group.

Early in June, 1959, this committee concluded its work when the founding congress of a new Peasants Federation was held in Caracas. Ramón Quijada, principal peasant leader of Acción Democrática, was elected its president, and another AD leader, Pedro Torres, was chosen as secretary-general.

The Venezuelan agrarian reform is unique among those that have been attempted in Latin America in that it is in a real sense a national effort. This was clear from the membership of the Agrarian

Reform Commission, which included not only representatives of the four political parties but also leaders of the Confederación de Trabajadores de Venezuela, the Peasants Federation, the landlords' organization, the business and banking communities, and organizations of agricultural experts and technicians.

The report of the Agrarian Reform Commission was published in several volumes. It included a very extensive economic survey by a subcommission headed by Dr. Tomás Enrique Carrillo Batalla, one of the country's leading economists, former head of the Agricultural Landlords Federation, and some time later Minister of Finance of the Betancourt government. Similar studies of the agricultural resources of the country, the social problems of the rural areas, and of other aspects of the reform problem were drawn up by other units of the commission.

The Agrarian Reform Commission report was submitted to President Betancourt on May 29, 1959. He and his cabinet, in turn, elaborated a bill that was submitted to Congress a few months later. After long and sometimes bitter debate, the Agrarian Reform Law was enacted on March 19, 1960. Since this law encompassed not only the land of ex-officials of the dictatorship but also privately owned lands, the title of which was not in doubt, and sizable segments of government-held territory, reform measures could be undertaken on a large scale.

Among the fundamental principles that guide the Venezuelan agrarian reform, there are some that tend to differentiate it from land reform programs carried out in some other Latin American countries. They particularly set it apart from the analogous process undertaken in Cuba by the regime of Fidel Castro.

To begin with, the agrarian reform in Venezuela is being carried out in conformity with the law. It is being conducted by a constitutional government, duly elected. There is no arbitrary seizure of land, as in Castro's Cuba.

It is true that peasants impatient of what they conceived to be the slowness of the program sometimes occupied land illegally and that, in some cases, the seizures of estates were connived at by landowners who wanted to have the government buy their land; however, the Betancourt administration discouraged these illegal moves. The President himself appealed to the peasants to obtain land through the processes of the law. The IAN announced in August, 1961, that it would not grant land to peasants who had taken the law into their own hands. Leaders of the Peasants Federation and of the two government political parties made special trips to urge offenders to leave the land they had occupied, and in a few rare instances the police were called out to oust squatters.

The issue of illegal land seizure inevitably became a political problem. The opposition parties, particularly the Partido Comunista and the Movimiento de Izquierda Revolucionaria, encouraged peasants to take possession of the land illegally, and denounced government efforts to restrain the process. On the other hand, the Right-wing opposition used the scattered cases of illegal invasion of land to accuse the government of inability to maintain order.

In all expropriation procedures the government strictly adhered to the principle of making fair compensation to landowners. In the majority of cases, the amount to be paid was settled amicably by the landowner and the Instituto Agrario Nacional. Only if such an accord could not be reached was forcible sale resorted to, and then only after action in the regular courts. In spite of the legal safeguards, remarkably few landlords went to court over the issue of compensation, and the program suffered little delay because of recalcitrance on the part of the landowners.

Another basic feature of the Venezuelan agrarian reform is that ultimately the new landowner will receive virtually full title to his land. There are only three limitations on his ownership rights. First, he can sell the land he has received under the reform only after giving the Instituto Agrario Nacional sixty days' notice of his intention to do so, and then only if the buyer is attested by the IAN to be eligible to receive land under the agrarian reform law.[6] Second, a beneficiary of the reform may under certain well-defined circumstances be deprived of his land. Articles 83 and 84 of the law state these conditions:

"Article 83: In the title referred to in Article 75 it will state that the Instituto Agrario Nacional may by declaration of its directorate, with previous knowledge of the person involved, revoke the title for the following reasons:

"1) If the parcel is used for ends other than those of the agrarian reform.

"2) If the parcel or the beneficiary's family is unjustifiably abandoned. In this case, the IAN will give the parcel to the wife, or, if there is none, to the concubine, or, in the third place, to the child who has demonstrated greatest capacity in the judgment of the IAN. . . .

"3) If there is manifest negligence or ineptitude on the part of the beneficiary in the exploitation of the parcel or the conservation of the structures, improvements, or work tools which have been given to him and which belong to the organization.

"4) If the beneficiary does not himself cultivate the land, except in special cases provided for in this law.

"5) If there is failure, without justified cause, to pay back obligations entered into with the Instituto Agrario Nacional or with the Banco Agrícola y Pecuario or cooperatives and agricultural credit unions.

"6) If there is repeated failure to obey legal regulations for conservation of natural resources.

"In cases 1, 3, 4, 5, 6, a warning must have been issued and not been heeded and there must be an opinion on the part of the local administrative committee favorable to the revocation.

"Article 84: In cases of revocation of titles, the beneficiary will be paid the value of improvements which he has made and which still exist, according to the evaluation of experts. . . .

"In these same cases, the beneficiary will be repaid any sums that he has paid to amortize his property, minus up to 10 per cent of the amount of the amortization in cases covered in Article 83."

Finally, Article 73 of the law placed some small limitations on the right of inheritance of property granted under the agrarian reform. It provided:

"In case of the death of a beneficiary, whether he has paid for his parcel or not, if the heirs cannot come to an agreement for the administration and working of the farm, or decide to divide it, the Instituto Agrario Nacional, after a report of the administrative committee, will declare the grant revoked, and give the parcel in preference to a member of the family who fulfills the conditions established in Articles 62 or 67 and other parts of the present law. In these cases, the IAN will pay to the recognized heirs the price of the parcel and of the improvements, minus any debts due to administrative organizations of the agrarian reform."

An outstanding characteristic of the Venezuelan agrarian reform is its flexibility. The authors of the Venezuelan law did not adopt any hard and fast rules such as apply to the semi-communal *ejido* which has become the pattern of the Mexican land reform.

Basically, the Venezuelan Agrarian Reform Law is individualist in its approach. Land can be asked for either by individual peasants or by a group. By the end of 1962 most peasants had received individual rather than group titles; however, provisional titles were usually given first, while the peasants were getting started in the business of operating their new landholdings. During this period, elected committees of agrarian reform beneficiaries coordinated and in some cases supervised their work. The elected committee also served as a representative of a group of benficiaries in obtaining credit and technical assistance from government agencies.

In at least one case, the individualistic approach of the reform went further. This was in the state of Mérida, where the local authorities of the IAN merely invited peasants to occupy land, to which, after one year, they would obtain full title. The IAN made no attempt to provide credit, housing, technical assistance, or anything except the land. This program is as nearly like homesteading in the United States as can be found in the Venezuelan agrarian reform.

However, the leaders of the Venezuelan agrarian reform did not feel that the individualistic approach is always desirable. They pushed the establishment of cooperative settlements among the peasants on some lands that were better suited for livestock than for crop production. The cooperative approach was also applied on land producing certain types of crops.

Peasants were settled both on land expropriated from private holders and on that belonging to the government. A controversy persisted throughout the Betancourt administration concerning which method of peasant settlement was preferable. After the middle of 1961, the IAN concentrated most of its efforts on expropriation of private lands.

The Venezuelan agrarian reform was planned as a rounded effort, which would not only serve to bring about a more equitable distribution of wealth and income but would also have the effect of raising significantly the output and productivity of the country's agriculture. In this, it has not differed fundamentally from most other Latin American agrarian reform programs.

President Betancourt himself explained the "integral" nature of the Venezuelan agrarian reform in his speech to the founding congress of the Peasants Federation, on June 2, 1959: "The agrarian reform will be carried out in a comprehensive manner. It has been said, and I wish to repeat it, that it would be demagogic and irresponsible to consider this reform as a kind of hand-out which will give each peasant his little piece of land, and only that. We are not trying to perpetuate the conuco system, we are not trying to substitute for the unproductive latifundia the equally unproductive minifundia. What we are trying to do is to give the peasant not only land but modern implements, the security of credit, the assurance that minimum prices fixed by the Banco Agrícola will not benefit the fly-by-night trucker but rather the peasant. We are trying also to take the rural school to the country, along with a rural dispensary, a rural water supply, and to provide the peasant with construction materials to build his own house, so that there will disappear from Venezuela the shameful phenomenon of seven hundred thousand rural hovels."[7]

Various institutions were established or adapted to the purposes of the agrarian reform. The program of actual land distribution was placed in the hands of the Instituto Agrario Nacional. Governed by a five-man board of directors, in which the Peasants Federation was amply represented, it had a delegate in every state. The IAN decided what land should be expropriated or what government land should be turned over to the peasants in a given state. It negotiated with the landowners and, if necessary, took the expropriation problem to the courts.

Once expropriation was decided upon, the IAN paid the landowner for his land, usually giving about 10 per cent of the purchase price in cash and the rest in nontransferable agrarian reform bonds. Meanwhile, it also decided which peasants should be settled upon this land. Until the end of 1961 the IAN in some cases built houses for the new farmers, dug wells for them, and constructed neighborhood roads. In some isolated cases, the IAN also provided loans as well, though this was not normally supposed to be within its province. Late in 1961, however, the IAN decided to turn over these miscellaneous functions to other, more appropriate government agencies, and to concentrate the use of its limited funds on the purchase, delimitation, and actual transfer of land to the peasants.

The beneficiaries of the agrarian reform do not pay anything for the land they receive. Ramón Quijada, the Acción Democrática peasant leader who formerly headed the Peasants Federation, originally favored having the peasants pay a small amount, so as to give them a greater feeling of security in their new property. He succeeded in getting the federation to go on record in favor of such a procedure; however, his point of view was opposed by other AD peasant leaders, notably Armando González, AD leader in Carabobo State, and the party adopted the principle of free grants of land to the beneficiaries of the reform. This criterion was finally adopted by Congress in the Agrarian Reform Law. It was also provided that if peasants wished to buy land in addition to the amount the IAN granted them gratis, they might do so, if it was available, and provided that the total land area they held did not exceed the legal maximum of 150 hectares, or about 375 acres.

The Banco Agrícola y Pecuario, the credit agency of the agrarian reform, was established many decades ago for the purpose of lending money to large grazers and agriculturalists. During the Betancourt administration its funds were greatly increased, so that it could perform its part in the agrarian reform program. Thus in contrast to the 50 million bolívares available to the bank in 1957, the last year of the dictatorship, in 1959 it had 200 million bolívares available, in 1960 also 200 million bolívares, in 1961 some 100 million bolívares, and in 1962 it granted 224 million bolívares in loans. Its program for 1963 called for the granting of 47.1 million bolívares in loans to agrarian reform beneficiaries, 55.8 million bolívares to other landholders, and the concession of 49.6 million bolívares in loans connected with special government agricultural development projects, for a total of 152.5 million bolívares.[8]

The task of providing technical assistance and instruction to the peasants who receive land from the IAN was given to the Ministry of Agriculture. For this purpose, the extension service of the Ministry of Agriculture was raised to the status of a separate division. The technical assistance efforts of the Ministry were hampered not only by insufficient funds but also by a lack of adequate personnel. However, the number of agricultural extension offices rose from 23 in 1958 to 164 in 1963.[9]

Complementing the agricultural extension efforts of the Ministry of Agriculture was the program of the Instituto Agrario Nacional to provide agrarian reform beneficiaries with necessary agricultural equipment. In August, 1963, the first installment of 238 tractors belonging to the IAN were given to groups of peasants. At that time the IAN was reported to have 1,200 tractors on hand for distribution.[10]

Another government agency of key importance in the Venezuelan agrarian reform is the Ministry of Education, which has responsibility for extending school facilities to agrarian reform settlements. State departments of education also participate in this campaign.

The Malaria Section of the Ministry of Health, the principal organization involved in rural housing activities, has placed some of its projects in agrarian reform settlements. Water supply and sewerage programs of the Instituto Nacional de Obras Sanitarias have also been coordinated with the reform in some cases; and the Ministry of Public Works has built some roads in these settlements.

Chapter Thirteen

The Agrarian Reform: Some Specific Examples

The agrarian reform was well advanced during President Rómulo Betancourt's five-year term of office. Although the President and other leaders of the government had no illusions that they could complete even the land redistribution program, let alone other aspects of the agrarian reform, in a single administration, they had made the reform a basic part of the country's social and economic fabric by the end of Betancourt's term.

In the first phase of the reform the objective of the Instituto Agrario Nacional was to concentrate its efforts in sections where the social and population pressure was most intense. As a result, the first states to receive large benefits from IAN's operations were the central coastal states of Miranda, Aragua, and Carabobo in the vicinity of Caracas. In these three states, the agrarian reform transformed the social and economic structure. For instance, around Lake Valencia (including parts of both Aragua and Carabobo), the agrarian settlements came to occupy most of the arable land. Only a few private landholdings of some size continued to exist as enclaves within the land that had been expropriated under the agrarian reform by the end of the Betancourt regime.

The state of Carabobo had forty-three peasant settlements by August, 1961, when the author visited the area, and the government had spent some 30 million bolívares in buying land for them.

By that time, some 13,000 families had been settled on the land in that state, of a total of some 30,000 peasant families in the state who needed land when the program began. Given the shortage of arable land in the state, it was impossible for all of the peasants needing land to obtain it within the state.

A major step in the agrarian reform in the Lake Valencia region was the expropriation of the Pimentel property. This landholding, consisting of over 15,000 hectares, or approximately 38,000 acres, had originally been acquired by Antonio Pimentel during the dictatorship of Juan Vicente Gómez. During the Acción Democrática administration of the 1940's, the land had been confiscated and peasants had been settled upon it; however, the Pérez Jiménez regime restored the land to its owner. During this dictatorship, Antonio Pimentel died, and his property was inherited by his son. The latter sold small portions of the property, but most of it was still in his hands when Pérez Jiménez was overthrown.

As soon as the Agrarian Reform Law was passed, the Instituto Agrario Nacional began negotiations concerning the expropriation and purchase of the Pimentel property. Pimentel demanded some 76 million bolívares, but finally agreed to accept 26 million. The sale went through even though the payment of this much to the heir of one of the chief associates of Juan Vicente Gómez became a subject of bitter political dispute. Upon its acquisition by the Instituto Agrario Nacional, the Pimentel property was turned over to some 3,000 families, most of whom had received the titles to their new property by the middle of 1961. Most of the settlements on the Pimentel property were economically successful, and the peasants worked their new land conscientiously. The government constructed several small housing groups, a vocational school, one six-grade primary school, and numerous three-grade primary schools. Besides a full-scale dispensary, several small health centers were started.

In the central coastal states, the main emphasis of the agrarian reform in its first phase was on redistribution of privately held estates. However, in the states southwest of this region, between the great plains of llanos and the Andes Mountains, the agrarian reform was of a somewhat different nature. In Portuguesa and Barinas the work of the IAN involved a good deal of colonization work, for very little of the land had previously been used to raise either crops or livestock, and much of it belonged to the federal, state, or local government. This is almost virgin territory, and the problem has been to open up new lands. In time it is hoped that many of the landless peasants of Carabobo, Lara, and Yaracuy, and perhaps even of a state as far east as Aragua, can be offered land in Portuguesa and Barinas, and thus can be induced to settle here.

The kind of pioneering required in these states is difficult for the peasants concerned, and it involves a larger capital investment than the agrarian reform projects in the central coastal states, though less money will have to be spent on land purchase. The peasants who cut off the primeval forest in Barinas and Portuguesa have had to deal with large poisonous snakes and alligators, and numerous other wild beasts. They have had to travel long distances to get to market, and being farther from the seat of government than the peasants in Carabobo or Aragua, they have had more difficulty in presenting their problems to the appropriate officials.

On the other hand, peasants who move into Portuguesa or Barinas have the advantage of farming in rich and virgin soil. They have been able to obtain considerably larger grants of land than those available in the more heavily populated sections of the republic. Being at some distance from the population center of the country has even been of some advantage in terms of lack of government interference in their affairs.

During the first phase of the agrarian reform, the IAN did not give as high priority to Barinas and Portuguesa as to the central coastal states; however, by the end of 1961 there were already twenty-four agrarian reform settlements in Portuguesa and seven in Barinas. Three of the latter were old settlements, started during the first Acción Democrática regime. Five of the thirty-one settlements, totaling 363 families, were made in November, 1961. The peasants in many of these projects received little more than land, since credit and other help were not forthcoming.

One large IAN project in the state of Mérida involves some 1.25 million acres along the Pan American Highway in the western part of the state. On the invitation of the IAN to choose plots of land and settle on them, more than 5,000 peasants took up land near the highway and some local roads. About 70 per cent came from the Andean states of Trujillo, Mérida, and Táchira, and the other 30 per cent from the Lake Maracaibo area, eastern Venezuela, and Colombia. Of these settlers, 978 had already been granted provisional land titles as early as August, 1961. The process of granting permanent titles to homesteaders who had shown that they intended to stay on their plots began in October, 1961.

This homesteading program was bitterly attacked, particularly by Copei political leaders in Mérida, but there is no doubt that it resulted in the settlement of a large group of peasants on the land very quickly, and at little expense to the government.

This experimental program could prove to be of great importance. One of the difficulties of the agrarian reform program has been the tendency of the beneficiaries of the agrarian reform to look to the government to provide them with everything—not only land, but credit, housing, technical help, machinery, aid for every aspect of their work and life. In talking with peasants on agrarian reform settlements in many of the Venezuelan states, the author observed an unfortunate lack of initiative on the part of the peasants to help themselves, without government aid and direction. The Mérida homesteading project represents an entirely different approach to the problem of the agrarian reform, for the peasants are given land but promised nothing else. From the very beginning, they know that their success or failure as independent farmers depends upon their industry and initiative. They clear the forest, plough their fields, get in their crops, construct their meager homes. The only IAN aid to these peasants was the digging of fresh-water wells, for which the peasants were more grateful than those in other settlements in which the IAN attempted to do everything.

Agrarian reform had had relatively little impact in some other parts of the country by the middle of the Betancourt administration. By August, 1961, only some thirteen peasant settlements had been established in the large, oil-rich state of Zulia, around Lake Maracaibo in the northwestern part of the country. However, during the last three months of 1961, the IAN made a significant advance in the agrarian reform program for that state, with the establishment of four new settlements totaling 1,100 peasant families, and further projects were established in Zulia during the following two years. The nearby state of Lara had a somewhat larger number of agrarian reform settlements, but the magnitude of the reform operations was in no way comparable to that in Carabobo, further east.

The easternmost states of the country had been affected least by the agrarian reform by the end of the Betancourt regime. There were only seven settlements, for example, in Anzoátegui State and eight in Sucre by August, 1961, and only a handful of others were established during the subsequent two years. A few of these settlements dated from the 1945 to 1948 Acción Democrática government, although most were established between 1959 and 1961. One or two of these were very successful colonization projects.

In the southern states of Bolívar and Guárico there was somewhat more evidence of the reform than in the east. Bolívar had thirty-three settlements by September, 1961, though most of these were very small. Guárico, in the heart of the llanos, had twenty-five settlements. Both Bolívar and Guárico were to be specially noted because the various organizations associated with the agrarian reform were much better coordinated than they were in most of the other states.

Although most of the agrarian reform settlements were established on an individualist basis, with each peasant getting his allotment of land, and being set up as an independent farmer, the IAN undertook several cooperative projects. Description of two of them will suffice to give an idea of their nature.

The Unidad de Producción Monterrey, near the city of Mérida in the state of the same name, was set up by thirty-six families. Although fourteen of the original families withdrew within a few months, twenty-eight new ones joined the group, and there were fifty families when the author visited there in August, 1961.

An administrative committee of five members of the community was elected to supervise the day-to-day management of the cooperative. The director of the grazing programs of the office of the IAN in the state of Mérida served as technical director of the project, and lived there during the first year of its existence. The work force of the settlement was divided into five sections: dairy farming, agriculture, truck gardening, flowers and fruit, and land rehabilitation and miscellaneous work. Individual members chose the sections in which they wished to work. Since at the time the cooperative was established most of the buildings were in a state of considerable disrepair, the initial task of the members of the cooperative was to rehabilitate their capital equipment. Although the purpose of the cooperative was to produce a profit for its members, they remained satisfied temporarily with a mere subsistence income during the early months, and most of the profits of the enterprise were ploughed back for the acquisition of machinery and other basic needs.

The cooperative started with a herd of 123 dairy cattle, which had increased to 160 by the end of six months. These included thoroughbred imported Holsteins and some of the native stock descended from animals brought over from Europe in colonial times. The people working in the dairy barn were given tuberculosis tests, as were the cattle, and the cattle were bathed and treated for ticks twice a month. The Ministry of Health gave the cooperative a high rating on its milk supply.

The agricultural section of the cooperative grew principally Irish potatoes and peas. The seed for the latter was provided by the Heinz Company, which also agreed to buy much of the crop for its canning and freezing plant near Valencia. The potatoes were graded according to size and sold in Mérida.

The flowers and fruit section concentrated on growing flowers, which had a good market in Mérida. Some were available for sale every day.

The truck gardening section of the cooperative grew a wide variety of vegetables, including lettuce and onions. The fields were rotated between truck garden products and root and leguminous vegetables. Most of the land for all sections of the cooperative was irrigated by overhead spraying.

The land rehabilitation section of the work force was of particular importance, for when the cooperative was established, the land was exceedingly rocky. Under the supervision of the technical director, the workers undertook to clear the fields of stones, at the same time building stone fences to terrace the land and prevent the erosion of the top soil. Fruit trees were planted along the terraces. The technical director estimated that it would take two and a half years to clear the cooperative's fields of stone.

The settlement consists of 249 hectares, of which 149 were being used for agriculture when the author visited it in August, 1961. A large forest reserve on a hill across a small valley from the principal fields and pastures of the cooperative was the source of the ample water supply that the settlement enjoyed. The water was distributed by a series of pumps and irrigation pipes throughout the settlement.

A small retail store maintained by the cooperative sold only groceries and a few other items in the beginning, but planned to add clothing and other general store supplies that the peasants need.

The cooperative started out in converted buildings or modified stone ranchos, but by the end of the first six months, the members were building thirty stone houses, each with three bedrooms, a

Leo Matiz, PIX

Raúl Leoni, as President of Congress, places presidential sash on Rómulo Betancourt at the inaugural ceremonies in 1959. Rafael Caldera, President of the Chamber of Deputies, looks on.

Peasants of Turén in the state of Portuguesa gather to receive land titles under the agrarian reform.

Embassy of Venezuela

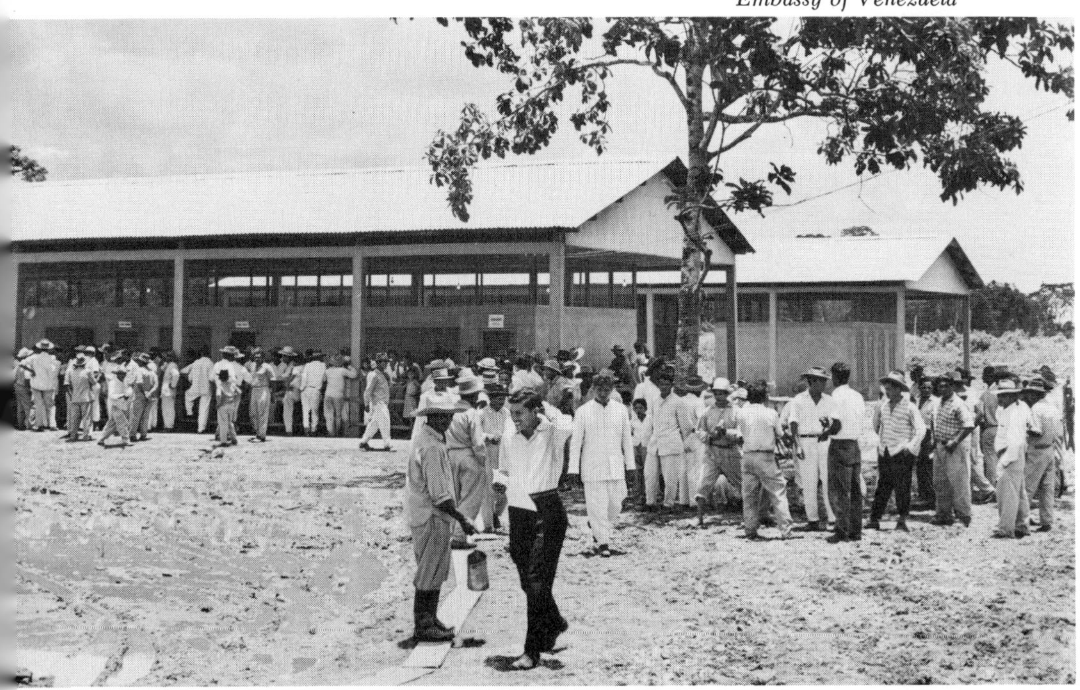

Creole Petroleum Corporation

The Caroní River Dam, near Santo Tomé de Guayana.

The health center at Río Caribe, state of Monagas.

Embassy of Venezuela

Embassy of Venezuela

A typical rural primary school at Las Morochas in the state of Miranda.

The crafts school at El Macaro, state of Carabobo.

Creole Petroleum Corporation

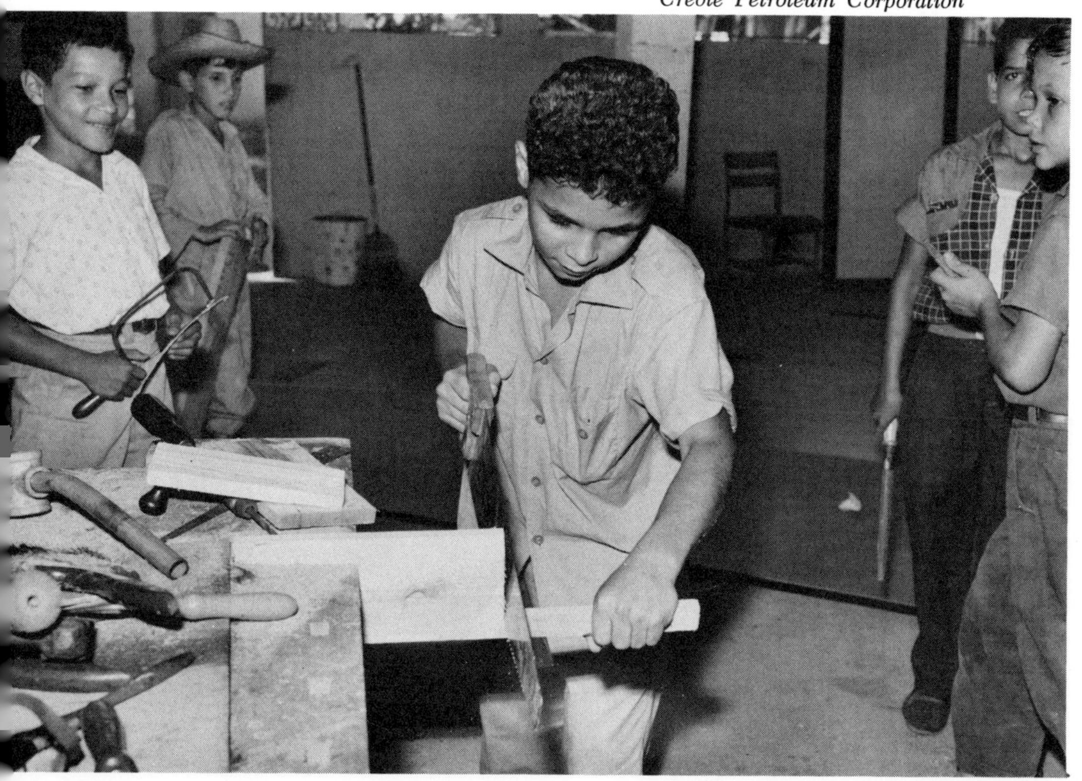

Creole Petroleum Corporation

The national Capitol in the center of Caracas.

Presidents Betancourt and Kennedy in the White House, February 19, 1963.

City News Bureau, Washington, D.C.

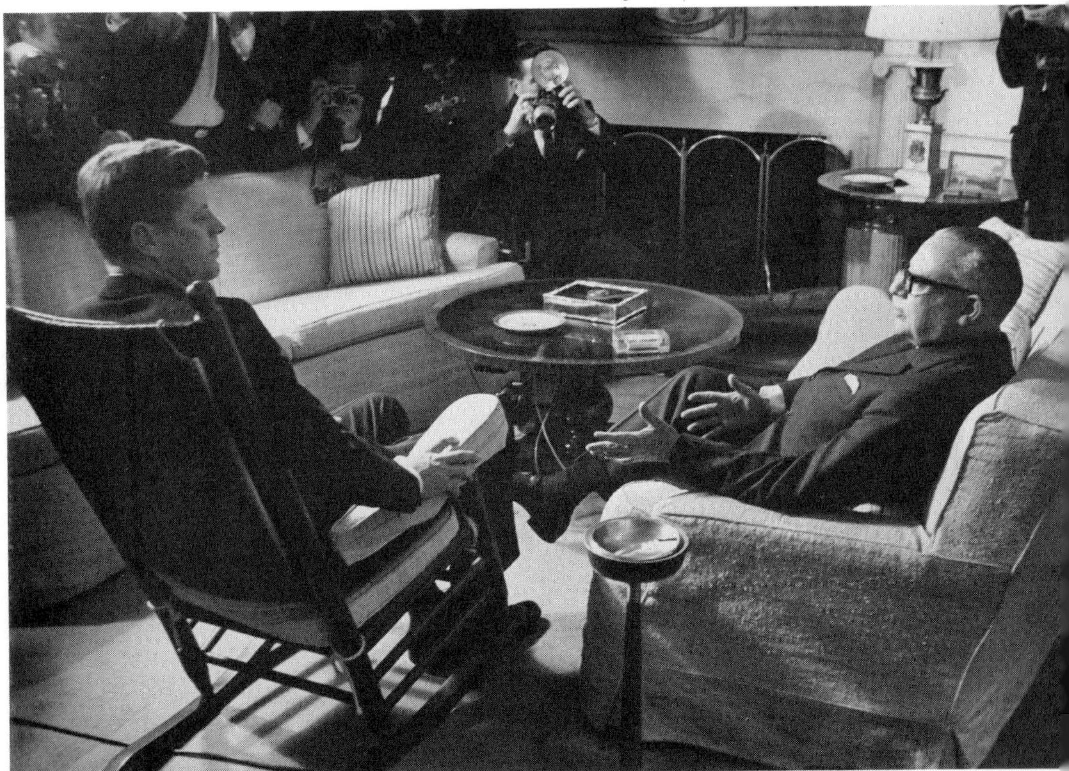

kitchen, bathroom, and dining-living room. Steel rails donated to the cooperative were used for the skeleton of the buildings, the walls being constructed of stone collected on the cooperative itelf.

The new housing development was built overlooking an artificial lake that members of the cooperative had formed by damming up a stream. The lake was stocked with trout. The technical director of the cooperative was planning the construction of a hydroelectric plant, to be run by a water wheel built out of wood by the members of the cooperative. Meanwhile, a small diesel engine plant supplied the electricity for the cooperative.

Each peasant on this cooperative received a regular daily income derived from the profits of the enterprise. Workers in each section received a different income, varying from 8 to 10 bolívares a day.

The second cooperative visited by the author was the Unidad de Producción Cascarí in Táchira State, which in August, 1961, consisted of eighty-four families. At that time most of them were living in the nearby town of Rubio, since they felt that it made more sense to build up the agricultural and productive units of the community before building a village. They concentrated on painting, reconstructing buildings, putting up fences, cleaning and repairing machinery in the coffee and sugar processing center of the cooperative. They had built three hundred chicken coops.

Members of the Unidad received an advance on profits of 8 bolívares a day each. They did not work any fixed number of hours per day, but rather worked until the day's job was completed. The executive committee of the cooperative, consisting of five persons elected by a general meeting of the community, assigned the members to the work that needed to be done each day. They also had disciplinary powers over the members, in accordance with the statutes that had been adopted by a general membership meeting. If a member did not do his assigned task, if he came to work drunk, or otherwise violated the rules, sanctions were applied to the erring member.

The Cascarí cooperative received a loan of 80,000 bolívares from the Banco Agrícola y Pecuario when it began. Members paid this back within a few months, and had a profit of 20,000 bolívares, which they invested in the cooperative.

Several massive colonization schemes form a part of the Venezuelan agrarian reform program. They were a feature of the program undertaken during the first Acción Democrática government of 1945 to 1948, and were the only elements of this program that were continued under the dictatorship. The IAN took over these projects and undertook to establish several more; however, in the middle of 1961 it decided to halt work on the new projects, at least for the time being.

The largest colony is at Turén, in the state of Portuguesa. Although the planning for this colony was carried out during the first Acción Democrática regime, it was built by the dictatorship, beginning in 1950, on rather different lines. The AD government had intended to settle small peasant farmers, but the dictatorship laid the project out on the basis of grants averaging about 125 acres, which is large for Venezuela. Also, grantees paid for their newly acquired land instead of receiving it free, as had originally been planned.

By the middle of 1961, when the author visited the Turén colony, it consisted of approximately 110,000 acres. The 629 farmers in the older part of the colony had grants of from 100 to 425 acres. There were also some 300 small peasant plots, 12.5 to 25 acres each. These settlements had been made before the overthrow of the Pérez Jiménez dictatorship. Between 1958 and 1961 some 793 small parcels of approximately 25 acres apiece were carved out of a new section of the colony established by the IAN.

The main crops cultivated at Turén are rice, corn, sesame, and cotton. The colony was producing in 1961 about 80 per cent of the country's total output of sesame seed. Sesame has the advantage of being a reliable crop with only such variation in yield as is determined by the weather.

The Turén colony is generally regarded as the most successful enterprise of its kind in Venezuela. Others have been less profitable from the point of view of both the settlers and the government. For instance, the Unidad Agropecuario de los Andes, in Táchira State, on which the government had spent some 30 million bolívares by the middle of 1961, was considered a failure. It was settled by people who were not peasants, but favorites of the Pérez Jiménez dictatorship, principally people of the cities, many of whom promptly hired others to work their land for them and used their land for week-end visiting.

The IAN undertook to establish another large colonization project, El Guapo, in the state of Miranda, some fifty miles from Caracas. At the end of August, 1961, the executive committee of the IAN decided to discontinue this project, in which several million bolívares had been invested.

Chapter Fourteen

The Agrarian Reform: Success or Failure?

Has the Venezuelan agrarian reform been a success? It is too early to give a definitive answer to this question, but some of the important positive and negative aspects of its operations during the Betancourt administration can be discussed.

A basic question concerning any attempted land reform is the speed with which it is being accomplished. Is it being carried out quickly enough to achieve the stated economic and social objectives? Is it going forward with sufficient rapidity to meet the aspirations and hopes of the peasantry, and to sustain their faith in those who are in charge of the program?

Plainly, the Venezuelan agrarian reform did not move as fast under Betancourt as its leaders had hoped it would, although statements by some of them that the process of redistributing the soil would be completed by the end of the Betancourt administration can be chalked up to excessive optimism or public relations.

Various estimates were made by spokesmen of the regime during the five years of President Betancourt's term concerning the amount of land the administration intended to distribute. In a speech he gave at Quito, Ecuador, on September 2, 1960, Rafael Caldera expressed the hope that between 120,000 and 150,000 families would be settled on their own land by the end of the Betancourt administration. President Betancourt himself, in his fourth annual message to Congress in March, 1962, set the number of families he hoped to have settled by March, 1964, at 150,000. However, as a result of the capture of control of the Chamber of Deputies by the opposition after the defection of the ARS faction of Acción Democrática, Congress severely cut the budget of the IAN in 1962 and 1963. Hence, President Betancourt in his fifth annual message to Congress in March, 1963, reduced his land distribution target to 100,000 families.

A survey made by the IAN in August, 1961, showed that three hundred and seventy-one groups of peasants had been settled on a total of 1,445,569 hectares (approximately 3.5 million acres). The number of peasant families settled on the land was 35,662. Some 70 per cent of the peasant settlements were on level land, 24 per cent had all-weather drainage, and 72 per cent required irrigation. Two hundred and eight of the settlements used machinery to prepare the soil, but only 106 used it for sowing; seventy-three used machines for cultivating, but only twenty-nine used it for harvesting.[1]

The speed of land redistribution was stepped up after September, 1961. According to Luis Piñerua, president of the IAN, whom the author interviewed on August 2, 1962, some 36,295 families had received land by December, 1961, out of a total of 84,676 families which had asked for land since the passage of the Agrarian Reform Law twenty-one months before. By the beginning of August, 1962, the number of recipient families had risen to 50,155. Of these, some 38,037, or 75.8 per cent, had been settled on land expropriated from private landholders. In his fifth annual message to Congress in March, 1963, President Betancourt reported that by that time his administration had settled some 57,000 families on 1.5 million hectares (3.75 million acres).

One indicator of the success of the agrarian reform is the degree to which the parties leading the government were able to keep the loyalty of the peasantry. Judged on this basis, the agrarian reform could be considered successful. The overwhelming majority of the peasant unions throughout the country remained under the control of Acción Democrática, and the attempt by the ARS to take the peasant movement out of AD control failed. The only states in which the AD was not in control of the majority of organized peasants were the two Andean states of Mérida and Táchira, where the local units of the Peasants Federation were led by elements of the Copei, which shared government responsibility with Acción Democrática. Certainly the peasant reaction against attempts of extreme Leftists to launch guerrilla activities in isolated rural areas beginning in 1962 and 1963 showed that the peasants continued to regard the Betancourt regime as the guarantor of effective agrarian reform.

A decline in agricultural output and productivity frequently occurs when an agrarian reform is undertaken because the peasantry who benefit from the reform do not know how to use the land, or they are unaccustomed to living in a money economy, and find little incentive to produce goods to sell in the market. They are content to grow enough for their own small wants, without producing a surplus that can be sold to the people of the cities.

Such evidence as there is available indicates that this has not occurred as a result of the Venezuelan agrarian reform. Quite to the contrary, there is some evidence that land redistribution was accompanied by increases in output. Although no cause and effect relationship can be proved between the agrarian reform and increases in output of key crops between 1958 and 1963, it is certain that the two phenomena took place at the same time.

Rafael Silva Guillén, member of the directorate of the Instituto Agrario Nacional, writing in the daily *El Nacional* on August 4, 1961, discussed the increases in agricultural production that had occurred during the constitutional government: "Any examination . . . must start with an analysis of maize production, the staple peasant crop. During 1959, when the Congress was still discussing the Agrarian Reform Law, some 280,000 hectares were cultivated in maize in the country, with a yield of 336,000 metric tons; in the following year, the first of the reform, it was possible to sow 120,000 additional hectares, with which production rose to 440,000 metric tons, or 30 per cent more corn than was produced the year before."

Production in 1961 was reported to be somewhat less than in 1960 because of adverse weather conditions. There was also a shortage of maize in the country in 1961, resulting from a spectacular increase in the demand for it. During the previous three years, the production of animal feed made from maize had risen sharply. The demand for maize by the newly established liquor industry for use in manufacturing whisky also rose dramatically.

Silva Guillén went on to discuss the output of other products: "The case of rice is much more astonishing: from an area of 28,500 hectares under cultivation, which yielded 38,500 metric tons of rice in 1959, the area rose to 42,000 hectares (a 48 per cent increase), which yielded 72,000 metric tons of rice (an 86 per cent increase) in 1960, the first year of the agrarian reform. . . .

". . . in 1959 some 14,500 hectares in potatoes yielded 93,000 metric tons of potatoes, while in the first year of the agrarian reform 18,200 hectares (a 25 per cent increase) were cultivated, to produce 133,600 metric tons (a 43 per cent increase). Although we did not succeed in fully meeting our consumption needs, it cannot be denied that the advance is substantial and that we shall soon achieve self-subsistence."

In his fifth annual message to Congress, President Betancourt noted that in 1962 there had been an 8 per cent increase in agricultural output, and that between 1958 and 1962 the average increase had been 6.9 per cent, compared with a rise of 5.1 per cent in the 1950 to 1958 period. He noted increases from 357,000 to 550,000 metric tons in maize production between 1958 and 1962; from 19,000 to 100,000 metric tons of rice; from 21,000 to 28,000 metric tons of sesame; from 21,000 to 40,000 metric tons of cotton; from 2 million to 3 million metric tons of sugar; and from 5,000 to 9,000 metric tons of tobacco in the same period. He also noted the rise in dairy production, from 139 million liters of pasteurized milk in 1958 to 162 million liters in 1962. Finally, he cited a decrease of 10 per cent in agricultural imports and a rise of 15 per cent in agricultural exports between 1958 and 1962.

The Betancourt government considered the problem of conservation to be closely associated with the agrarian reform. The elimination of the conuco system was designed in part to end primitive farming practices which caused erosion of extensive areas of the agricultural and forestry lands of the nation. However, the regime went much further than this, and for the first time in Venezuela's history established the basis for a rational policy of conservation of the nation's resources.

In August, 1961, President Betancourt established the National Council of Hydraulic Resources. The purpose of the new organization, which consisted of representatives of the Ministries of Agriculture and Public Works, the president of the Instituto Agrario Nacional, and other appropriate government officials, was stated in Articles 4 and 5 of the decree by which it was established:

"Article 4: The National Council of Hydraulic Resources will be the advisory, coordinating, and consultative organism . . . in everything regarding the use and conservation of publicly owned waters, for human, industrial, and irrigation use.

"Article 5: The National Council of Hydraulic Resources will serve as the coordinator of the programs, projects, and budgets of different parts of the public administration which are related to the use and conservation of waters, so as to propose necessary reforms."

Another step in the direction of conservation was taken with the establishment of the National Forest Products Laboratory by the Ministry of Agriculture and the Universidad de los Andes in Mérida. This laboratory was to have as its function the study of the forest reserves of the nation.

In July, 1961, the directorate of the Instituto Agrario Nacional was reorganized. The new administration undertook as its first act a general survey of what had been accomplished by the agrarian reform to date. This did not mean that they intended to slow down the process of land redistribution, but only that they felt that it was time to assess the program and decide how it could be improved.

The Venezuelan agrarian reform operations were inevitably affected by the fierce political crosscurrents, the constant threats to the security of the regime, the economic-financial crisis, and the lack of sufficient skilled man power.

One initial problem of the agrarian reform operations was the nature of the implementing agencies. The Instituto Agrario Nacional, the Banco Agrícola y Pecuario, and the Ministry of Agriculture were all inherited from the dictatorship. They had been designed by the Pérez Jiménez regime for purposes very different from those for which the Betancourt regime needed them, and the process of transforming them into organizations capable of carrying out a fundamental change in the economic and social structure was not easy. Nor were these organizations free of the evils of excess bureaucracy which plagued all agencies of the constitutional regime.

Coordination of the activities of the agencies administering the program presented other problems. Partly this situation arose from different political control in the three institutions. The Instituto Agrario Nacional was dominated from the beginning of the Betancourt regime by Acción Democrática, though the Copei was represented in its directorate. The Ministry of Agriculture, on the other hand, was from the beginning of the constitutional regime in the hands of the Copei party. The Banco Agrícola y Pecuario was headed for the first two and a half years of the Betancourt government by an independent, under whose administration the Communists and their fellow travelers had a great deal of influence; then in the middle of 1961 the bank passed into AD hands.

Aside from political considerations, the bureaucratic separation of the three chief organs of the agrarian reform was bound to lead to considerable confusion. The jobs that they were doing needed to be closely coordinated, and failing this, difficulties occurred on both state and national levels.

In only a few states did the state governor undertake to coordinate the agrarian reform program in his area. Governor José Regino Pena of the state of Carabobo established in July, 1961, a coordinating committee composed of the principal state representatives of the IAN, the Banco Agrícola y Pecuario, and the Ministry of Agriculture, as well as of officials of other federal and state agencies involved in the agrarian reform, and of the state unit of the Peasants Federation. This committee met regularly to iron out details of the reform on a state level. Similar local committees were established in several subdivisions of the state. The governor of the state of Bolívar met weekly with an economic and social development committee composed of the top state officials of the groups mentioned in the case of Carabobo, plus representatives of all the other important dependencies of the state and national governments dealing with economic and social problems. The scope of this group went further than, but included, agrarian reform activities in the state.

As the program progressed, the need for closer coordination among the organizations working on the agrarian reform was better understood. After the installation of the new directorate of the IAN in July, 1961, the President ordered the formation of an informal national committee consisting of the top people in the IAN, the Banco Agrícola y Pecuario, and the Ministry of Agriculture to bring into line the policies of these three key institutions. Further measures to achieve over-all coordination of the agrarian reform effort were taken in the following years, but the problem was by no means solved at the end of 1963. Ideally, when the Instituto Agrario Nacional decides upon the expropriation of a given unit of land, the Banco Agrícola y Pecuario should be ready at the same time to extend the credit needed by the peasants who are to be settled, and the Ministry of Agriculture should have its technicians immediately available to advise and direct the planting efforts of the new landholders. At the same time, the Ministry of Education, the Rural Housing Division of the Ministry of Health, the Instituto Nacional de Obras Sanitarias and all of the other institutions concerned should be ready to go to work on the new agrarian reform settlement. Unfortunately, such unified effort was seldom possible.

It was the author's observation during July and August, 1961, that adequate credit for the beneficiaries of the agrarian reform was available in only a handful of states, and scarcely anywhere was sufficient technical help being given to agrarian reform settlements by the Ministry of Agriculture. The difficulties of the Banco Agrícola y Pecuario in providing credit for the beneficiaries of the agrarian reform were several. The bank did not have sufficient funds to fill all of the demands made upon it, and was also trying to adapt itself to a job in the agrarian reform field for which it was not originally intended. It was the site of much political bickering during the first two years of the Betancourt regime.

Although the principal political problems of this bank were resolved by the middle of 1961, it continued to suffer from the financial crisis, because the government was unable to allocate the full amount of money needed, though the bank did receive much more than it had under the previous regime. The bank was also hampered by the failure of its debtors to pay back loans. Both the large landholders and to a smaller degree the agrarian reform beneficiaries were at fault. The delinquency of many large landholder debtors reached the point of scandal years before Betancourt became President. This situation encouraged deliquency on the part of smaller borrowers. With the installation of a new management in the bank in the middle of 1961, the directorate ordered that no further loans be advanced to any individual or group in arrears in payment of outstanding debts. A concerted effort was launched also to collect sums still owed to the institution.

The Banco Agrícola y Pecuario was not originally intended to do the kind of job that it was called upon to perform in the agrarian reform. Beneficiaries of the agrarian reform exhibited considerable resentment over the fact that the institution that they thought should be designed primarily to serve their interests continued to give large loans to large landholders, the purpose for which it was in fact set up. The possibility of establishing a separate lending institution to meet the needs of the agrarian reform was still under study by the end of the Betancourt administration.

The Banco Agrícola y Pecuario was not alone in its financial troubles. Like most other branches of the government, the Ministry of Agriculture did not receive the funds that it needed to do an adequate job in the agrarian reform field, or, for that matter, in any other area in which it was active. But more serious was the lack of trained members of the extension service of the Ministry. Even had it had all of the funds that it wished, the Ministry would not have been able to muster the personnel to provide advice for all of the peasants who received land. The Venezuelan universities had never offered training courses in agricultural extension work, and the few hundred people who were available had been trained largely in the institutions of higher learning of the United States.

In seeking to recruit agronomists and extension agents, the Ministry had to compete with other institutions involved in the land reform program. The Instituto Agrario Nacional selected considerable numbers of the trained agricultural technicians as its state and local delegates. Although their knowledge and training were of great value for these jobs, they were not available for the detailed programing of production and instruction in new techniques that were needed by the new settlements of the IAN.

Another weakness of the land program was the slowness in providing the peasant families with final titles to their new holdings. By August, 1962, only about 5,000 of the 50,155 families which had been settled on the land had actually received such documents. This is partly because the law wisely requires that one year pass after a peasant has been settled on land before title can be issued; at the end of this trial period it should be clear whether he intends to stay on the holding or not. Another cause of slowness, however, was undoubtedly the lack of sufficient technical personnel to carry out the work of delimiting the new peasant holdings.

It soon became evident that one of the principal handicaps of the agrarian reform program was inadequate marketing facilities for the products grown by the new settlements. In the state of Carabobo, for example, peasants of the La Linda agrarian reform settlement at Güigüe planted a large number of tomatoes and had a bumper crop in 1960; however, since no precaution had been taken to assure a market for this highly perishable product, most of the harvest was lost. The next year the peasants of La Linda returned to growing cotton and corn, the traditional crops of the area.

By 1961 the Instituto Agrario Nacional was giving more attention to the marketing problem. A large outlet for fruits and vegetables, at least insofar as the central coastal states of the republic were concerned, was created with the building of a sizable cannery near Valencia by the Heinz Company. Heinz was one of several manufacturing firms that took the initiative in providing markets for the produce of the beneficiaries of the agrarian reform. Two others were the manufacturers of tobacco and cotton textiles, who not only encouraged the growing of raw materials they needed but also sought to get the farmers, whether peasants or large producers, to improve quality and to grade their output.

A key element in marketing was the provision of local roads to connect the peasants with the nearest highways. By the middle of 1963 the Betancourt government had built some 10,000 kilometers of such roads, compared with only 2,900 constructed between 1955 and 1958, inclusive.[1]

Political rivalries and quarreling between members of the different political parties and within Acción Democrática greatly complicated the agrarian reform. In some states members of the government parties were at odds with those of the opposition in the rural areas. In the few places where the Communists or other opposition parties had some influence in the peasant movement, they attempted to use their peasant followers to embarrass the Instituto Agrario Nacional and the government.

The Left-wing opposition parties violently attacked the agrarian reform program of the government, and sought to discredit it in the eyes of the peasants. They accused the government of lack of sincerity in its land redistribution efforts, and violently criticized the failure of the regime to provide sufficient credit or technical aid to the beneficiaries of the reform. Frequently they went too far, and accused the local peasant union leaders of Acción Democrática of stealing and misusing such loans from the Banco Agrícola y Pecuario as they did receive. Typical of the attacks on the agrarian reform by the parties of the extreme Left is an article by Domingo Alberto Rangel, principal figure in the Movimiento de Izquierda Revolucionaria, which appeared in the newspaper *El Nacional* of Caracas on July 25, 1961. Entitled "Without Maize, Without Potatoes, Without Beans," it said in part:

"The scarcity of maize and beans underscores the government's policy and is evidence of the disaster toward which we are being taken by a group without firmness, without vision, and without backbone. We Venezuelans are paying in the high prices of maize and beans for the result of two years and a half of irresponsible demagoguery. The leaders of the government look upon the peasants only as electoral tools. Complacency is their weapon. They flatter in the peasant exactly those bad qualities that an effective agrarian reform would try to overcome. . . . Very seldom have the leaders of the IAN or of the peasant unions tried to establish solid bases of efficiency in the agrarian colonies, or to orient the conuqueros to make best use of their credits. Malice, waste, and the absence of administrative norms in the colonies of the IAN have never been dealt with with the vigor that they warrant, by government people concerned with the countryside. Insofar as credits are concerned, more than one local "leader" has squandered the money in drinking bouts with masses of peasants who because of being disoriented and poverty-stricken cannot by themselves find the right road. . . . In Venezuela, this agrarian reform of the constitutional government is going to repeat the Mexican experience, where the masses, still frustrated, only serve to support small local "caudillos" who flatter them to assure their own personal domination. As long as this continues, we will have scarcity of food in the cities, as testimony of the existing mess. . . ."

The Communists and Right-wing opponents of the regime likewise denounced the reform, the latter from a somewhat different point of view. The Rightists tended to exaggerate the number of cases in which peasants had illegally seized the land, and argued that the way in which the agrarian reform was being carried out was undermining the confidence of the business community in the country's future.

None of these attacks had made much impression on the peasants by the end of the Betancourt administration. Although critical of the slowness with which the land distribution was moving, and of their failure to receive adequate credit and technical assistance, the great mass of the peasants continued to support the agrarian reform and the government that was carrying it out.

Some of the worst political quarreling took place in the mountain states of Mérida and Táchira between members of the coalition parties, Acción Democrática and the Copei. Rivalry between these two parties was the main cause of failure of the Río Chama agrarian reform project, which was supposed to be a broad gauge program for land redistribution and agricultural development of a major part of the state of Mérida. The Copei leaders who controlled the local unit of the Peasants Federation in the state of Mérida declared their intention to sabotage the project because they felt they were subject to discrimination at the hands of the predominantly AD-controlled state delegation of the Instituto Agrario Nacional.

Even more disconcerting for the agrarian reform were rivalries within Acción Democrática. In the early months of 1961 the work of the IAN was endangered by a bitter feud between Ildegar Pérez Segnini, president of the IAN, and Ramón Quijada, president of the Peasants Federation, both members of Acción Democrática. Various issues were involved in this dispute. On the one hand, there were the personal ambitions of Quijada, who was rumored to be anxious to become head of the IAN. In the second place, there was controversy over the emphasis to be given the IAN's work. Quijada argued that the IAN should concentrate on expropriating privately held land and distributing it among tenants and agricultural workers. Pérez Segnini, on the other hand, sought to have the IAN complement this approach to the problem by colonization schemes on government-owned land in relatively unpopulated parts of the country. Early in July, 1961, Pérez Segnini resigned, and although Quijada did not become head of the IAN, the policy he had advocated was adopted by the new directorate.

An even more difficult situation developed at the end of 1961, when the Peasants Federation was split as a result of AD internecine quarrels. This was dangerous because of the key role representatives of the federation played in the directorate of the IAN, and because of the chance it offered extreme Left elements to penetrate the peasantry for the first time. However, by the end of the Betancourt regime, it was clear that these dangers had been overcome. The pro-government faction of the federation, which was the group represented in the IAN directorate, represented the great majority of the peasantry, and it was obvious that the extreme Leftists had been unsuccessful in seeking support among the rural populace.

I may observe once again that among the greatest handicaps to the full development of the Venezuelan agrarian reform has been the tendency of the peasants to look to the government for everything. Spanish colonial administrations sought to regulate minutely every aspect of their subjects' affairs, including their religion, their economic life, even their reading habits. The dictators who ruled the country subsequently did little to change the customs established during colonial days. Furthermore, during the boom of the twentieth century a large part of the country's national income began to pass through the government's hands, converting the public administration into the source of rapid profits, large fortunes, and tens of thousands of jobs, the latter constituting a high percentage of the nation's well-paid jobs.

The peasant, who traditionally was dependent upon the landlord for whatever meager public services he enjoyed, tended to turn to the IAN and other government agencies with the change in the pattern of landownership, just as he had turned to the landlord in the past. The peasant thus expected that the IAN and other agencies of the agrarian reform would supply him not only with land and credit, but with housing, local roads, water supplies, and practically everything else that he needed. From conversations with many beneficiaries of the agrarian reform, the author gained the impression that it had not dawned upon many peasants that they might through their own efforts, or through cooperation with their fellows, build the roads, construct the houses, and provide some of the other things that they all need. This pressure of the peasantry upon the government strained the administration's financial resources.

Although the Venezuelan agrarian reform has been beset with problems, its significance in the general pattern of the country's Democratic Revolution is unquestionably great. The land distribution program had already brought about long overdue improvement in the economic and social structure of the country by 1964. It had established a class of small landholders who will be able to put into production large parts of the nation's arable land never before used. These small holders will in many cases have a money income for the first time, and will constitute a sizable increase in the market for the goods manufactured by new industries established as a result of another phase of the democratic government's program. Available figures indicate that the agrarian reform has already brought a noticeable increase in the output of agricultural products.

The agrarian reform measures were instituted in a constitutional manner and without disorganizing the economy. The majority of the landlords acquiesced in the expropriation proceedings and some in fact were eager to get the government to purchase their holdings.

The agrarian reform is essential to the stability of a democratic regime in Venezuela. By the end of 1963 it was progressing with sufficient rapidity to maintain the loyalty of the peasantry in the democratic regime, and particularly in the Acción Democrática party.

Chapter Fifteen
Industrialization: Aid to Private Enterprise

President Rómulo Betancourt and his associates favored the development in Venezuela of a mixed economy in which private Venezuelan entrepreneurs, foreign investors, and the state would all have important roles to play. In conformity with this objective, industrialization was regarded as a fundamental part of the program of the Venezuelan Democratic Revolution. Not only is it an essential means of bringing about the desired alterations in the country's economic and social structure, but it is also a basic part of the program of economic nationalism advocated by Betancourt and Acción Democrática ever since the party was organized in 1937.

Some progress in industrialization had been made during the nine years of the Pérez Jiménez dictatorship—largely in spite of the actions of that regime. The oil boom of those years resulted in a considerable increase in the Venezuelan internal market, and a number of new firms were established to make products used by the construction industry, in the food processing field, and in some other industries. However, the dictatorial regime did little to encourage this development. It allowed the Corporación Venezolana de Fomento, which had been established by the Acción Democrática government in 1946 to spur agricultural development and industrialization, to become inactive. It signed a commercial treaty with the United States which, as long as it was enforced, served to prevent the extension of protection to a wide variety of industries.

The only positive action of the dictatorship in favor of industrialization was to launch two government-owned heavy industry projects: a steel mill in the Orinoco River Valley and a petrochemical plant near Puerto Cabello in the central part of the country. Both of these enterprises were masterpieces of misplanning and were designed more to make a profit for government officials involved in working on them than to establish viable industries.

Once again in power, Betancourt reasserted his determination to push forward the development of Venezuelan manufacturing. Thus, in a speech he made on June 18, 1959, the President commented: "We are concerned that the country not continue investing the dollars that petroleum produces for it in bringing from abroad those things which we can and must and will produce within the national boundaries. In this regard, the industrialists of Venezuela need not have the least doubt concerning the defined and clear policy of the national government." [1]

In his 1960 New Year's message, President Betancourt explained the nature and projections of the government's industrialization policy: "There is going forward a structural change in the national economy, and we are beginning to break our dependence on foreign production. This has been possible because of the joining of forces by the state and private enterprise. The state is orienting credit toward industries and agricultural and livestock enterprises, and halting importation or regulating it, so that we do not destroy ourselves through the cut artery represented by purchase abroad of luxury articles or articles that could be produced in the country, thus diverting foreign exchange that is needed to bring from abroad machinery and raw materials, the latter transformable by national labor into products of domestic manufacture.

"Private firms are orienting their investments more toward industry, agriculture, and livestock raising, instead of merely toward distributing foreign merchandise, or toward speculation in real estate.

"This change in orientation of the nation's economy, a change which is the only one that can assure a solid base for real independence for the fatherland, brings difficulties and transitory maladjustments. . . . But in Venezuela these difficulties will be fewer than in other countries, because industrialization will not be realized at the cost of the consumer and of the workers; but rather, through the decided action of the state and the receptive attitude of the most dynamic and modern sector of the capitalist classes, the benefits obtained from protected industries will be equitably divided among the consumer, the workers, and the peasants who work for them. . . .

"In summary: In Venezuela there will be a maladjustment which is foreseeable, inevitable, in certain sectors of the economy; but there will be no crisis in the country as a whole. The contrary will be the case because the nation is ceasing to be, and definitively will cease to be, dependent on foreign production of those things which can be produced with the national capital, technique, and labor, and because the time is past when we were a sure market for any costly gewgaws from abroad. We are a country of limited resources, in spite of the marvelous gift of petroleum and iron that nature has given us. We must dedicate those resources to forging a permanent economy, to attending to many of the unsatisfied needs of a nation where millions of families live without the advantages of civilization."[2]

The Betancourt regime chose three methods to stimulate the industrialization of the country. First, it adopted a policy of protection to manufacturing, through the device of high tariffs, where that was possible, through absolute prohibition or limitation of imports by decree, and through the establishment of exchange controls. Second, it reactivated the Corporación Venezolana de Fomento, and through it extended considerable sums to aid private investors in various manufacturing fields. Third, it caused the government itself to carry out the work of a catalyst by supplying the principal elements of the "infrastructure" of the economy—electricity, transportation, and others—and establishing and maintaining the principal heavy industries of the nation, including steel, petrochemicals, and aluminum.

Different approaches to the problem of protection were needed for different industries. Since in a number of cases, the commercial treaty with the United States prohibited the raising of customs duties, which would serve to keep United States products from entering the Venezuelan market, other means of protecting local industries from foreign competition were resorted to. With the introduction of exchange controls late in 1960, an additional protective device came into use—the legal rationing of foreign currency.

Characteristic of the methods used for protecting Venezuelan industries by the Betancourt regime was that applied to the automobile industry. In July, 1961, Director de Industria Manuel Delgado Rovatti announced that after December 31, 1962, no further importation of assembled automobiles would be permitted. The purpose of this move was quite frankly stated to be to force the Volkswagen, Fiat, Renault, and Mercedes Benz companies, which had expressed interest in establishing plants in Venezuela, to make up their minds. Ford and General Motors were already building assembly plants in Valencia.

Several industries were particularly favored by the protection policy of the Betancourt government. During the first two years or more textiles and food processing enterprises were the principal beneficiaries. In the middle of 1961 the government turned its attention to the pharmaceutical industry.

The Dirección de Industrias of the Ministry of Development, which administers the policy of protection, used various criteria in deciding whether or not an industry deserved protection. These included the amount of raw material from Venezuela that would be used, the number of people who would be employed, the value that would be added to products by the industry to be protected, as well as the costs of the industry seeking protection.

The increase in price that may be passed on to the consumer by protected industries was controlled by the Dirección. Usually, protection was extended to an industry only if the cost of its product to the consumer was not more than 10 to 30 per cent higher than that of imported products; however, this varied with the case. For instance, industries that used a lot of local raw materials and added a large amount of value to the product in the manufacturing process were allowed a higher price increase than those which added little and did not use Venezuelan raw materials.

In his fifth annual message to Congress on March 12, 1963, President Betancourt underscored the importance of this factor in the government's decisions to defend particular industries. He noted that in the previous year some one hundred and fifteen industrial projects had been registered with the Ministry of Development, representing a total investment of 256 million bolívares. These industries used some 255 million bolívares worth of raw materials, of which 56 per cent were produced in Venezuela.

One of the cases that was most criticized was that of copper electric wire. The Dirección allowed a 300 per cent increase in price in that case; however, it did so with an eye to the future. As of 1961, when protection was extended to that industry, the only manufacturing operation carried out in this field in Venezuela was the twisting and finishing of copper wire. The industry was using wire imported from abroad. It was expected that with protection, the next step would be taken, that is, the importation of copper sheets and the making of wire in the country. In time it seemed likely that the country might develop an integrated copper industry, since there are various copper mines in Venezuela that have not hitherto been exploited, largely because they had no domestic market.

Another consideration of the Dirección de Industrias was the amount of foreign exchange an industry would save if it were given protection. This assumed importance particularly after the imposition of exchange controls.

In extending protection, the government took steps to prevent excessive price increases. Thus, in August, 1961, when further protection was offered the textile industry, this was made dependent upon the textile manufacturers' being willing to sign an agreement limiting price rises. This agreement included a promise not to increase prices over those in effect on June 30, 1961, unless absolutely forced to do so by increases in costs. It was agreed that the Dirección de Industrias would investigate hardship cases, and if it found that price increases had not been justified, they would be abolished. The agreement also called for reinvestment of profits in the industry, use of domestic raw materials, cooperation in improving the quality of Venezuelan cotton and output increases so as to make Venezuela completely self-sufficient in textiles.[3]

The quality of Venezuelan products was also taken into account in determining whether or not protection should be given a national industry. Thus, when the Dirección de Industrias began to plan for limiting foreign competition with the national pharmaceutical industry in the middle of 1961, it established prerequisites to be met before additional import restrictions would be imposed. One of the most fundamental of these was that the Ministry of Health must be satisfied that the quality of the goods produced by the Venezuelan industry would be as high as that of imports. Likewise, the textile agreement provided for the labeling of all textiles, to indicate quality and raw material content, as a protection for the consumer.

The extent of protection offered to industry by the government since the fall of the Pérez Jiménez regime, and particularly since the advent of the Betancourt regime, has been considerable. The principal private organization pushing the industrialization program, the Asociación Pro-Venezuela, estimated in the middle of 1961 that some eight hundred industrial categories had been protected during the previous three years. The industries thus favored were estimated by Pro-Venezuela to have turned out 1,300 million bolívares worth of goods during that period.[4]

The commercial treaty signed with the United States during the dictatorship did not prove to be as great a handicap to the Betancourt regime's protectionist policy as had been anticipated. In the first place, the measures adopted by the Venezuelan government in many cases consisted, not of raising tariffs, but rather of imposing physical limitation on the import of foreign goods, or an absolute prohibition of such imports; thus the treaty did not apply. In the second place, the United States Embassy tended to close its eyes to specific encroachments on the provisions of the treaty as long as United States exporters to Venezuela were not discriminated against as compared with exporters from other countries. Where discrimination was involved in a protectionist decree, the Embassy pointed out to the Venezuelan government that this involved a violation of a basic aspect of the commercial treaty, and in each case an amicable solution of the problem was agreed upon.

The program of protection not only aided the development of Venezuelan-owned industrial enterprises, but also encouraged the establishment of a number of foreign-owned manufacturing firms in the country. Peter Wenzl, Venezuelan manager of Pan American Airways, speaking on February 14, 1961, to the School of Advanced International Studies of The Johns Hopkins University, summed up this result of the Betancourt government program as follows: "So as to maintain their markets, North American firms found that they could diminish the effect of these moves by sending in semi-finished products, or packaging or converting them in the country. . . . An impressive number of North American firms came to Venezuela in 1960, principally in the fields of canning, foodstuffs, clothing, automobile tires, paint, cigarettes, glass, aluminum, and automobile assembly plants. In addition to Chrysler and General Motors, Ford recently joined this group."[5]

Through the Corporación Venezolana de Fomento, another basic agency in the industrialization program, the Betancourt regime achieved several objectives. Not only did it extend very large sums of money to private investors in the manufacturing field but also it reorganized and decentralized the administration of several key industries that were in the hands of the state.

As originally constituted, the Corporación de Fomento was supposed to aid the development of both agriculture and industry; however, its activities were subsequently confined to the urban economy, largely to manufacturing and power.

During the Betancourt regime the Corporación concentrated its lending activities on long-term loans of from five to twelve years to industrial enterprises. These loans were given at 8 per cent interest, which is very low in Venezuela, where most commercial banks lend at from 9 to 12 per cent—and will not make long-term loans in any case.

There was a dramatic increase in loans by the Corporación Venezolana de Fomento after the overthrow of Pérez Jiménez. Some 77 per cent of all its loans as of July 1, 1961, were made before or after the nine-year dictatorship. Between July 1, 1956, and June 30, 1957, the last full year of the dictatorship, the Corporación made loans of only some 2,575,956 bolívares. Subsequently, the rate of lending increased almost fifty-fold.

Table II shows the number of loans given and the total value of loans during various periods in the history of the Corporación, that is the period of the first Acción Democrática regime, the dictatorship, the provisional government, and the first years of the Betancourt regime.

Dr. Luis Valenilla, president of the Corporación Venezolana de Fomento, in an interview that appeared in *El Nacional*, on July 31,

TABLE II

Corporación Venezolana de Fomento Loans, 1946 to 1962

Period	*Number of Loans*	*Value of Loans*
July 1, 1946–December 31, 1948	108	Bs. 38,290,259.91
January 1, 1949–March 30, 1957	209	102,735,983.37
March 1, 1958–February 12, 1959	192	107,642,028.03
February 13, 1959–April 30, 1961	266	205,505,422.23
January 1, 1962–December 31, 1962	–	281,000,000.00

Sources: CVF–15 Años de una labor patriótica, Imprenta Nacional, Caracas, 1961, p. 44, and *V Presidential Message, 12th March 1963.* Imprenta Nacional, Caracas, 1963, p. 52.

1962, outlined the loan policies that the corporation had followed since he had taken over the leadership of it on January 1, 1961:

"Dr. Luis Valenilla, president of the CVF, explained that the present directorate of the development organization during the period of his administration, between January 1, 1961, and June 30, 1962, had approved 240 long-term industrial loans, compared with 407 granted in the three previous years (1958 to 1960). Of these 240 loans . . . 92.5 per cent, or 222 loans, were for less than 1 million bolívares. Likewise, of the 240 loans, 99, or 41.26 per cent of all loans approved, were for less than 100,000 bolívares. And 65 loans, or 27 per cent of all of them, were for less than 300,000 bolívares. Four loans, or 1.67 per cent, were for 1 to 1.5 million bolívares. The directorate approved 5 loans, or 2 per cent of the total, for from 1.5 to 2 million bolívares; 4 loans, or 1.6 per cent, for from 2 to 2.5 million; one loan for 2.5 to 3 million; one loan for 3 to 3.5 million; and one loan for 4,690,586.25 bolívares.

"The president of the CVF also noted that . . . the loans of less than 1 million bolívares accounted for a total of 59 million bolívares, or 53 per cent of the total in bolívares. . . ."

Until 1961 the Corporación helped principally firms that were already established and sought out its aid; however, early in that year it started a program of promotion of new industries. First, the Corporación worked out with the Oficina de Coordinación y Planificación, of the Office of the Presidency, and the Ministry of Development, a survey of industries that they felt could and should be developed to supply products previously imported and to develop new exports. The Corporación then established a promotion office which sought to interest businessmen in starting new industries. A technical assistance department was set up to help firms establish efficient operations in all phases of their work. The members of this department included industrial engineers, accountants, economists, and other technical experts. The promotion department copied some of the methods of the Economic Development Administration of Puerto Rico.

In 1961 the Corporación de Fomento extended the scope of its activities in another way. Instead of confining its financial operations to lending funds to firms receiving its help, it decided to invest directly in certain enterprises. Dr. Luis Valenilla announced this new program in the following terms: "In synthesis, it will permit anyone who has an industrial project which has been thoroughly studied by the promoter or which the Corporación may elaborate with him . . . to provide only the working capital, with the Corporación financing the land, the buildings and machinery, and renting this fixed capital to the firm, with an option to the stockholders to purchase it. This will permit the promoters in some cases to provide a minimum of 20 to 25 per cent of the total investment. . . ."[6]

Under the Betancourt government, the Corporación concerned itself with aiding small producers, and particularly the nation's artisans. The need for this kind of a government-sponsored credit program arose from the same causes that made necessary the large-scale efforts of the Corporación Venezolana de Fomento. The Venezuelan banking system is not equipped to provide working capital for the local artisan or very small entrepreneur any more than it has been able to lend larger sums to more substantial manufacturing enterprises.

The idea of a special effort to aid very small manufacturers and artisans originated with Governor Rafael Solórzano Bruce of the state of Anzoátegui soon after the constitutional government was inaugurated. He presented the idea to President Betancourt, who was impressed with it, and included funds for the project in succeeding budgets.

It was felt that to be effectively administered, such a program had to be locally run. As a result, the state governments were given the principal responsibility in this field. Although the funds for the program came from Caracas, each state governor was instructed to name a special committee of local citizens to pass on all applications for small loans of up to 25,000 bolívares. This committee was also charged with the job of supervising the use of the loans, to make sure that they were spent for the purposes for which they were intended.

Relatively small but important sums were spent by the Betancourt regime on this program. By March, 1961, some 9.5 million bolívares had been thus expended.[7] The budget of 1962 provided for the expenditure of an additional 25 million bolívares in this field.[8] By the end of 1962, some 1,806 loans, amounting to 25 million bolívares, had been dispensed in this program.

The effectiveness of the program varied from state to state, depending in large part on the personal interest that the governor took in it. Some states chalked up a very good record of stimulating new small-scale enterprises, with a high rate of repayment of loans. Firms aided by these small loans included clothing shops, tile-making establishments, machinery repair shops, tire recapping enterprises, and carpentry shops. The program provided employment for several thousand people, and undoubtedly aided many small businessmen who could not otherwise have made a start for lack of capital. The program also helped to slow down the drift of rural folk to Caracas and other major cities, for since the loans were given only in the provinces, they served to give an appreciable number of artisans, small entrepreneurs, and workers remunerative employment in their home towns. A few employees were even recruited in Caracas for work in the small provincial shops.

The Betancourt government counted a good deal on the cooperation of the local and state governments in its industrialization efforts. Although in many cases this cooperation left a lot to be desired, some examples of very effective action on a municipal or state basis may be noted.

A praiseworthy move was made in the city of Valencia, capital of the state of Carabobo, to stimulate the development of industries within its city limits. The municipality owned a sizable amount of land on the edge of the city, and set aside some 800 hectares (about 2,000 acres) as an industrial park. The city authorities paved the streets of the area and provided water, sewerage, and other facilities. These improvements were paid for from the sale of land to new enterprises.

The industrial park was divided into two sections, one for relatively large plants, the other for small firms with comparatively few workers. Among the large firms which bought land in the industrial park were the Ford Motor Company; a subsidiary of the Container Corporation of America; Industrias Integradas, a firm to produce refrigerators, automobile parts, air conditioners, and other metallurgical products; and a sizable vegetable oil firm.

The municipal council coordinated this program with a more general effort to modernize Valencia. Two main avenues were constructed, the sewerage system was renovated, and the old public market in the center of town was razed, its functions being taken by four newly constructed markets in outlying parts of the town. Although the municipality received help from several organs of the national government in this face-lifting operation, the initiative for all of it came from the local leaders.

Another outstanding municipal program was carried out in the town of Cagua, in the central coastal state of Aragua, which grew very rapidly from a primarily rural area to one of the country's important industrial centers.

A joint approach to the industrialization problem was represented by the establishment of the Comisión Pro-Desarrollo Industrial de Estado Zulia, set up early in 1961 to further the development of the Zulia region. It consisted of thirteen members representing the Corporación Venezolana de Fomento, the state government, the labor federation of Zulia, the industrialists, the merchants, and the agricultural landlords.

The three committees into which the commission was divided dealt with plans for the location of industry in the region, publicized the needs and opportunities for industrialization, and promoted the establishment of industry. The first committee had the job of analyzing the resources, markets, raw materials, and other factors influencing the location of industry in the region. The second conducted a series of lectures and discussions on the problems of industrialization, while the third worked with the municipal council of Maracaibo in developing an industrial park somewhat smilar to that of Valencia. The commission also undertook to negotiate with firms that might be interested in locating there.

A representative of the Corporación Venezolana de Fomento served as secretary of the Comisión Pro-Desarrollo Industrial de Estado Zulia. The Corporación hoped that if this approach proved successful in the Maracaibo area, it could be applied to other parts of the country.

A regional organization set up to seek the cooperation of local interests in economic development was the Corporación Venezolana de los Andes. This organization resulted from the First Economic Congress of the Andes, held in the city of Mérida in August, 1961, which was attended by state officials and representatives of industrial and commercial groups, labor organizations, and educational institutions in the states in or bordering the Andean region of the republic.

The functions of the Corporación de los Andes, as they were spelled out in the Mérida conference, were somewhat vague, and at the same time all-inclusive. Basically, however, the purposes of the new group were to arouse local interest and participation in both industrial and agricultural development in the area, and to decentralize some of the government help to this process in the Andean states. If initial enthusiasm is any indication of success, this program is likely to have a bright future.

The Betancourt regime thus sought to stimulate the contribution of private entrepreneurs to the industrialization of Venezuela. Through a policy of protection for new industries, through the lending program of the Corporación Venezolana de Fomento and other government credit agencies, and through the efforts of state and local governments, the revolutionary democratic administration sought to create the conditions that would make such a contribution possible. In this policy, the Betancourt government did not discriminate against foreign enterprises, nor did it especially favor them.

Chapter Sixteen

Industrialization: The State-Owned Sector

The nationalism of the government of the Venezuelan Democratic Revolution was reflected in its approach to economic growth and industrialization. Hence, in looking at the industrialization program of the Betancourt regime, one must take into account not only the efforts of the government to stimulate private investment but also its administration and development of the public segment of the economy. This segment includes two basic parts, heavy industry, and power and light. To get the best possible allocation of the country's scarce resources, leaders of the regime felt that economic planning and management would be considerably facilitated if these key sectors of the economy were to remain in government hands.

The government accordingly began working on a program to develop iron and steel, heavy chemicals, and aluminum enterprises. At the same time, in part for similar reasons of nationalistic policy, it laid the basis for a government-owned national electricity network, and likewise stimulated the development of natural gas resources under government auspices.

Present-day Venezuelans are convinced that Guayana, the large eastern region of the country comprising the valleys of the Orinoco River and its tributaries, holds vast promise for the economic future. It is known to possess large reserves of several minerals, notably iron, diamonds, and gold, and is presumed to contain other large resources. Hence a considerable part of the state-controlled industrialization effort was placed under the newly formed Corporación Venezolana de Guayana.

The possibilities of the Orinoco River Valley as "The Ruhr of Venezuela" were first visualized by the Acción Democrática government of the 1940's. Negotiations begun with foreign steel firms at that time concerning the exploitation of the iron resources of the region were conceived of by the AD government leaders as the first step toward the integral development of the area as a center of heavy industry. In their preliminary talks about the iron mining problem, the AD leaders were anxious to link the export of iron ore with investment by the exporting companies in a joint enterprise with the government for the establishment of an iron and steel plant.

The dictatorship was indecisive in its attitude toward this problem for several years; however, before it fell, it had begun building a steel plant near the confluence of the Orinoco and Caroní rivers and a large hydroelectric installation at the falls of the Caroní in the same region. Although both were held up for some time after the overthrow of the dictatorship because of difficulties with the contracts under which they were being built, by the second year of the Betancourt administration, work was again going forward at high speed.

That the Betancourt regime did not regard these projects as two isolated development efforts, but rather as key parts of an over-all program for the development of the Guayana area, was made clear when the government established the Corporación Venezolana de Guayana at the end of 1960. President Betancourt described his vision of the future of the work of the Corporación thus:

"The Corporación de Guayana is another fundamental instrument for the industrial development of Venezuela. The development of the steel plant is going to permit us to locate in Guayana a large nucleus of heavy industry and associated enterprises. In the government, we are studying with much interest the agreements for a Latin American Common Market signed in Montevideo, because we think that within a few years Venezuela will be able to compete in the Latin American common market with automobiles, with tractors, with agricultural machinery produced in Guayana. These are not illusory aspirations, but concrete possibilities, as estimated by national and foreign technicians. . . . We are already the leading exporter of iron to the United States, but we wish to be, and we shall be, exporters of machinery produced in Venezuela.

"The Corporación de Guayana does not propose to convert itself into a state super-monopoly. It will maintain control of the steel plant and of the hydroelectric works of the Caroní. All the subsidiary industries may be developed by private capital, or through mixed firms, such as that formed with Reynolds Metal to produce aluminum, in which the Corporación is associated with a manufacturing enterprise of the United States."[1]

The scope of Corporación's activities is tremendous, at least potentially. Although initially it was given control over only a relatively small area around the confluence of the Orinoco and Caroní rivers, it was empowered to undertake the mining, industrial, and agricultural development of this region. Ultimately it is foreseen that the whole valley region will probably come under its sway. Besides the supervision of the steel plant and the Caroní hydroelectric project, the Corporación de Guayana was at the outset given the task of beginning the development of an aluminum industry through its own efforts, as well as that of encouraging private enterprisers to undertake projects in the region. It was also to plan for the development of a city of 250,000 people as the heart of what many Venezuelans hope will become the country's major industrial area.

The steel plant was only about 20 per cent completed when the Betancourt regime came to power early in 1959. To complicate matters, the dictatorship had dropped the idea of the Acción Democrática regime of the 1940's of tying in a steel enterprise with the iron exporting activities of the two United States firms which received mining concessions in the area. Furthermore, in the early 1950's a combine of Venezuelan business groups, including those of Eugenio Mendoza and Gustavo Vollmer, became interested in constructing a small steel plant, with a capacity of 150,000 metric tons, and had pushed the planning aspects of this enterprise to completion by 1955. At that point, the Pérez Jiménez regime stepped in and forbade the further development of this steel firm, on the grounds that the government was planning a much larger enterprise of the same nature.

Whereas its first projects called for a plant of 300,000 metric tons capacity, even before construction had begun, these plans were revised to provide for 600,000 metric tons output, with the possibility of later expansion to 1.2 million tons. The Pérez Jiménez regime signed contracts with the Italian firm of Innocenti—which had never before constructed a steel plant—for the planning and supervision of this enterprise. Construction got under way during the last two years of the dictatorship, but was suspended with its overthrow. Throughout the year 1958 the Innocenti contract was submitted to minute study and investigation for possible fraud, and it was only after the inauguration of Betancourt that negotiations with Innocenti were again renewed. In 1960 construction work recommenced on the enterprise.

A part of the plant began producing seamless steel tubes in July, 1961, using imported steel bars as raw material. It had been set up for an output of 280,000 metric tons a year, but had in prospect during its first year of operation orders for only about 100,000 metric tons. The original planners had anticipated that the feverish oil exploration of the middle 1950's would create a large demand for such pipe, but by 1961 exploration by the major companies was almost at a halt.

In September, 1961, the steel wire mill began operation, and in mid-October the first of nine electric furnaces for turning out pig iron was opened, and by early 1963 eight of the nine planned furnaces were functioning. The first open-hearth furnace began operating at the beginning of July, 1962, and by March, 1963, a second furnace was in full operation.

The Corporación de Guayana made market surveys of the products that the steel plant was expected to produce, and there was little doubt that the plant would turn out, at the beginning at least, more than the local market could use. Ability to export the surplus depended upon the cost structure of the industry. In 1962 some 80,000 metric tons of cast iron and steel were exported, and the mill was producing all of the country's requirements for barbed wire, which had formerly been imported.

The Corporación de Guayana signed a contract with the Koppers Company of the United States for management of the steel plant for a period of six years. Koppers named twenty-five people to act as advisors to Venezuelans at various levels of management. If a Venezuelan proved inadequate to do his job, his Koppers counterpart would step in until a replacement was found.

The Macagua electric plant, at the mouth of the Caroní River, which was planned as the first installation in a much larger project, was completed by the end of 1961. In its first phase, it was designed to produce 300,000 kilowatts of electricity, but ultimately was to have a generating capacity of 1 million kilowatts. Going beyond that, the Betancourt government entered into negotiations with the International Bank for Reconstruction and Development in 1961 concerning a larger hydroelectric enterprise at Guri, higher up on the Caroní, with an installed capacity of 4 million kilowatts, more than Egypt's Aswan Dam project.[2] Late in 1963 Venezuela received the first loan of $85 million from the International Bank for this project.

The aluminum firm, the third large project under control of the Corporación de Guayana, was set up as a joint enterprise of the Corporación and the Reynolds Metal Corporation of the United States. It will utilize power from the Caroní plant to refine bauxite obtained from neighboring British Guiana. The Venezuelans hope that bauxite will bc discovered in the Guayana area of Venezuela. Stock ownership is on a 50-50 basis, with the technical direction in the hands of Reynolds, at least in the beginning, but the general control is in the hands of the Corporación de Guayana.

The Corporación sought to attract other industries to the Orinoco area. The first to come was the Phillips Petroleum Company, which established a tank farm at Puerto Ordaz, the river port built by the United States Steel Company's Orinoco Mining Company to handle its iron ore shipments. Woodworking and lumbering industries are expected to be among future bulwarks of manufacturing in the area. The Corporación began a survey in 1961 of the woods in the area in conjunction with the Universidad de Oriente and the Universidad de los Andes, which has a school of forestry engineering and good laboratories for analysis of wood and wood products.

A key element of the Corporación's planning for the Orinoco area was the new city of Santo Tomé de Guayana, located at the confluence of the Orinoco and Caroní rivers and straddling both sides of both rivers. It was projected as an urban center of some 250,000 people, among them, steel company employees, aluminum company workers, and those working for the Phillips Petroleum Company and the Caroní electric plant.

Santo Tomé de Guayana was formally incorporated in July, 1961. At the end of the year it was converted into a separate municipality, with its own representatives in the Bolívar state legislature.

Planning was done by a group of Venezuelan architects, advised by experts from the Joint City Planning Center of Harvard University and the Massachusetts Institute of Technology. Ultimately it will become the third largest city of Venezuela.

Another aspect of the industrialization of Venezuela that the Betancourt government regarded as the primary responsibility of the state was the establishment of a petrochemical industry. President Betancourt expounded the government's point of view in his annual message to Congress on April 29, 1960, in the following terms:

"A country that is an exporter of petroleum cannot adopt a policy of monopoly over the refining of oil or the petrochemical industry. This would be self-defeating. However, a country which produces and exports petroleum can limit the participation of private industry in the concessions for producing the raw material, which is the source of many types of petroleum products and processing industries. And it can, as has this nationalistically oriented government, create a petroleum corporation belonging exclusively to the state to begin direct participation in the production of petroleum, and can foster an industry such as the Instituto Venezolano de Petroquímica, also belonging exclusively to the state, to participate directly in an industry basic to the establishment of other industries that are necessary for the economic development of Venezuela. Installing government enterprises for petroleum and similar enterprises for the petrochemical industry, we can insure their development as successful and growing enterprises. . . . If the national interest, which is not challenged publicly by anyone, demands the continuation of private enterprises in petroleum production, the basis of the economic life of the country, it requires as a consequence that is equally necessary for the national interest that the petroleum that is produced be refined or converted into petrochemical products in Venezuela, insofar as the international markets permit." [3]

A bit later in this same speech, Betancourt added:

"The potential capacity of the petrochemical industry to produce raw materials, and the prospect for selling these products, are such that the government cannot supply financial support for the necessary operations. Hence, the government believes that in the development of the chemical industry based on Venezuelan petroleum the operations of the Instituto Venezolano de Petroquímica should be supplemented by the establishment of new, privately owned plants, with or without participation by the government, whenever it is of no real advantage for the Instituto to build plants to produce other products.

"The orderly development of this industry requires close coordination between the government and private entrepreneurs, keeping always in mind the greatest interest that the nation may derive from their operations."[4]

The establishment of a petrochemical complex had been undertaken by the Pérez Jiménez regime, but like most of the things started by the dictatorship, it was planned principally with an eye to making the most possible profit for insiders in the regime. It was built at an inconvenient site on land belonging to a principal figure of the Pérez Jiménez government. It was located some distance from a port, with the arrangement that another insider of the regime would transport the raw material for the plant by tank truck from Puerto Cabello. Furthermore, those who approved the order of priorities in the construction of plants were little concerned with efficiency and economy in getting the enterprise into full production.

The project called for a complex of plants, including an oil refinery, several fertilizer plants, an explosives factory, and others to make plastics, synthetic rubber, and other commodities. However, the construction was so planned that even by the middle of 1961, when we visited the plant, after some 850 million bolívares had been spent upon it, only a small part of the complex had been constructed and put into operation.

Those put in charge of the petrochemical installations by the Betancourt regime estimated that the cost was about double what should have been spent by 1961. They also estimated that some 70 million bolívares more investment would be required before the plants could be fully operative. The provisional government had added to the confusion and expense engendered by the dictatorship by employing some seven hundred additional workers who were not actually needed for the construction work.

According to President Betancourt, "the fundamental activity of the directorate of the Instituto Venezolano de Petroquímica designated at the beginning of the constitutional period was that of evaluating the current situation and orienting the organization toward the basic objectives of the enterprise, which in its present state does not possess any characteristics proper to a petrochemical industry. To this end, programs for improving the administrative efficiency of the plants, for raising production, for promoting markets for present and future products, and for accelerating the fertilizer complex were carried out." [5]

The heart of the petrochemical installations, the plants to process raw materials for plastics, synthetic rubber, and other products, did not exist even in blueprints during the dictatorship, and the plans were not finished until the last months of 1961.

On the other hand, considerable progress was made during the Betancourt regime in putting the plants that had been built into production. The small pilot-plant oil refinery went into operation, as did the sulphuric group of the fertilizer complex, which by August, 1961, was producing sulphuric acid, phosphates, phosphoric acids, and superphosphates. Most of these products were being sold in Venezuela, though small amounts were being exported to Brazil, some Caribbean areas, and Europe. The fertilizer complex also includes a nitrate group, a urea group, and a synthesis group. Although the nitrate and urea plants were completed by the middle of 1961, they could not start working until the synthesis plant was completed; however, by early 1963 the full fertilizer complex had been brought into production. During 1963 the explosives plant also began operation.

The Betancourt government also succeeded in building collateral parts of the complex. Thus the government-owned electricity firm finished a 50,000-kilowatt electric plant, run by gas, which would provide much more electricity than the petrochemical complex itself could ever require. The Instituto Nacional de Obras Sanitarias completed a dam on the Morón River to supply water for the petrochemical complex and the new town around it.

The housing needs of the complex also received attention by the Betancourt administration. Under the dictatorship a handful of very expensive *quintas* were built along the ocean front. These ultra-luxurious houses included one for Pérez Jiménez himself, who made infrequent visits to the complex. Subsequently, a trailer camp was constructed, with several hundred trailers, each supplemented by an additional room in front, to make it more livable. In addition to these temporary dwellings, the Banco Obrero constructed during the Betancourt regime some seven hundred houses, and the government rural housing program built several score more. A section of the property was set apart for workers to build ranchos by their own efforts, along well-planned streets, provided with running water, electricity, and other conveniences. These huts are slowly converted into decent homes by the savings and effort of the workers themselves.

The Betancourt regime regarded adequate electrical power as a prerequisite to the industrialization of Venezuela. In a speech in Maracaibo on October 25, 1960, the President explained this point of view:

"Also closely allied with industrial development is electrification. Without cheap electricity neither prosperous industrial development nor a civilized life is possible in our contemporary era. . . . We must accept the principle that public service industries managed by the state must not operate at such large losses as to make them bankrupt; but they must also behave as firms with a definite mission of public service, always taking into consideration the needs of economic development and of the collectivity." [6]

With this in mind, the government not only pushed forward the development of the projects under the control of the Corporación de Guayana, but also fostered the extension of the activities of CADAFE, the government-owned electricity firm, in the central and western parts of the country.

The Compañía Anónima de Administración y Fomento Electrífico, to give CADAFE its full name, was established by the provisional government in 1958; however, its roots go back perhaps as far as the dictatorship of Juan Vicente Gómez. He built an electric plant in Maracay as his private property. Upon his death, it was taken over, along with the dictator's other possessions, by the Office of Restitution, set up by General López Contreras, and during the succeeding administration of President Medina Angarita it was turned over to the Ministry of Development. During the Acción Democrática administration of the late 1940's the Maracay plant and another electricity enterprise, La Cabrera, became the property of the newly formed Corporación Venezolana de Fomento, which established an electricity department to plan for and undertake the development of the country's power resources. In 1947 the CVF drew up the first National Electrification Plan. By 1958 the CVF had some fifteen small electric plants under its supervision, and the provisional government brought all of these together to form the CADAFE, a corporation the stock of which continued to be owned by the CVF.[7]

CADAFE has the job of organizing a national electricity network. Ultimately this is likely to mean its taking over the privately owned companies that serve Caracas, Maracaibo, Valencia, and Barquisimeto, and perhaps also its acquiring title to the big projects being built by the Corporación de Guayana. Meanwhile, however, the CADAFE manages a growing number of thermoelectric plants serving small towns and cities of the interior; it cooperates with privately owned firms whenever this is necessary, and is planning to purchase power from the Caroní projects for redistribution to the central and western parts of the country.

The CADAFE plants are almost all thermoelectric, using principally natural gas as their fuel; however, the firm constructed one small hydroelectric plant in the Andean area of western Venezuela, and surveyed the possibilities for a more general development of the water power resources of that area during the Betancourt regime. The company had on hand projects for one 300,000-kilowatt installation, and was studying the possibility of others by the time Betancourt went out of office.

CADAFE has absorbed numerous small plants built by municipal and state governments because they did not want to wait for CADAFE to extend its transmission lines to their areas. As the opportunity presented itself, CADAFE coordinated these new installations with its own facilities, often keeping the small local diesel motor plants as standby resources for emergency use.

Since its establishment, CADAFE has greatly augmented its facilities and its service. In 1958 it had an installed generating capacity of 204,000 kilowatts, and was serving some 175,545 customers. In 1961 its capacity had reached 365,133 kilowatts, and it was serving 274,478 subscribers. It was estimated that some 1.34 million Venezuelans in more than five hundred cities, towns, and villages were being served by the CADAFE network. During this same three-year period, the capital of CADAFE had increased from 424.5 million bolívares to 612.1 million bolívares.[8]

One major problem facing CADAFE has been that of finding sufficient personnel to service its small local plants. In an attempt to meet this difficulty, CADAFE entered into an agreement with the Instituto Nacional de Cooperación Educativa in 1961 for a program for training rural electricians. It was hoped that this would provide sufficient personnel to keep the CADAFE plants operating smoothly.

CADAFE does not operate solely as a business concern, although it has showed a profit every year and reinvests these profits in extending its services. CADAFE has frequently gone into rural areas that would be unprofitable for private utility companies. The social benefits of bringing electricity to these isolated areas are considered more important than the profitability of the operations.

The firm has acquired a reputation for efficiency and good organization. Thus, although the Federation of Chambers of Commerce and Production, in its seventeenth assembly at Puerto Cabello in April, 1961, generally condemned the inefficiency of most government-owned businesses in Venezuela, it specifically praised CADAFE for the way in which its operations were conducted.[9]

By the end of the Betancourt regime, substantial progress had been made in the process of industrializing the country, one of the basic objectives of the government of the Democratic Revolution. The textile industry was nearly able to meet the country's total needs, and food processing plants were set up to handle a great variety of foodstuffs that were not being produced in Venezuela before the fall of the dictatorship. Certain cities of the interior, such as Valencia, Cagua, and Barquisimeto, enjoyed an industrial boom during the Betancourt regime. The process of establishing a base of heavy industry in the Orinoco Valley and in the central state of Carabobo went ahead, albeit with considerable difficulty.

That the general economic crisis through which the country passed in 1960 and 1961 was a hampering factor to industrialization is clear from the figures available for the first two years of the constitutional administration. Industrial progress was marked during 1959. The increase of output in the industrial sector during that year was 17 per cent, the greatest rise in five years, since the height of the oil boom. In the same year there was recorded the largest volume of capital investment in manufacturing firms in the history of the country.[10] In contrast, in 1960 the increase in the value of industrial production over 1959 was only 0.5 per cent, the smallest rise in several years.

In 1961 the rhythm of industrial development picked up once again. President Betancourt, in his fourth annual message to Congress, summed this up as follows: "In the three-year period 1959 to 1961 the value of industrial production, at 1960 prices, was 26.9 billion bolívares, as opposed to 21.2 billion bolívares in the three-year period 1956 to 1958, which represents an increase of 27 per cent. However, the really important fact is that in 1961 the value of industrial production was 486 million bolívares more than in 1960, and 284 million bolívares more than in 1959, the highest figures hitherto achieved by the industrial sector of the Venezuelan economy."[11]

The relative slump in 1960 was due principally to a decline in demand, and not at all to inability to produce. That it reflected in large degree the crisis in the construction industry was clear from the fact that there were severe decreases in output of paint and cement, as well as in wood products, furniture, and nonmetallic mineral products, all of which are related to the construction trades. There was also a considerable decline in output in amount and value of both passenger and commercial vehicles, reflecting the decline both in the oil and construction industries and in the general demand. In contrast, there were, as might have been expected, sizable increases in output of foodstuffs, beverages, tobacco, paper and paper products, and most textiles. There was some decline in the production of woolen clothing and of shoes.[12]

Table III indicates the increases in production of some of the country's principal manufactured products in the consumers' goods

TABLE III

INDEX OF INCREASE IN OUTPUT OF CONSUMERS' GOODS IN VENEZUELA, 1956 TO 1960 (1958 = 100)

Product	*1956*	*1957*	*1959*	*1960*
Sugar	127	123	112	123
Processed Rice	90	103	129	126
Cigarettes	86	89	112	174
Candy	79	94	115	119
Processed Meat	78	88	105	109
Soap	91	104	102	109
Canned Milk	66	72	118	153
Pasteurized Milk	80	91	107	112
Butter	73	88	97	108
Spaghetti, Macaroni, etc.	85	94	99	99
Textiles	86	93	104	106
Beer	74	81	114	134
Soft Drinks	64	79	112	123
Fruit Drinks	54	62	124	131

Source: Article by Héctor Stredel in *La República*, Caracas, August 19, 1961.

field from the end of the dictatorship through the second year of the Betancourt regime.

The textile industry made spectacular advances under the Betancourt government's economic development program. José Gerbasi, writing in *El Nacional* on July 29, 1962, summed up these advances thus: "the productive capacity of the national textile industry has reached 100 per cent for cotton textiles, 95 per cent for artificial silk and synthetics, and 85 per cent for woolen cloth. . . . In 1958, production of cotton textiles was 29,736,477 meters and in 1961 exceeded 56 million meters, thus almost doubling. In 1961, there were also produced 27 million meters of synthetic fibers and 1.4 million meters of woolen cloth.

". . . The textile industry in the metropolitan area had in 1958 some 77,890 spindles and now has 175,002. In 1958, it had 12,384 spindles for synthetic fibers and in 1962 has 16,730. In 1958, there were no spindles for woolen textiles, and now there are 8,800. . . .

". . . The number of workers directly employed in the textile industry was 6,500 in 1958 and in 1962 reached 12,800. . . . The average daily wage of these workers is 22 bolívares, and employment is governed by a collective contract which establishes numerous social benefits. . . ."

In his fifth annual message to Congress, President Betancourt noted that the increase in industrial production in 1962 had been 11.8 per cent. He added that "many of the principal items of the manufacturing industry in the country show a distinct tendency towards high levels of production. This means a gradual transformation of the one-staple economy in the country into a diversified economy using with ever more intensity domestically produced raw materials and offering greater employment opportunities." He pointed out that the rate of increase in industrial production during the first four years of his administration had been 7.7 per cent a year.

There is little doubt that the policies of the Betancourt regime in terms of protection for national manufacturing, loans to industrial entrepreneurs, and strengthening of the infra-structure of the economy helped to create a solid base for a diversified economy in which a wide variety of manufacturing industries in both the heavy and consumers' goods fields will play a fundamental role. To the degree that this program succeeds, the excessive dependence of Venezuela upon petroleum production will be lessened, and the economic independence of the nation will be strengthened.

Chapter Seventeen

Petroleum, Mining, and Conservation Policy

The nationalist aspects of the Venezuelan Democratic Revolution were most clearly revealed in the policies adopted for handling the nation's subsoil resources. The basic objective of these policies was to make these resources serve to the greatest possible extent the interests of Venezuela, rather than the interests of some other country.

Venezuela, like most of the countries of Latin America, became excessively dependent during the early decades of the twentieth century on the exploitation and export of a single raw material, in this case, petroleum. Thus, by 1938, official figures showed that 93.4 per cent of all of the country's exports came from this single source.[1] This situation led to the development of what many Venezuelans call a semicolonial economy. By this, they mean that their economy became excessively dependent on foreign countries and foreign firms, and that this dependence tended to limit the effectiveness of the nation's political sovereignty.

The semicolonial nature of Venezuela's economy was evident from the fact that the prosperity of the Venezuelan economy depended very heavily on the willingness of a very few countries to purchase a single Venezuelan export product. Furthermore, the exploitation of this basic industry was for the most part in the hands of companies owned outside of Venezuela, and the finances of the government itself depended very heavily on the level and price of petroleum exports.

Table IV analyses the imports of the fourteen nations that have been purchasers of Venezuelan petroleum in recent years.

Table IV shows that Venezuela's export of its principal product depended very heavily on the willingness of the United States and a few other countries to buy; however, the country's reliance on the United States as a source of imports was much greater. In 1957 some 63.5 per cent of all Venezuelan imports came from that country, and in 1959 and 1960 this percentage was 52.9 per cent and 51.7 per cent, respectively.[2]

Until the advent of the Betancourt regime, all Venezuelan oil production and export was in the hands of United States and British companies. The principal firms were the Standard Oil Company of New Jersey subsidiary, the Creole Petroleum Corporation, the Compañía Shell de Venezuela, Ltd., and a Gulf subsidiary, the Mene Grande Oil Company.[3]

The reliance of the government upon the oil industry for its own revenue is evident from the fact that in 1958 some 3,226,780,000 bolívares of the total government revenues of 5,441,820,000 bolívares

TABLE IV

VENEZUELAN OIL EXPORTS, 1955 TO 1960

Country	*Percentage of Oil Exports* 1955	1957	1959	1960
United States	39.58	41.88	43.97	44.56
Canada	10.85	10.49	10.65	9.99
Great Britain	6.77	9.52	8.38	9.60
Brazil	5.94	4.53	4.92	5.08
British West Indies	3.08	2.60	3.53	4.40
Puerto Rico	0.87	1.67	3.23	3.37
Argentina	4.23	4.44	4.56	3.31
France	1.10	2.13	2.94	1.94
Netherlands	3.96	3.92	1.58	1.61
Germany	1.58	1.03	1.63	1.49
Sweden	1.99	1.79	1.39	1.39
Cuba	1.50	2.36	3.23	1.34
Uruguay	1.17	0.98	0.81	1.04
Others	17.34	12.72	9.88	10.68

Source: Banco Central: *Memoria correspondiente al ejercicio anual 1960,* Caracas, 1961, p. 231.

came from oil. In the following year petroleum revenues amounted to 3,002,190,000 bolívares, out of a total of 4,960,890,000 bolívares.[4]

Of the several basic objectives in the policies that were followed by the Betancourt regime in the petroleum and mining field, foremost was that of exerting effective national control over the exploitation of the mining and petroleum resources of the country. Second, the Betancourt regime sought to get the best possible return from this exploitation, without "killing the goose that lays the golden eggs." Third, by joint action with other petroleum-producing nations, it sought to stabilize world oil prices at as high a level as possible. Fourth, it followed policies designed to convert Venezuela from a mere exporter of raw materials to a producer and exporter of semifinished and manufactured products derived from the national mineral resources. Last, but of great concern to the democratic regime, was the conservation of the nation's natural resources, including petroleum.

Two aspects of the general economic policies of the Betancourt regime were closely associated with the problem of oil and minerals, but go beyond them. These were the attempt to use the sales returns received by the country in the most economical and socially useful manner, and the effort to make the country less dependent than it had hitherto been upon its raw material exports.

In the platform that it adopted at its 1958 convention, prior to the elections that made Rómulo Betancourt President, his Acción Democrática party summed up the policies that it would follow were it to acquire the responsibility of governing the nation:

". . . It is necessary that the party support a petroleum policy . . . which will really integrate the industry in economic development based on the following general propositions:

"1) To create a national, integrated petroleum agency to produce, refine, transport, and sell;

"2) To create a national oil fleet and adopt legal means to impede the abuse of the tankers flying flags of convenience;

"3) To revise the tax system of the petroleum industry, to obtain a larger and juster participation by the state, demanding from the firms that their profits be limited to a reasonable return on invested capital;

"4) To ratify the principle of no new petroleum concessions to private firms and to study various aspects of the concessions given during the years 1956 and 1957, so as to adopt a definitive position;

"5) To ratify the policy of industrializing the largest possible part of petroleum and gas production in Venezuela;

"6) To establish, as a permanent part of the Venezuelan government's economic policy, the systematic study of world petroleum markets so as to plan national petroleum exploitation and production;

"7) To establish the participation of the Venezuelan state as essential in all conversations of governments and firms concerning the division of markets and establishment of production and import figures;

"8) To demand greater collaboration of the petroleum firms in plans for economic development of the country;

"9) To provide means to carry out the requirement that 75 per cent of all workers in all levels of employees of petroleum firms must be Venezuelans, including technicians and members of boards of directors. . . .

"This is only a program for a period of transition. We do not believe that this program represents a 'revolution,' because the latter would have to be broader; however, this program is of a revolutionary nature, because it accepts and recommends changes in the national economic structure, and could be converted into a really revolutionary program if it were made more precise in the long run."[5]

In summary, when the Betancourt regime took office, it again made it clear that it would grant no new private oil concessions. It maintained the high level of taxation established just before Betancourt was inaugurated, but opposed the raising of taxes to the point of making Venezuelan oil uncompetitive with exports from other parts of the world. It took steps to establish a government-owned petroleum firm, and sought to establish an international organization to keep up world petroleum prices. Finally, the Betancourt regime made it clear that it had no intention of nationalizing the oil industry.

Acción Democrática has been opposed to further concessions to private oil companies for more than two decades. During the discussions in Congress of a new Petroleum Law in 1943, the handful of AD members sought to have such a prohibition of new concessions written into the new statute. Their efforts were unsuccessful. During the Acción Democrática regime of the 1940's the government would grant no new concessions. When the dictatorial regime did invite the international oil firms to seek new grants of oil lands during 1956 and 1957, Acción Democrática protested strongly.

Both President Betancourt and Minister of Mines and Petroleum Juan Pablo Pérez Alfonso, the principal architect of Acción Democrática's oil policy, insisted over and over again after February, 1959, that their government would not grant new concessions. Dr. Pérez Alfonso spoke at length concerning this aspect of the government's oil policy in an interview published in the Caracas magazine *Elite* in its issue of July 8, 1961:

"The stimulation of investment in exploration still has extensive possibilities, and there is plenty of time for this. With such stimulation or without it, new concessions cannot be considered an urgent problem. Since less than a tenth of the concession area which the petroleum industry controls has been exploited or explored or proved by drilling, the other nine-tenths being untested, development requires extensive investment.

"As far as time is concerned, leaving out of consideration the concessions of 1956 and 1957, which have thirty-seven years to run, there is plenty of time for exploration and exploitation in the rest. The twenty-three years they have to run represent a longer period than typical concessions agreed on in Canada and other parts of the world. Furthermore, when ten or fifteen years have passed, depending upon the state of exploitation at that time, the national administrations which will then have responsibility will have to study what is best for the country and may perhaps find the economic solution to be the extension of the concessions for the most efficient exploitation of the fields then in production.

Many local officials of the international oil companies operating in Venezuela agree that existing concessions are sufficient for their companies' needs; however, the situation varies with different companies. Most of the large ones, such as Creole and Shell, have ample reserves. On the other hand a number of the small operators are faced with possible exhaustion of their reserves in the proximate future.

The no-concessions policy appealed to the nationalistic fervor of the Venezuelan people, and few opposition politicians dared to come out openly against it. Among the few who criticized the policy obliquely was independent Senator Arturo Uslar Pietri, who in an interview in the Caracas monthly *Mundo Económico* of July-August,

1961, laid stress on the alleged decline of the petroleum industry, and particularly of investments in the industry:

"The petroleum industry of Venezuela is the fundamental economic activity of the country. For historic reasons that everyone knows, it has come to be the master wheel. . . . Anything that affects it, that makes petroleum activity decline in Venezuela, is reflected immediately in other aspects of our economic life. And the petroleum industry in Venezuela has entered a period of frank decline and of no new investment. Here are some figures that demonstrate this. . . . There is a relationship which is very important, a vital relationship for judging the future of the petroleum industry in any country, that is, the relationship between discovery of new reserves and production. Here is our situation between 1955 and 1959. In 1955, new discoveries of petroleum reserves, that is, newly explored fields, represented 190 per cent of petroleum production of that year. This is to say that in 1955 Venezuela not only discovered as much new petroleum reserves as the amount of oil taken out that year, but 90 per cent more than that amount, or almost double what was extracted. That signified assurance that there would be more petroleum for the future. In 1956, the relationship was 174 per cent. In 1957, it was 157 per cent. In 1958, it was 126 per cent. In 1959, it was 107 per cent. That is to say, in the year 1959 Venezuela discovered only a little more oil than the amount which left its wells during that year. Exploration had been suspended."

Senator Uslar Pietri did not draw the logical conclusions from his comments—that is, that new concessions should be granted, as was being done in the 1955 to 1959 period. Privately many politicians associated with business interests drew these conclusions. This fact did not change the position of the Betancourt regime, however.

A little more than a month before Rómulo Betancourt became President, the provisional government enacted an income tax law intended to raise the total share of the government's share of petroleum industry profits from a minimum of 50 per cent, which it had been since the Acción Democrática regime of the late 1940's, to 60 per cent. In fact, this law, which was retroactive from the beginning of 1958, increased the state's participation in these profits to 65 per cent in 1958.[6] In subsequent years the state's proportion is said to have risen to about 70 per cent, although the law was not changed.[7]

The increase in income taxes was partly responsible for a substantial decrease in the return on capital invested in the oil industry. In most of the 1950's this return was 20 to 32 per cent; however, in 1958 it was 17.02 per cent, in 1959 was 13.44 per cent, and in 1960 had fallen to 11.96 per cent.[8]

The Betancourt administration, although its leaders had probably not been consulted when the new income tax law was imposed in December, 1958, favored the increases incorporated in this law. Furthermore, in February, 1961, it successfully urged Congress to pass another law providing for payment of some taxes in advance. This added to the charges on the oil companies for the following three years. However, when the opposition suggested further taxes on the oil industry during the discussion of the stabilization law proposed by President Betancourt in May, 1961, the administration opposed additional levies. President Betancourt argued thus: "Insofar as taxes on the petroleum companies are concerned, it must be pointed out with clarity that this fundamental sector of the country's economic activity was especially affected by the reform of the income tax law of 1958, which was principally directed at the petroleum firms, elevating substantially their taxes, and thus the participation of the Venezuelan state in the profits of the industry. . . . For this reason it is felt that the present conditions of the market and in the face of international competition, it is not to the best interests of the country to continue increasing the tax level of the petroleum industry, because of the negative effects this would produce on production, on the market, and on investment, and thus on the share of the state in the profits of the industry." [9]

Although not willing to grant new concessions to the international petroleum companies operating in the country, the Betancourt government encouraged these firms to invest some of their profits inside Venezuela in economic activities not connected with petroleum. This had long been the policy of Acción Democrática. During the late 1940's, the AD had favored the establishment of the Venezuelan Basic Economy Corporation (VBEC), headed by Nelson Rockefeller, much of the capital of which came from the Creole Petroleum Corporation. Through the Corporación Venezolana de Fomento, the government in that period entered into partnership with VBEC in a number of enterprises of considerable importance to the development of the agricultural, industrial, and commercial sectors of the economy. The same attitude was taken by the second Betancourt government. Thus in the middle of 1961 the administration welcomed the initiative of the Creole Petroleum Corporation to establish the Creole Investment Corporation to invest in nonpetroleum enterprises. This firm, which started out with an initial capital of $10 million, proposed to enter into partnership with Venezuelan entrepreneurs on the basis of the Venezuelan interests holding a majority of stock in the new enterprises. By the time the Creole Investment Corporation was formally launched in September, 1961, it had already received some eighty proposals from Venezuelan business interests for joint enterprises. About 60 per cent of these proposals were in the field of manufacturing, the rest being in agriculture and the livestock industry.[10] Creole's initiative had obviously aroused a good deal of interest not only in government circles but in the business community.

When the proposal to form the investment company was announced by Creole officials, they let it be known that if the venture was successful, they would be disposed to invest further sizable sums in the new venture in the near future. Furthermore, the initial $10 million was to be a species of revolving fund, since Creole expressed its willingness to sell out its interest in the new enterprises once they were well established.

Although some opposition spokesmen saw in the Creole proposition a new "invasion of Yankee imperialism" in the economy of Venezuela, the government leaders saw the matter in a different light. It came at an opportune moment, when the government itself was making strenuous efforts to stimulate recovery from the recession of 1960 and 1961, and it promised to make a significant contribution to the industrialization of the country and the general diversification of its economy. Whatever dangers might be involved in extending the foreign oil companies' influence into sectors of the country's economic life that they had not hitherto touched, government spokesmen felt were mitigated by the willingness of Creole to become a minority stockholder in the new firms to be established, and by its willingness to get out of these firms entirely once they had been put solidly on their feet. Far from decrying the initiative of the Creole Petroleum Corporation, government leaders expressed hope that other oil companies would follow Creole's lead.

A fundamental part of the petroleum policy of the Betancourt regime was the establishment of a government-controlled oil company, something that Acción Democrática had been urging since the party was established. As leaders of the democratic regime pointed out, most of the oil-producing countries of Latin America have a government-owned firm which produces some—and in some cases all—of the country's petroleum. This is the case in Mexico, Bolivia, Colombia, Ecuador, Chile, Argentina, and Brazil, among others.

The Corporación Venezolana del Petróleo (CVP) was established in conformity with already existing laws. The Petroleum Law of 1938 had provided for the possibility of organizing such a firm, and this power had been continued in the Law of 1943; however, no government previous to that of President Betancourt had actually undertaken to set up such a firm.

The Corporación was established by a cabinet decree of April 19, 1960. In July of the same year Congress granted the new company the right to exploit some 141,000 hectares of concession land returned under terms of their concessions by the international oil companies, most of which was located around or in Lake Maracaibo. The value of this area was estimated at about 600 million bolívares, in the light of the proved resources it was known to contain.[11]

The Corporación Venezolana del Petróleo has two executive bodies. The first is the directing council of seven members, named by the President of the Republic, the chairman of which is the Minister of Mines and Petroleum. A smaller executive committee consists of a director-general and three members of the directing council. The director-general is responsible for the day-to-day operations of the company.[12]

The scope of operations of the CVP was supposed to be limited in the beginning, but no bounds were established in the decree as to possible expansion. An official pamphlet describing the CVP sketched its field of operations: "The Corporación will begin to operate on a small scale, and will gradually expand its field of action, until it becomes a firm which engages in all phases of the petroleum business. In the development of these diverse phases it might be convenient to have collaboration of private capital. If the directing council thinks that such is the case, the Corporación may subscribe or acquire shares or other securities in firms which have the same purposes. For this reason its objectives will include: (a) carrying on all of the operations of an integrated industry: exploration, exploitation, refining and transport of hydrocarbons, as well as the purchase and transformation of the same; (b) the promotion of firms with the purpose of developing industrial or commercial petroleum activities, with the government able to contribute to the capital of these firms as deemed advantageous, and the subscription or acquisition of shares or other securities in firms which have the same purposes; (c) the carrying out of any other activities which contribute to the fulfillment of the purposes of the Corporación."[13]

The organizers of the Corporación Venezolana del Petróleo foresaw a wide perspective for the future operations of the company. In the immediate future it proposed to enter into competition with the international oil companies in both the domestic Venezuelan market and in the world markets. Nevertheless, the government firm was not to enjoy any special privileges not available to the international companies.

By the end of the Betancourt administration the company had established a network of gas stations throughout Venezuela. The problem of obtaining markets abroad was more difficult, since the government did not wish to have its company interfere with the already established channels for disposing of Venezuelan oil. However, a number of oil companies in the United States have distributing agencies, but inadequate sources of supply. The CVP began negotiating with these companies in 1961. By the end of 1962 it had signed service contracts with the Mobil Oil Company and the Mene Grande Oil Company to help in the exploitation and marketing efforts.

Drilling operations by the Corporación began in 1961. Its first successful well was brought in in June, and the second one in September. Both of these were closed down temporarily until marketing problems had been overcome.[14]

Officially, most leaders of the Betancourt administration left open the question of whether the Corporación Venezolana del Petróleo would ultimately take over the bulk of the country's oil industry. There seems little doubt, however, that one of the basic functions of the CVP is to prepare the way for the government's taking over of most if not all of the existing concessions when they begin to expire in the early 1980's. This view is shared by at least some of the officials of the international oil companies operating in Venezuela. AD leaders foresee the time when the CVP will be the largest if not the only producer of oil in Venezuela, although they seem to feel that even then the selling of petroleum in foreign markets might best be left in the hands of the international companies, functioning as agents of CVP.

The Betancourt government favored the employment of Venezuelans in the foreign-owned oil industry. From the fall of the dictatorship, there existed a tacit prohibition on the employment of new foreign personnel in the oil firms in Venezuela, except in those cases in which there was clearly no capable Venezuelan to fill the position.

Some of the international oil companies themselves promoted the policy of recruiting Venezuelan personnel. This is particularly true of the Creole Petroleum Corporation, subsidiary of the Standard Oil Company of New Jersey, and the largest firm in the Venezuelan oil business. For many years all manual workers hired by the firm have been Venezuelans, and increasingly the company has incorporated Venezuelans into the supervisory personnel in the operating departments. The public relations department was almost completely Venezuelan by 1961, and the labor relations department was completely so by the end of that year. Creole brought two Venezuelans into the company's five-man board of directors in 1960.

Thus, when the concessions begin to run out in the 1980's, the Venezuelan government should be in a position to take over the ownership of the country's petroleum industry with little or no interference with its efficiency and smooth functioning. Venezuelans, both in the Corporación Venezolana del Petróleo and in the private companies, should by that time have sufficient experience to make the transition to national ownership a smooth one. Furthermore, the existence of the Corporación should provide an administrative organization with sufficient background and wisdom to manage the country's principal source of foreign exchange.

Whatever the long-run perspectives with regard to the ownership of the Venezuelan oil industry, the Betancourt government made it very clear that it had no intention of expropriating it, that is, seizing ownership of the existing concessions. President Betancourt and Dr. Pérez Alfonso reiterated this position over and over again. In the interview with a representative of the magazine *Elite*, which appeared in the issue of July 8, 1961, Dr. Pérez Alfonso explained the government's position in this regard:

"The policy of the President, which is the policy of Acción Democrática, the party to which we both belong, has never favored the nationalization of the petroleum industry. Furthermore, nationalization has not been advocated by anyone here, not even by those Venezuelans who might be considered to have extremist ideas. This general position is explained by the role which petroleum plays in the economy of the country, and by its international ramifications.

"Our petroleum wealth is so great that we cannot limit its production only to our own consumption. We must export on a large scale, and in the world markets it is convenient for Venezuela to use the services of the international firms. Such services are offered with greater interest and efficiency when they are linked to the basic activities of exploration and production."

The Betancourt regime sought to reduce the danger to the Venezuelan economy from violent changes in the demand for and prices of petroleum. One of the basic approaches that it used for obtaining this objective was promotion of the establishment of the Organización de Países Exportadores de Petróleo. (OPEP; or Organization of Petroleum Exporting Countries, OPEC.)

This organization was established in September, 1960, at a conference in Baghdad. The countries attending this conference—Iraq, Iran, Kuwait, Saudi Arabia, and Venezuela—decided to establish OPEC, with "the principal objective . . . the unification of the petroleum policies of the member countries and the determination of the best means of safeguarding the individual and collective interests of the member countries."[15]

This conference adopted three resolutions. The first expressed the solidarity of the countries attending the meeting, exhorted the oil companies to "maintain their prices stable and free from all unnecessary fluctuation," and pledged all of the attending countries to "attempt to re-establish prices . . . at the level prevailing before reductions," and urged that before companies decided to change prices, they should consult the governments of all of the countries involved. The second resolution established OPEC, and the third provided for exchange of ratifications of the other two.[16]

The resolutions of the first conference of OPEC were ratified by the Venezuelan Congress on May 22, 1961. Meanwhile, the second conference of the OPEC had met in Caracas in January, 1961. The second meeting adopted a much more complicated series of resolutions. It set up a permanent headquarters for the OPEC in Geneva, and adopted the statutes of OPEC. The Arabian country of Qatar was admitted to the group.[17] The conference provided for a study of the financial return to concessionaires from the oil industry in the various member countries.

The projections of the OPEC are broad, and the Venezuelan government officials involved in its establishment have great hopes for using it as an effective weapon to keep up oil prices. The attitude of the oil companies so far has been noncommittal. They are not opposed to maintaining prices, but they are somewhat dubious about the viability of the OPEC for this purpose. The author tends to share their skepticism, largely because of the avariciousness of the rulers of several of the key Arab states whose cooperation is essential for the success of OPEC, and the possibility that the Soviet Union and other nonmember Eastern European producers could flood West European markets with oil at prices below those set by OPEC.

The threat of competition from the Soviet Union was a major problem facing OPEC almost from the beginning. Minister of Mines and Petroleum Pérez Alfonso visited Moscow in the summer of 1961 to discuss this problem with the Soviet leaders. He returned officially optimistic about the willingness of the U.S.S.R. to cooperate with OPEC, and said that it was improbable that the U.S.S.R. would be in a position to dump sufficient quantities of oil on world markets to imperil the operations of the organization. In private conversations, some knowledgeable Venezuelan officials are not so optimistic. Minister Pérez Alfonso sought to make Venezuelan participation effective. Thus, on at least one occasion he forbade oil ventures at prices which he felt would undercut OPEC's stabilization efforts.

As the world's second largest exporter of iron ore, Venezuela was greatly concerned with the price situation in the iron mining industry. In the summer of 1961 Dr. Pérez Alfonso took the first step toward forming an equivalent to the OPEC for the iron mining industry. He discussed the possibility of such an organization with Swedish officials, and upon returning home he expressed the opinion that the chief countries in an effective international group would have to be Sweden, Venezuela, Liberia, Brazil, and Chile.[18] However, by the end of 1963 no concrete steps had been taken to establish an iron mining cartel.

Finally, mention should be made of the projections of the government's oil policy in the general economy. The policy of making sensible and economic use of the sizable resources provided by the oil industry was an integral part of the Betancourt government's approach to the problem of oil. The President and other leaders of the democratic government stressed many times the exhaustibility of the country's oil resources, and the dangers involved in the nation's excessive dependence upon their exploitation. They stressed the need for making the best possible use of these resources so that Venezuela would have a viable and nationally controlled economy once the oil boom slackened.

In his speech opening the Fourth Convention of State and Territorial Governors in Caracas on February 15, 1961, President Betancourt summed up the concern of the government with this problem: "We must dispel the happy theory that the oil derricks are producing an inexhaustible quantity of dollars and bolívares. The truth is that we are spending the proceeds of unrenewable, perishable wealth, and that we must spend it well, taking advantage of the extraordinary current situation of Venezuela to establish solid and durable bases for the Venezuelan nation. We are investing the funds that oil brings us to obtain increasingly greater returns from this marvelous wealth. . . ."[10]

The Betancourt regime sought to develop a nationalistic policy for handling its oil and mining industry, but a policy such that it would not destroy or seriously impair the productiveness of the industry. The government's purpose was to bring the industry as much as possible under the control of the nation, without immediately transferring full ownership from the foreign companies to Venezuelans. Through establishing the Corporación Venezolana del Petróleo, it prepared the ground for smooth conversion of the oil resources into national property when the existing concessions run out.

The government of the Venezuelan Democratic Revolution also sought to reduce the danger to the national economy from rapid and frequent changes in demand for oil. To this end, it promoted the formation of an organization of governments of oil exporting countries to stabilize prices, and applied the sizable income from oil to diversify the economy and to increase the material and social well-being of the people of Venezuela.

Chapter Eighteen

Labor Policy and Organization

During the years following the overthrow of the Pérez Jiménez dictatorship the organized workers demonstrated on many occasions that they were of key importance to the success of the Venezuelan Democratic Revolution. They constituted a powerful group for the defense of the democratic regime, and their solid support was one of the strongest guarantees that the government would be able to complete its constitutional term of office and carry out its program of social and economic change.

When upon two occasions in 1958 dissident military elements attempted to carry out *coups d'état* against the provisional regime, the Coordinating Committee for Trade Union Unity of the labor movement called a nation-wide general strike, the absolute effectiveness of which was a major factor in the government's ability to thwart the insurrectionary efforts. The same thing occurred in April, 1960, when General Castro León seized the city of San Cristóbal and from there sought to launch a nation-wide revolt against the Betancourt government.

The support of organized labor also constituted one of the government's principal assurances against attempts by the extreme Left to launch a popular insurrection. The workers refused to heed a Communist–MIR call for such an uprising in November, 1960, and the successive defeats that the extreme Leftists suffered in the trade unions during 1961 and succeeding years indicated that the great majority of the workers had faith in the government's willingness and ability to carry out the program to which it was pledged. They supported its efforts to bring about economic and social improvements by democratic means.

Although organized labor was thus a key to the stability of the democratic regime, the leaders of the Venezuelan Democratic Revolution made no pretense of being the exclusive spokesmen of labor or any other single class. Even less did they believe in or advocate the idea that they were the "vanguard of the proletariat," and, as such, knew better than the proletariat itself what the working class wanted.

The Acción Democrática party from the beginning looked upon itself as a "multi-class" party, appealing to and seeking to speak for not only the urban workers but also the peasantry, the intellectuals, and the progressive middle class. The Copei also thought of itself as a multi-class party, although it did not state its philosophy in terms of being representative of a particular class, or group of classes, but rather founded its philosophy and program on its interpretation of the social teachings of the Roman Catholic Church.

The organized labor movement emerged from the Pérez Jiménez dictatorship in a very weak condition, because the regime had tried to divide and disorganize unions that were not completely under its control, while at the same time organizing a pet Confederación Nacional de Trabajadores to serve the political purposes of the dictatorship. Although this Confederación had little support among the workers, the Pérez Jiménez government made it very difficult if not impossible for unions to function effectively if they were not part of the regime's apparatus. The exception was the Black Communists' union movement in Caracas. During more than nine years of the dictatorship, the great majority of the organizable workers were not in unions at all. Those who were organized were split among a group of small, informal federations, organized along political lines. Acción Democrática, the Copei, the URD, and both the Red and Black Communists had such small central labor groups under their influence. All of these, except that of the Black Communists, were bitterly persecuted by the Pérez Jiménez regime, with their leaders being arrested, tortured, sent to concentration camps, and sometimes killed.

From the moment that the dictatorship fell, the leaders among the workers were agreed on the necessity of combining forces to rebuild a united trade union movement. All of the politically oriented labor groups had participated in the final struggle against the Pérez Jiménez regime, though the Black Communists had joined this struggle very tardily.

Insofar as the labor movement was concerned, the first effect of the end of the dictatorship was the disappearance of the Confederación Nacional de Trabajadores. In its place was established a Coordinating Committee for Trade Union Unity, composed of workers representing Acción Democrática, the Copei, the Unión Republicana Democrática, and the Communists (the distinction between Reds and Blacks disappeared at this point).

The Coordinating Committee agreed on several principles to be followed in rebuilding the labor movement. First, it was agreed that where the various political groups had competing unions in the same field, these unions would be merged into single organizations. Second, all local unions in a given trade or industry were to be brought together into a national union or federation. Third, the apportionment of offices in unions on all levels would be in accordance with agreements reached among the four principal political groups active in the labor movement, that is, AD, the Copei, the URD, and the Communists.

As a consequence of these agreements, the individual local labor groups under control of the four parties were merged in nearly all cases. In most instances, the local unions that had belonged to the Confederación Nacional de Trabajadores had ceased to exist with the fall of Pérez Jiménez; but where these locals had enjoyed some support among rank and file workers, they were included in the mergers to form single unions in every field in each locality.

Among the few unions that were not merged into the *sindicatos únicos* established under the direction of the Coordinating Committee were those organized by an independent Catholic group that had emerged after January 23, 1958, from the Catholic Workers Circles movement. These Circles, which had the official patronage of the Church hierarchy, were strictly religious groups which trained workers in Catholic doctrine, public speaking, and other subjects, and did not function as unions. In a number of places throughout the country, however, the Circles helped to establish genuine unions soon after the establishment of the provisional government. These unions were independent of the influence of the Copei party. The objective of their organizers was the establishment of a Catholic labor confederation, and as a result, they refused to have their groups merge with those of the political parties in the general unification movement.

In conformity with the policy of the Coordinating Committee, national unions were formed in every major branch of the Venezuelan economy. Some important national unions had been established before 1948, notably the Federación de Trabajadores Petroleros (Fedepetrol) (Petroleum Workers Federation), in the oil industry. This type of organization now became the national pattern. At the same time, the Coordinating Committee also undertook to re-establish the regional labor federations that had existed in each state before 1948. During the first year and a half after the fall of the dictatorship, national and regional conventions were held in various industries and trades and in the twenty states, and by the latter part of 1959 most had duly constituted organizations.

Several of the national industrial federations were of particular importance. One key group was the reconstituted Fedepetrol. Likewise of importance was the Federación de Trabajadores de la Construcción (Construction Workers Federation), an organization which had also existed before 1948. A new national group of major importance was the Federación de Trabajadores del Transporte (Transport Workers Federation). Among the other national federations of significance were the Asociación Nacional de Empleados (ANDE) (White Collar Workers Association), the Federación de Trabajadores Textiles (Textile Workers Federation), and the Federación de Trabajadores Portuarios (Port Workers Federation).

One of the most striking results of this trade union movement was the establishment of a large number of unions of agricultural workers and tenants. Such organizations as had existed in this field between 1945 and 1948 had been destroyed by the dictatorship, and the work of organization had to be undertaken all over again. Success came with the re-establishment of the Federación Campesina (Peasants Federation) during the first year of the Betancourt administration.

The united front policy agreed upon by the Coordinating Committee was also followed throughout the reorganized labor movement. Although elections were held on local, national, and regional levels, there were scarcely any open party contests. Agreement was reached beforehand, with the offices on the executive committee of each union being apportioned roughly in proportion to the supposed strength of each party.

As a result of this arrangement, Acción Democrática, though the largest single group in the leadership of the majority of the unions, was considerably weaker in the trade union movement than it had been between 1945 and 1948. The reunited Communists were recognized to be the second most important element in the reorganized labor movement. There is little doubt that both the Copei and the Unión Republicana Democrática were given representation on union executive committees out of all proportion to their rank and file following.

The work of the Coordinating Committee was not confined to formal re-establishment of the local and national units of the labor movement; it also undertook to recruit rank and file membership for these organizations. Since there was widespread enthusiasm for the unions among the country's workers, this was not a difficult problem. By the end of 1959 the Venezuelan labor movement probably had within its ranks some 300,000 to 400,000 members.

The government played an important part in this process of reorganizing the labor movement. Under the country's Labor Law, every union had to be officially recognized by the government in order to be able to bargain collectively and otherwise function effectively. Under both the provisional government and the constitutional regime of President Rómulo Betancourt the Ministry of Labor moved with considerable rapidity to give the necessary legal standing to the workers' organizations on all levels. During its first year in office the Betancourt regime legalized seven hundred new local unions.[1]

The newly constituted unions entered into collective bargaining negotiations with their respective employers or groups of employers. During the first year, until national federations had been generally organized, most of these collective agreements were negotiated by individual local unions, but the policy of the Coordinating Committee, and of the Confederación de Trabajadores de Venezuela after it, was to sign national collective agreements wherever this was feasible.

One of the first national groups to sign collective agreements for all categories of its workers throughout the country was the Federación de Trabajadores de la Construcción. Even before the federation had been officially re-established, the various local construction workers' unions agreed to allow a specially elected committee to sign agreements with the Ministry of Public Works and with organizations of private contractors.

The most important national collective contract was that between Fedepetrol and the oil companies. Both the union and the employers made extensive use during the negotiations of skilled professional people, not only lawyers, but economists, engineers, and others with special knowledge of the petroleum industry. This agreement was widely considered to be one of the most advantageous, from the workers' point of view, to be found any place in the world. However, as noted elsewhere in this volume, this contract provoked serious political disagreement, notably a split in Acción Democrática.

By the middle of 1960, it was estimated that some 200,000 workers were organized in legally recognized unions, besides those in the peasant field. There were in effect by September, 1960, some 1,109 collective agreements throughout the country.[2]

The work of rebuilding the Venezuelan labor movement was nearly completed with the meeting of the Third Congress of Workers in Caracas in December, 1959, ten months after the inauguration of President Betancourt. This congress, called by the Coordinating Committee for Trade Union Unity, re-established the Confederación de Trabajadores de Venezuela.

This congress of the CTV was a study in compromise by the democratic elements. Although Acción Democrática had a majority of the delegates in the meeting, they went out of their way to avoid giving offense to other elements, particularly the Communists. As a result, the AD people not only failed to push their point of view on some key issues but also permitted the Communists to use the meeting as an occasion for extensive propaganda, and accepted smaller representation on the CTV executive than was justified by their representation in the congress.

A United States observer of the Third Congress of Workers, writing in the AFL-CIO's *Free Trade Union News* of January, 1960, explained the cautious attitude of the AD and Copei delegates:

"During the one year that the new government has been in power, it has had to face several crises, for the military are still in the strongest force and many in their ranks are far from satisfied. The small clique, loyal to the deposed dictator, is still active. The minority parties are continuously pressuring for a larger share in the government.

"In these troubled waters, the Communists, with their strength concentrated in the capital and surrounding industrial areas, are in their element, shifting their support as each new crisis develops, initiating a crisis when the necessity arises, threatening to overthrow the democratic applecart if their demands are not met.

"Whether such a crisis had existed or was artificially stimulated by the Communists just prior to the CTV congress, is immaterial. It was there, and the need for more time for the democratic regime to consolidate its position, for democratic processes, which are so new to Venezuela, despite its one hundred and fifty years of republican life, to be understood and accepted, precluded a showdown with the Communists at this moment.

"The democratic forces in the CTV retreated on the labor front in order to save the political battle line. . . ."

One of the questions about which there was a strong difference of opinion among the trade unionists of different political groups was that of the international affiliation of the reconstructed Venezuelan labor movement. This was one of the issues left unresolved by the Third Congress of Workers. During the years following the overthrow of the Pérez Jiménez regime four different points of view were discernible among the country's trade union leaders.

During their period in exile, the Acción Democrática trade union leaders had been closely associated with the Inter-American Regional Organization of Workers (Organización Regional Interamericana de Trabajadores) (ORIT) and its parent body, the International Confederation of Free Trade Unions (ICFTU). Several of them had served as officials and organizers for the ORIT, and when they returned home after the fall of the dictatorship, they had at least a tacit agreement with the ORIT and the ICFTU that they would try to bring the reconstituted labor movement into the ranks of the world and hemisphere free labor movement as soon as this proved practicable. President Betancourt also strongly favored such a course of action.

Several of the Communist trade unionists, notably Rodolfo Quintero, had worked with and for the Communist trade union apparatus, the Confederación de Trabajadores de América Latina (CTAL), during the period of the dictatorship. The Black Communists' Federación de Trabajadores del Distrito Federal, which functioned quite openly during most of the Pérez Jiménez period, was officially affiliated with the CTAL and with its parent body, the World Federation of Trade Unions (WFTU). Quintero worked for some of this period in the CTAL headquarters in Mexico City.

The Communists would certainly have preferred to bring the CTV into their Latin American and world-wide trade union groups if this had proved feasible. Since the AD and the Copei trade unionists were unalterably opposed to affiliation with the CTAL and the WFTU, the Communists in the Venezuelan trade unions fell back on a second proposition, which for a while had a certain attraction for the Acción Democrática people and even for some Copei leaders. This was to have the CTV participate in an attempt to form another Latin American labor confederation which would be ostensibly neutral politically, and, for the time being at least, would not join either the WFTU or the ICFTU. This idea had first been launched by the Communist-dominated but internationally unaffiliated Central Única de Trabajadores of Chile, early in 1959. At that time it aroused little enthusiasm among those labor groups which were outside of the CTAL and ORIT, and none at all among the affiliates of the ORIT.

The Catholics in the trade unions were divided concerning what policy the CTV should follow on international affiliation. A few of the Copei-controlled unions had joined the International Trade Secretariats closely associated with the ICFTU, and were therefore disposed toward joining the ORIT and the ICFTU. Another group of Copei adherents and all of the independent Catholic trade unions outside of the CTV favored affiliation with the International Federation of Christian Trade Unions and the Confederación Latino Americana de Sindicalistas Cristianos (CLASC), or, if that proved impossible, preferred the Venezuelan labor movement to remain independent of any international body.

Although the CTV was committed throughout 1960 to cooperation in establishing a new Latin American labor group, little concrete progress was achieved in this direction during that year. Finally, after the break with the Communists at the end of 1960, the AD leaders of some of the national unions took a step that seemed to presage the affiliation of the CTV with the international free labor movement. Fedepetrol and the Federación de Trabajadores del Transporte joined their respective International Trade Secretariats in the middle of 1961. Other AD-controlled national groups were contemplating taking the same step. The Fourth Congress of Workers, which met in Caracas on December 9, 1961, gave up completely the idea of forming a new Latin American labor confederation. Rather, it resolved that the CTV would affiliate with the ORIT and the ICFTU. The CTV joined both free labor groups early in 1962.

The united front in the Venezuelan labor movement fully crumbled in November, 1960. At that time the Communists and the MIR members of the executive committee of the Confederación de Trabajadores de Venezuela issued a call for a revolutionary general strike against the Betancourt regime. Although the strike failed to materialize, the attempt by the extreme Leftists was a declaration of war on the AD and the Copei inside the labor movement. The AD took up the challenge, and there began an intense struggle for control of the rank and file unions throughout the country. Starting in February, 1961, elections were held in most of the country's important unions. Unlike the situation in previous years, when single lists of candidates had been put up jointly by all of the parties, there were now bitterly competitive slates. In most cases, the three opposition parties—the Communist, the MIR, and the Unión Republicana Democrática—put up a joint ticket; and in most cases, too, the Acción Democrática had its own separate list. In a few cases, AD and the Copei joined forces in a joint slate, and in others the three opposition parties ran separate lists.

The outcome of these elections was an overwhelming victory for the trade union forces of Acción Democrática. Between February and July, 1961, Acción Democrática won elections in one hundred and thirty-six of the one hundred and forty-eight local unions in which they were held. Most of the rest were won by the extreme Left coalition. The AD also won ten of the twenty-five held during August, 1961. The net result was that by the end of 1961 Acción Democrática by itself controlled from 65 to 70 per cent of all of the unions in the country.

In the oil fields Acción Democrática came out as victor in all but one of the major local unions. It also obtained a sizable majority in the key transport and construction workers' organizations. It had about half of the port workers' groups under its control, and all but one of the mining unions. It was weakest in the factory workers' organizations in the Maracay and Valencia areas, where the Communists were strongest and the URD also had considerable influence, and in ANDE, where the MIR was the largest element.

The struggle for power was also reflected in the regional federations of the CTV. In state conventions held in the states of Lara and Portuguesa, where the MIR and the Communists, respectively, had been in control before 1961, Acción Democrática acquired a majority. They also won control of the labor movements in the states of Guárico and Bolívar, where, through defection of the MIR group, AD had lost control of state federations in 1960.

Finally, AD won the power fight within the CTV itself. Although the AD-Copei alliance and the extreme Leftists each had seven members in the fourteen-man executive committee of the CTV, AD held the top posts of president and secretary-general. However, AD waited for six months after the break with the extreme Leftists before taking action against them in the top echelon of the labor movement.

In May, 1961, a bitter public controversy occurred between the two groups in the executive committee of the CTV. The PCV-MIR-URD group issued a proclamation "in the name of the CTV" denouncing measures that President Betancourt had submitted to Congress for the purpose of stabilizing the economy. CTV President José González Navarro immediately responded, supporting the government program and denying the right of the extreme Leftists to speak in the name of the labor movement as a whole. Furthermore, the AD-Copei members of the executive committee called a meeting of the Confederación's disciplinary committee, on which they had a majority, and presented charges to this committee against the extreme Leftists on the executive committee. After due deliberation, the disciplinary committee suspended the Communist and MIR members of the executive committee, pending the holding of a special convention of the CTV at the end of 1961.

The Fourth Congress of Workers, which met in 1961, reflected the complete break in the unity of the labor movement which had occurred during the previous year. It completely reorganized the leadership of the Confederación de Trabajadores de Venezuela, naming only AD and Copei members to the new executive committee. For practical purposes, labor organizations under the control of the Communists and their allies were excluded from the CTV.

Delegates from a total of thirty-three federations, including nine industrial groups and twenty-one state and territorial labor federations, attended the congress. The great majority of the delegates belonged to AD, the only other political group with sizable representation being the Copei. The unions and federations dominated by the parties of the extreme Left coalition boycotted the meeting.

Among the federations that did not attend the congress was the Federación Campesina. Its absence reflected the strained relations then existing between Ramón Quijada, president of the peasants' group, and the leadership of his party, Acción Democrática. The decision of the Federación Campesina not to send delegates to the Fourth Congress of Workers provoked the executive committee of the CTV to intervene in the affairs of the federation, officially ousting its leaders, and establishing a temporary committee to reorganize it. This committee, headed by Armando González as president, called a congress of the federation during the first week of June, 1962, which was attended by delegates from a large majority of the local peasant unions.

In 1962 the dissolution of trade union unity became complete. A number of URD labor leaders still holding office in federations affiliated with the CTV were removed, as were the handful of secondary trade union officials who had joined the ARS split in Acción Democrática. Trade unionists of the URD, the ARS, the MIR and the Communist party formed what they called the Unofficial CTV, which held a convention in March, 1963, at which a new central labor group, the Confederación Única de Trabajadores de Venezuela, was established. It claimed "more than four hundred" of the country's more than 3,600 trade unions then enjoying legal recognition. Meanwhile, the AD had organized a rival Asociación Nacional de Empleados to that controlled by the MIR and the Communists. The ANDE had been the only national federation under extremist control.

By the last months of 1963 the CTV claimed that thirty-seven of the thirty-nine legally constituted labor federations were affiliated with it. They also claimed 3,211 local unions and peasant leagues, and 1.3 million workers of an estimated 2.8 million working population.[3]

The split in the labor movement did not alter the basic labor policies of the Betancourt administration. President Betancourt stated very early in his regime what these policies were to be. In his May Day message in 1959, he stated:

"With the new regime after January 23, this nightmarish situation of the people began to change. The urban and rural workers set out to rebuild their organs of economic defense, and there began a process of readjustment of wages, salaries, and social benefits. I have said, and I want to repeat, that both employers and workers have demonstrated understanding and a patriotic spirit in reaching labor-management agreements and in seeking the normal path of discussion and compromise to adjust their difficulties. Thus collective contracts have been signed for whole industries, and only on rare occasions has the strike been resorted to. Strikes always have a perturbing effect in a country such as ours where there are shortages in so many areas of production. I must insist here that the government guarantees and will guarantee the right of unionization, a social gain incorporated in legislation throughout the world. Concurrent with and complementing the right to form a union is the right to strike, which is assured in our Labor Law. The government will seek to intervene in a friendly way in order to avoid strikes, but if one takes place, the government will act in conformity with the law. A reckless strike before legal procedures have been exhausted is illegal, and the government has declared such strikes illegal, and will do so in the future . . . the government seeks to keep labor problems within legal channels, guaranteeing rights to all three interests involved: the employers, the workers, and the general public."[4]

In spite of the bitter strife in the ranks of the trade union movement after 1960, the government continued to follow much the same policy, and the general labor relations situation remained relatively calm. For example, there were three legal strikes between January and September, 1961, and three illegal ones. Attempts by the Communists and the MIR to stir up trouble for the government among the workers were unsuccessful. The extreme Leftists overreached themselves, and as a result, tended to alienate large elements among the workers.

During this critical period, the Minister of Labor, Raúl Valera, adopted a steady but flexible attitude. He was violently attacked by the Communists as the "Anti-Labor Minister," although they had worked closely with him in 1958 when he held the same post in the provisional government (which the Communists supported). At the demand of the opposition deputies, Valera was summoned to be interrogated on his policies by Congress. They accused him of violating trade union immunity. According to the law, trade union officials cannot be dismissed except for grievous cause, and their dismissal must be authorized by the Minister of Labor personally. Valera was able to demonstrate that of the 20,000 workers enjoying trade union immunity, employers had sought the dismissal of eighty during the first six months of 1961, and he had authorized the firing of only thirty-seven, an insignificant number. He also pointed out that when one of the oil companies dismissed a Communist union leader and refused to restore his job, he threatened to order the arrest of the oil company official involved, whereupon the unionist was put back to work.

Valera handled illegal strikes very cautiously. He refused to take any measures against an illegal walkout of oil tanker crews, on the grounds that there was plenty of oil available, whereupon the strike collapsed. In another case, in July, 1961, in which three Communist-influenced oil field unions walked out shortly before the eighth anniversary of Fidel Castro's attack on Moncada Barracks, and sought to snowball this into a general strike on that anniversary, July 26, the Ministry of Labor left the settlement of the problem up to the Fedepetrol. The national organization succeeded in getting the men in the three unions back to work without further repercussions. On the other hand, the Ministry insisted on the enforcement of the law, whereby workers who participate in illegal walkouts lose their pay for the days they are off the job. This policy was continued by Valera's successors in the post of Minister of Labor.

In spite of the turbulence caused by the attempts of the extreme Leftists to arouse popular insurrection after 1960, the labor scene remained relatively calm. Thus, during 1962 there were only eight strikes, although some 642 collective contracts were signed. These new agreements brought union members an average salary increase of 61.5 bolívares per month for white collar workers and 1.83 bolívares per day for manual workers, as well as extensive fringe benefits. During the first four years of the Betancourt regime, there were only thirty-eight strikes, although 2,665 collective agreements were signed.[5]

Chapter Nineteen
Primary Education

Although faced with monumental problems of both quantity and quality in the elementary and secondary schools, the Betancourt regime in five years made spectacular advances in improving and expanding educational services for the Venezuelan people. Leaders of the regime were acutely aware that in the long run the success or failure of their efforts to establish a stable democratic form of government and a healthy economy depended on their ability to educate as well as govern the people.

So great was the neglect of the school system during the nine-year dictatorship of Pérez Jiménez that less than half of the school-age population was in school in 1958. Little of the large oil returns that accrued to Pérez Jiménez and his cohorts had been expended on public education, although by the end of the 1950's the population explosion was such that half of all Venezuelans were less than eighteen years of age. The number of classrooms, teachers, and students increased so slowly during the dictatorship that the percentage of the country's school-age population in school dropped. Indeed, in the last years of Pérez Jiménez' incumbency primary schools were closed down, and by the end of his regime the number of normal schools had also decreased.

Building schools for the children was only a small part of the problem. An intensive campaign had to be undertaken to train teachers capable of maintaining and improving the quality of instruction. Furthermore, a more diversified educational system was required if there were to be enough skilled technicians and craftsmen to man the wheels of expanding industry and commerce. For adults who had missed out on the benefits of even an elementary education, adult schools were needed. In other words, it was no longer enough to offer merely a standard classical curriculum designed for the few who would succeed in obtaining higher academic or professional degrees, often in foreign universities.

The first Acción Democrática government of 1945 to 1948 had begun to enrich the nation's educational system by establishing a considerable number of crafts, industrial, and commercial vocational schools, as well as expanding and diversifying university facilities. This program, all but abandoned by the dictatorship, was renewed by the government of the Democratic Revolution, and special attention was given to the development of agricultural vocational education.

The amount of money allocated for education by both national and state governments was augmented to such an extent that the Ministry of Education came to spend the second largest amount of money of all of the government departments, following only the Ministry of Public Works, a fair proportion of whose efforts were devoted to school construction and repair. For the first time, educational expenses exceeded those of the armed forces.

Juan Ramón Bucce, writing in the weekly newspaper *A.D.* of September 13, 1961, summarized the increase of expenditures on education by the Betancourt regime:

"It is important to note that the last budget for education of the dictatorship provided for 178 million bolívares, and that the present government—without counting the investments in school construction by the Ministry of Public Works, the 20 per cent of the budget of each state which is assigned to educational ends, the amount spent on special schools and scholarships by other ministries, autonomous institutes, and municipal councils—has given education a budget of 461 million bolívares for the 1959 to 1960 period, and 541 million bolívares for that of 1960 to 1961.

"Now, the budget assigned the Ministry of Education for the six-month period July to December, 1961, is 276,925,564 bolívares, or 12,851,128 bolívares more than that of the year just ended. It is estimated that for the fiscal year 1961 to 1962 the budget of the Ministry of Education will be once again increased, and will come to something in the nature of 696 million bolívares."

To ensure wise use of the new funds, the Betancourt regime established within the Ministry of Education a section to study and plan for the long-range needs of the country's educational system. The Oficina de Planamiento Educacional Integral, established by a decree of August 7, 1959, was empowered to study the over-all educational needs of the country in collaboration with the Oficina de Coordinación y Planificación (Cordiplan) of the President's office, and to make the appropriate recommendations to the Minister of Education and his associates. It was given advisory powers, but was not authorized to put plans into execution by itself.

More important than these specific aspects of the educational policy of the government of the Venezuelan Democratic Revolution was the spirit that it brought to the country's educational effort. The Ministry of Education was controlled by a group of dedicated teachers, who were for the most part disciples of Luis Beltrán Prieto Figueroa, mentor of the post-Gómez generations of Venezuelan teachers, Minister of Education of the 1945 to 1948 Acción Democrática regime, and senator after February, 1959. The second man in the Ministry, the Director General de Educación, was Reinaldo Leandro Mora, who had held the same position when Prieto Figueroa was Minister from 1945 to 1948. Upon the reorganization of the government in November, 1960, Reinaldo Leandro Mora became Minister of Education. Others who had played a leading part in the educational efforts of the first AD government returned to the Ministry after 1959.

All of these men believed that the teacher has a key role to play in the transformation of society and the development of the nation. He must be not only an instructor of the young but a leader in the community. Luis Beltrán Prieto Figueroa is the author of a book entitled *El Maestro como líder* ("The Teacher as Leader").

Under the Venezuelan system of education, children start to school at about seven years of age. After six years of primary school, they may go on to five years of secondary school, and then to the university. Although the government has for many decades assumed the principal responsibility for education in Venezuela, private organizations are permitted to maintain schools as long as these institutions conform to standards established by the government. In fact, less than 10 per cent of the primary schools were private at the end of the Betancourt administration. Most of these were under the control of the Roman Catholic Church, though there were also some secular private schools, particularly in the field of vocational training.

The federal, state and municipal governments all have schools under their control, although since 1959 the tendency has been to centralize the government educational system under the Ministry of Education. By the 1963 to 1964 school year about two thirds of the children in the primary grades were attending schools directly run by the national government. There tends to be a division of labor between the state and national governments in the educational field. Increasingly, the states are concentrating their attention on construction and maintenance of institutions in the rural areas where prior to the Betancourt regime there were very few schools of any sort. The federal government, on the other hand, has assumed primary responsibility for the schools in the urban centers.

The Ministry of Education is not the only national agency that has educational institutions under its control. The Ministry of Agriculture operates schools, as do other institutions such as the Venezuelan Children's Council (Consejo Venezolano del Niño), the Ministry of Health, and the Ministry of National Defense.

Whereas at the time of the overthrow of the Pérez Jiménez dictatorship, considerably less than half of the children of primary school age were actually attending school, during the succeeding years, the number of children registered in primary educational institutions increased by about 80 per cent. Almost all of the new enrollment was in government institutions. By the beginning of the school year 1961 to 1962, Ministry of Education officials reported that classes were available for virtually all children of an age to enter first grade. This was the first time in the country's history that this had been the case.

Table V presents detailed information on the increase in the number of students, teaching staff, and buildings of the primary school system, from the year 1957 to 1958, the last of the dictatorship, to the year 1961 to 1962.

This rapid expansion of the primary school population required extraordinary efforts to recruit new members of the teaching staff. Inevitably it became necessary to employ thousands of individuals who did not have proper teacher training. During the year of the provisional government, although over 4,000 new teachers were employed in the country's schools, the shortage of teaching staff

TABLE V

INCREASE IN PRIMARY EDUCATIONAL SYSTEM IN VENEZUELA, 1957-58 TO 1962-63

	STUDENTS			TEACHERS			SCHOOLS		
Year	Public	Private	Total	Public	Private	Total	Public	Private	Total
1957-58	608,428	143,133	751,561	14,912	6,002	20,914	5,606	1,070	6,676
1958-59	775,586	141,178	916,754	19,247	5,609	24,856	6,577	899	7,476
1959-60	933,441	161,163	1,094,604	24,788	6,101	30,889	5,727	923	9,650
1960-61	1,084,631	169,624	1,254,255	28,997	6,440	35,437	10,920	943	11,863
1961-62	1,185,200 *	—	1,354,824 *	—	—	—	—	—	—
1962-63	—	—	1,357,000	—	—	—	—	—	—

* Estimated.

Sources: Based on *Memoria que el Ministerio de Educación presenta al Congreso Nacional de la República de Venezuela en sus sesiones de 1961,* page E-2; article in *La República,* by Juan Ramón Bucce, September 6, 1961; and Rómulo Betancourt: *V Presidential Message,* Imprenta Nacional, Caracas, 1963.

was not as serious as it became later. This was because at the time of the overthrow of the dictatorship some 3,000 teachers were unemployed, and with the beginning of the new school year in September, 1958, it was possible to give all of them jobs. Subsequently, however, people who did not have proper accreditation as primary school teachers had to be used. In the school year 1959 to 1960, only 10,901 of the 24,788 teachers employed in the government primary schools had proper accreditation. Of the rest, some 13,767 had graduated from a secondary school other than a normal school, while apparently 106 had not completed their secondary education.[1]

The new regime immediately took steps to enable the unprepared teachers to complete their training and also established new normal schools. The number of government institutions for training primary school teachers increased from ten in the last year of the dictatorship, to sixteen in the year of the provisional government, to thirty-one in the school year 1959 to 1960, the first of the Betancourt regime. The increase in normal school students is described in the Ministry of Education's 1961 report to Congress (p. E-8):

"The enrollment of normal school students in the year 1959 to 1960, in relation to the previous year, showed 8,029 more students (104.4 per cent in public schools); 3,191 more in the private ones (48.1 per cent), for a total of 11,200 (78.3 per cent). The number of teachers in these schools increased by 423 in the public ones (128.2 per cent), and 137 in the private ones (18.8 per cent), or a total of 560 (52.9 per cent).

"Comparison of beginning and final enrollment in the normal

schools in the year 1959 to 1960 shows that 2,783 students in all, or 10.9 per cent, dropped out. The public schools showed 12 per cent dropouts, the private ones 9.09 per cent. . . ."

After the school year 1959 to 1960 no new normal schools were started. It was felt that in view of the efforts being made to give in-service training to qualified teachers who were already on the job, the thirty-one existing institutions were sufficient to meet the country's needs. By the school year 1960 to 1961 competition for teaching posts in the primary schools was becoming keen, and there were some qualified teachers who, being unwilling to take jobs in rural schools, were without employment. During the 1961 to 1962 school year some 32,400 students were in Venezuelan normal schools, compared to only 8,300 during the 1957 to 1958 period.

The program for training teachers on the job was the primary concern of the Instituto de Mejoramiento Profesional del Magisterio. Its work was described by Juan Ramón Bucce, in his article in *A.D.* on September 13, 1961: "The Instituto de Mejoramiento Profesional del Magisterio organizes resident courses and correspondence courses so that untrained teachers can obtain their certificates without giving up their teaching jobs. Other Teacher Improvement Courses were established for those holding certificates. At the present time 2,200 trained teachers and 9,000 untrained ones are taking these courses." By the 1962 to 1963 school year some 9,300 untrained teachers were being trained in the Instituto. Over 4,000 teachers had by that time received their certificates.

Although initially no untrained teacher was forced to take courses in the Instituto in order to hold his or her job, the Ministry of Education decreed that after the school year 1963 to 1964 no more teachers without certificates would be employed. It was planned to close the emergency courses of the Instituto at the end of that school year, and after the year 1961 to 1962 the Instituto did not take any more teacher-students for the three-year certificate course.

The Ministry's intensive training of teachers as well as the time limits it set were undoubtedly motivated by a desire to end as quickly as possible a situation in which such a large portion of the primary school staff did not have proper qualifications, and by its conviction that the regular normal schools would be able by 1964 to meet adequately the demand for additional teachers. The author suspects that the Ministry of Education leaders may be over-optimistic, for although it is true that there were enough teachers (trained and untrained) to provide classes for children old enough to enter the first grade in September, 1961, a large number of the schools then had only three or four grades. This meant that there was bound to be a large demand for additional teachers within three or four years to handle the upper elementary grades. Furthermore, the official target of fifty pupils per class means that the teacher cannot do an adequate job. Any attempt to reduce the pupil load would result in the need for a sizable increase in the teaching staff. Careful consideration of these two problems is needed on the part of the officials of the Ministry of Education before there can be any complacency concerning the adequacy of the primary education teaching staff.

The Ministry also has cause for concern about the large number of children who drop out after the first year or so of primary school. Furthermore, a great many fail to pass and must repeat a grade. In the school year 1959 to 1960 some 39.5 per cent of all of the students in the government-run primary schools were in the first grade. Thereafter, there was a very sharp drop, with only 19.7 per cent in the second grade, and only 5.8 per cent in the sixth or final primary grade. The Ministry of Education figures showed that of the 371,062 first grade pupils in 1958 to 1959, only 188,869 entered second grade in 1959 to 1960; 65,275 left school before completing the first grade, and 116,918 had to repeat the first grade.[2]

The rate of increase in number of children who have to repeat a grade has gone up in recent years. Venezuelan educationists attribute this in large part to the sizable number of untrained teachers employed in the primary school system. The large number of dropouts, on the other hand, is probably attributable chiefly to economic considerations. Particularly in the rural areas, the economic value of children in terms of work around their parents' farms is still very high, and it frequently happens that parents decide it is more important to have farm help than it is to let the children get an education. The vocational agricultural schools that are being established in large numbers on a primary level should help to convince the peasants of the importance of education.

That some progress was being made in dealing with the dropout problem was indicated by President Betancourt's fifth annual message to Congress on March 12, 1963. He noted that primary school attendance had risen from 22.6 per cent in 1958 to 1959 to 33.4 per cent in 1962, and commented that this "shows that the number of students who leave school without completing their educational training is steadily decreasing."

Also troublesome for the Ministry of Education are Venezuela's one-room schools, reminiscent of the "little red school house" of the rural United States of a couple generations ago. These schools, in which from one to perhaps three or four grades are taught by one teacher, dot the countryside. In October, 1959, there were 7,370 such schools,[3] and by the following year their number had increased considerably. Most are under the control of the state governments. Since these schools are likely to be located in areas far removed from centers of population, it is very difficult to exercise effective supervision over them. The living and working conditions of the teachers are trying, and there have been frequent cases in which they have been irregular in meeting their classes.

State and federal educational authorities who are concerned with these school problems try to consolidate two or three of the small schools into one if the student body is large enough. More generally preferred is the Rural School Nucleus, a "technical-administrative unit which groups a certain number of rural schools located in a homogeneous zone from the geographic, economic, and demographic points of view around a principal school that serves as guide and is called the Central School."[4]

By the 1960 to 1961 school year the Ministry of Education had established thirty-eight such units. Various state governments had set up others. The director of a Rural School Nucleus has no easy job, for he has to keep in close personal contact with each of the twenty or more school teachers in his nucleus. He not only supervises them but also helps them with problems they may have in their work. Also, he is responsible with the teachers for encouraging the interest of the parents and the community at large in the schools and their problems.

The government is also trying to give further help to the children who complete courses in the rural units. Where the student population justifies it, the state and national authorities add new grades as they are needed, and provide the teachers necessary to do the work.

Another type of school suitable to farming areas is the *escuela granja comunal,* or communal agricultural school. Although some of the institutions being established are secondary schools, others are set up as primary schools. In the latter, students who have gone as far as they can in a school close to home attend residential escuelas granjas comunales. There, besides their A B C's they are taught the rudiments of farming. Current running expenses of these schools are covered by sale of the crops, livestock, and other products grown by the students. Best of all, the escuela granja comunal is designed as a kind of demonstration farm, where the parents of the students and other peasants in the vicinity can be introduced to modern farming methods.

The escuelas granjas comunales are designed to limit the drift of the peasant population to the cities. Authorities feel that farm boys who have received training in agriculture will be more inclined to stay on the land than those who have not learned the principles of efficient farming. The program for establishing escuelas granjas comunales is regarded as a corollary to the agrarian reform program, which also has a primary concern with stopping the drift of the farmers to the urban centers.

Large sums of money were spent on the construction of school buildings during the Betancourt regime. The President, in his message to Congress in March, 1961, commented as follows:

"This signifies a net increase of 600,000 students over the number in the last year of the dictatorship, 1957 to 1958. It has been necessary to open more than 5,000 primary schools, 54 secondary schools, and one hundred buildings for vocational education, and practically to double the capacity of the universities.

"The conditions of the buildings in which public schools function are not satisfactory, especially in the field of primary education where more than 10,000 classrooms for some 500,000 children are needed, in spite of the fact that during the last two years there have been built classrooms for 200,000 students. . . ."[5]

Juan Ramón Bucce, writing in the newspaper *A.D.* of September 13, 1961, described the school-building efforts of the Betancourt administration:

"In order to incorporate these hundreds of thousands of children in the educational system, the democratic regime has built 2,952 schools—to make a total of 9,520—of which the Ministry of Public Works built 68 six-year schools in 1959 to 1960 and 138 in 1960 to 1961, for a total of 206. The state governments constructed 371 school buildings in 1959 to 1960, and 380 in 1960 to 1961, for a total of 751."

Both the national and state governments have had large school construction programs. It is our observation that the state governments have been more willing than the national Ministry of Education to experiment with new types of school construction. The Ministry has tended to stick by well-known formulas for the schools that it builds, which are frequently more expensive than those constructed by the state education authorities.

The state of Lara has been particularly successful in its school building program. By the beginning of the 1961 to 1962 school year the constitutional government of the state had built 180 new schools, and most of these had been constructed on a pre-fabricated basis, with the walls and ceilings of metal, in Barquisimeto, from whence they were transported to wherever they were needed. They were reported to cost only about a quarter as much as the Ministry of Education schools, and to take only fifteen days to construct. Education officials from half a dozen other states had studied Lara's school building program.

In his fifth annual message to Congress on March 12, 1963, President Betancourt said that the national shortage of primary school buildings had been reduced from 70 per cent in 1958 to 32.8 per cent at the end of 1962. He added that current school building plans would reduce the deficit to 24.5 per cent by 1966.

Those in charge of the Venezuelan educational program have been well aware that the success of their efforts depended basically on the cooperation of the teaching staff. They have been very much concerned, therefore, with improving the working and living conditions of the teachers. The dictatorship had had disastrous effects on the morale of the nation's teachers. They had been persecuted for political reasons, and many of them had been jailed or exiled. Their remuneration had been kept very low. But above all, they had been forced to function in an atmosphere of corruption and disrespect for things intellectual which was exceedingly demoralizing. Like other public employees, the teachers had those among their number who submitted to this aura of corruption, and generally the atmosphere was not conducive to the kind of professional dedication necessary for the development of an effective school system in Venezuela.

Basic to improving the well-being of the teaching staff was the democratic government's action in raising salaries. By the beginning of the 1961 to 1962 school year, Venezuelan educational authorities maintained that the salaries of the nation's school teachers were the highest to be found anywhere in Latin America.

The democratic regime also improved general working conditions of the teaching staff. It strictly enforced regulations with regard to stability of employment and orderly promotion procedures. In spite of the bitterness of political conflict that developed after October and November, 1960, few teachers were dismissed or otherwise punished because of their political affiliations. The author encountered several political opponents of the government, including some Communists, among officials of the Ministry of Education and in teaching staffs in various parts of Venezuela in the period July to September, 1961.

The social security system for teachers was also improved by the democratic administration. Symptomatic was the increase in budgetary appropriations for the Institute of Insurance and Social Assistance for Ministry of Education personnel from 1.6 million bolívares in 1957 to 1958 to 6.2 million bolívares in 1959 to 1960.[6]

Spectacular progress was made during the Betancourt administration in the field of primary education. Student attendance in government schools was almost doubled, as were the teaching staff and the number of schools. Emergency measures were taken for the training of unqualified teachers who were pressed into service during this period, while the normal schools increased from ten to thirty-one between 1957 to 1958 and 1959 to 1960. Finally, much attention was paid to improvement of the living and working conditions of the teaching staff.

Chapter Twenty

Adult, Vocational, Secondary, and University Education

A prime concern of the Betancourt government and of the provisional regime that preceded it was the development of a diversified educational system to serve the needs of citizens of all age levels and of every field of endeavor. With the tremendous increase in the number of primary schools, more secondary schools had to be established. Moreover, the government also took steps to expand the opportunities for vocational training and adult education, as well as higher education. Hundreds of thousands of Venezuelans have grown up without the benefits of even an elementary education, and many adults as well as young people require training in the mechanical and industrial arts and agriculture if Venezuela is to take its place as a progressive modern nation.

The new democratic government from the outset demonstrated a spirit of enthusiasm, a willingness to experiment, and an ability to get things done which are perhaps unequaled in the hemisphere. And it achieved its successes in the educational field without seeking to bend the school system to the political prejudices of any party or clique. To the contrary, it maintained academic freedom and protected the rights of the teachers and the students in the face of violent and persistent attempts on the part of the extreme Leftist opposition to mobilize the secondary school children and the university men and women to overthrow the regime itself.

In one of its major tasks, the campaign against illiteracy, the direction was in the hands of the Oficina de Educación de Adultos (Office of Adult Education) of the Ministry of Education. The Oficina worked through three types of schools, as well as through channels outside of the regular school system. Beginning classes in reading and writing were offered by *centros colectivos de alfabetización* (collective literacy centers), and for those adults who had achieved a basic knowledge in these centers, *centros de extensión cultural* were established to give them further training and keep them from slipping back into illiteracy. An already existing system of *centros de cultura popular*, which were night schools offering a regular primary school course, was considerably expanded.

The collective literacy centers were the most numerous of these three types of institutions. Not infrequently, the Office of Adult Education found that potential students, particularly in the cities, were reluctant to sign up for classes given in regular school buildings. Many people felt that if they were seen entering a school to go to these classes, they would be labeled "illiterate," and lose caste among their fellows. Therefore, many of the centers were opened in private homes in working-class and slum neighborhoods, or in some neighborhood building where class attendance would be more or less unnoticed.

The teachers of these adult classes were generally drawn from the regular staff of the public schools, although some additional personnel was recruited from outside their ranks. Unlike some of the other people working in the anti-illiteracy program, the teachers in the centers were paid for their services.

The country was divided into three zones, according to the type of campaign being conducted in them. Thus, in 1959 to 1960 what was officially called an "intensive" literacy effort was conducted in the states of Falcón, Guárico, Lara, Sucre, Yaracuy, and Zulia. The campaign in the Distrito Federal and the states of Aragua, Carabobo, Miranda, and Trujillo was classified as "semi-intensive," and the states of Apure, Barinas, Bolívar, Cojedes, Mérida, Monagas, Nueva Esparta, Portuguesa, Táchira, and the Federal Territories were the field of an "extensive" effort to teach the people to read and write.

During the year 1959 to 1960 there were some 2,928 collective literacy centers functioning in the area of the intensive campaign, with some 103,414 students receiving instruction. In the states in which the campaign was classified as semi-intensive there were 733 centers, with 27,343 students; and in the area of the extensive effort, there were 1,069 collective literacy centers and 42,203 students. The total for the country in that year, therefore, was some 4,730 local literacy schools, with 172,960 students.[1]

During the period July to December, 1960, the budget of the Office of Adult Education was reduced from 14 million bolívares to 9 million, and as a result the number of centers dropped to 2,294 and the number of students to 91,760.[2] No change was made in the budget for 1961; however, the budgets for 1962 and 1963 included a sizable increase for the activities of the Office of Adult Education.

Another method used by the Office of Adult Education to reach and instruct the illiterate is what the officials call "direct education." It consisted of sending sound trucks into a rural region or city ward to conduct propaganda for the anti-illiteracy campaign and at the same time to recruit volunteer teachers and potential students. Once lists were collected, "teacher-promoters" from the Office of Adult Education visited the area to match up teachers and students. In these cases, the teaching was on an individual basis instead of in classes.

Officials of the Office of Adult Education also carried the campaign into the factories of Caracas and other cities. They went to a factory, made a survey of how many illiterates there were, and then discussed with the owner or manager of the plant what he could do to help the campaign. Sometimes the head of the factory was willing to pay the expenses of a teacher or teachers. If not, the office employed the necessary teachers. Usually, the employers were willing to give the worker half an hour a day if he would spend an extra half hour from his own time for these classes. As early as the end of July, 1961, the officials of the Office of Adult Education had visited some 1,196 factories in the Caracas area. Of the 23,914 workers in these plants, they found some 924 who were illiterate, and had been able to get 496 into classes.[3]

School children of the fourth, fifth and sixth grades were also organized into "literacy legions" to participate in the program of teaching adults to read and write. The Office of Adult Education started organizing a literacy legion by having one of its officials visit a local school to talk to the principal and the student body and solicit volunteers. Those who volunteered were formed into a legion, with one of the teachers of the school as an adviser. The students elected their own executive committee, composed of a president, vice-president, and two secretaries.

Office of Adult Education officials talked with the volunteers to explain to them how to go about seeking students and how to use *Abajo Cadenas,* the basic textbook published by the Office. Then the children set out to find their students. Some already knew someone who wanted to learn to read. Others had to go from door to door, and many found this very hard to do and dropped out at this point. Once a child found his prospective student, he reported to the legion, and the Office of Adult Education sent someone out to confer with the young teacher and his prospective student, and to set up a schedule for the lessons. These were always held in the home of the student. The Office kept track of how the lessons were going, by keeping in touch with the members of the legions, and by visiting the students to make sure that the children were keeping their teaching appointments.

When a legion member reported that his pupil could read and write, there was an examination, with the legion members, someone from the Office, and sometimes the teacher-adviser giving the examination. This test consisted of writing nine lines and of reading a few paragraphs and explaining what they meant. The examination was certified by those who had given it, and record was made of the fact. The student was given a certificate attesting to his having learned to read and write.

In his fifth annual message to Congress on March 12, 1963, President Betancourt commented as follows on the results of the government's campaign against illiteracy: "Whereas the percentage of illiterates in the population fifteen years of age or older was 33.5 in 1961, that for 1962 was only 26.5 per cent. It is hoped that through the direct action of our literacy campaign and the indirect effect of the expansion of primary schools, the illiteracy rate will decrease sharply. This effort is the more significant, since, during the period between censuses taken in 1950 and 1961 the illiteracy rate decreased by 1.5 per cent annually, while the decrease for 1961 to 1962 was 7 per cent."

Until the Acción Democrática government of the late 1940's, Venezuela had only two types of secondary schools, *liceos,* or high schools of a pre-university type, and normal schools (which are secondary schools rather than university level institutions in Venezuela). That government took the first step to diversify the secondary educational system by organizing a number of vocational schools. However, during the nine years of dictatorship, little progress was made in this field, and the Ministry of Education had no special unit to supervise the existing vocational institutions. It was not until April 10, 1958, that the Directorate of Handicraft, Industrial, and Commercial Education was established by the provisional government.

After the fall of the dictatorship both the provisional government and the Betancourt regime devoted considerable attention to expanding the vocational education program of the Ministry of Education and the state educational authorities. Table VI gives the number of schools and students in various branches of vocational education in the year 1957 to 1958, and the increase in this number subsequently.

The Betancourt regime took another important step to set up facilities for training workers in the skills needed in Venezuela's increasingly industrial economy. This was the establishment of the Instituto Nacional de Cooperación Educativa (INCE), which set up an apprenticeship and on-the-job training program to supplement the vocational schools in the regular educational system.

The bill for the establishment of the INCE was presented to Congress by Senator Luis Beltrán Prieto Figueroa, and was supported by congressmen of all parties. It was passed on August 22, 1959, and the final regulations of the law were issued by President Betancourt six months later. The model for the Instituto was the Serviço Nacional de Aprendizagem Industrial (National Service of

TABLE VI

VOCATIONAL EDUCATION IN VENEZUELA, 1957-58 TO 1962-63 *

Year	*Handicrafts* *Schools*	*Handicrafts* *Students*	*Industrial* *Schools*	*Industrial* *Students*	*Commercial* *Schools*	*Commercial* *Students*	*Total* *Schools*	*Total* *Students*
1957-58	13	3,848	11	4,393	56	8,743	80	16,984
1958-59	15	1,730	17	8,308	70	12,035	102	22,073
1959-60	18	2,259	25	12,226	73	15,931	116	30,416
1960-61	—	—	—	—	—	—	203	42,230
1962-63	—	—	—	—	—	—		60,000

* Data not available for 1961-62.

Sources: *Memoria que el Ministerio presenta al Congreso Nacional de la República de Venezuela en sus sesiones de 1961;* article by Juan Ramón Bucce in *A.D.*, September 13, 1961; and Rómulo Betancourt: *V Presidential Message, 12th March 1963*, Imprenta Nacional, Caracas, 1963, p. 64.

Industrial Apprenticeship) of Brazil, and experts from this organization advised the Venezuelan authorities.

According to the law, at least 5 per cent of the total work force of each employer with more than ten workers must consist of apprentices between fourteen and eighteen years of age. These youngsters are given free time by their employers to attend training courses organized by the INCE.

During its first year of operation the INCE concentrated its attention on training instructors to teach the courses to be given to the apprentices. In four centers established for this purpose in various parts of the country, instruction was given in mechanics, electricity, boilermaking, and automobile mechanics; and a special course for rural electricians was conducted in cooperation with CADAFE, the government electricity company. Subsequently, a variety of on-the-job courses were organized for industrial workers. Early in 1963 President Betancourt announced a program for training 60,000 unemployed workers in various skills which would permit them to take their place in the country's growing economy.

The Betancourt government also started a system of agricultural education on the primary level. Juan Ramón Bucce described this program in the newspaper *A.D.* on September 13, 1961:

"The Directorate of Primary Education and the Directorate of Handicraft, Industrial, and Commercial Education have begun a new specialty in the country, Agricultural and Stock-Raising Education. With the collaboration of the state governments, agricultural schools are being created, where besides regular primary instruction, training in agriculture and stock raising is given, and also courses in arts and crafts. . . .

"The first school of this type was founded in 1959 in Bancos de San Pedro, near the Guárico dam, in cooperation with the Ministry of Agriculture, which ceded the land and buildings for classrooms and dormitories. This school has a capacity for 300 students, but in its first year, it had 153.

"For the school year which is about to begin, agricultural schools are being opened in Valle de La Pascua, San José de Guaribe, and Morotuco."

These schools were intended to supplement other rural primary schools which were established by the state governments.

With the great expansion of the primary school system, the demand for liceos, or high schools which prepare for university training, will rise sharply within a few years. Indeed, such was the neglect of academic secondary educational needs during the nine years of dictatorship, that the democratic government found itself hard pressed to keep up with the requests for additional space in the liceos.

Prior to the overthrow of the dictatorship, space available would permit only 54.5 per cent of the country's liceo students to attend public high schools; the rest were in private secondary schools. This percentage had risen to 74.7 per cent, however, by the 1960 to 1961 school year. The government had expanded existing schools and established many new ones, and of the 145 liceos open during the 1960 to 1961 school year, 48 were established during the government of President Betancourt. Of these, 15 were opened in new buildings, while the rest were installed in buildings that were not originally constructed for this purpose.[4]

The Ministry of Education's report to Congress in 1961 explained the scope of the work of the Directorate of Secondary Education: "The Directorate cooperates with the general effort of the Ministry to diversify secondary education; but it is conscious that this diversification will not only be the result of the plans drawn up by the educational authorities, but rather will depend upon a change in the ideas of the Venezuelan citizenry concerning the relation of productivity and education. This transformation in the way of thinking of our people will be the product of time, of the work of persuasion by social and educational leaders.

"For these reasons, the Directorate has heeded the increasing demand for enrollment in the national high schools and in some cases has given economic aid to schools established by the states and municipalities where national ones do not exist. However, it is worth noting that it has been agreed with the state and municipal governments that they will not open any new schools of this type without previous agreement by the Directorate . . ."[5]

In July, 1962, the Ministry of Education announced that when school opened in September for the 1962 to 1963 year there would be, for the first time in the country's history, enough room in the secondary schools to accommodate all primary school graduates seeking admission. This marked a major milestone in the educational history of Venezuela.

Table VII indicates the increase in secondary school enrollment from the last year of the dictatorship until the school year 1962 to 1963.

Training facilities for secondary school teachers also had to be expanded, for when the Betancourt government came to office, there was only one institution for their training, the Instituto Pedagógico de Caracas, which in 1957 to 1958 had only 346 students. In November, 1959, the Ministry of Education opened a second school, the Instituto Pedagógico Experimental in Barquisimeto, the capital of the state of Lara. During the 1960 to 1961 school year there were 2,157 students in these two institutions,[6] and in the following year, the number increased to 2,800.[7]

The Betancourt regime spent large sums to expand and diversify the Venezuelan university system and to improve the quality of higher education. At the time of the downfall of the dictatorship there existed only three national universities and two private institutions of university caliber. These were the Universidad Central in Caracas, the Universidad de los Andes in Mérida, the Universidad del Zulia in Maracaibo, the Universidad Santa María in Caracas, and the Universidad Católica Andrés Bello in Caracas. The provisional government established one additional institution of higher learning, the Universidad de Carabobo in Valencia, and authorized another, the Universidad de Oriente. By the end of the Betancourt

TABLE VII

INCREASE IN SECONDARY SCHOOL STUDENTS IN VENEZUELA, 1957-58 TO 1962-63

Year	*Students in Government Liceos*	*Students in Private Liceos*	*Students in Normal Schools*	*Students in Technical Schools*	*Total*
1957-58	30,095	25,009	3,844	17,239	76,187
1958-59	45,675	25,690	7,690	23,319	102,374
1959-60	65,005	24,923	15,719	31,992	137,639
1960-61	76,913	26,042	17,767	39,452	160,174
1961-62	84,673	—	17,150	41,324	169,189 *
1962-63	—	—	—	—	227,000

*Based on 1960-61 figure for private liceos.

Sources: Table constructed from data in *Memoria que el Ministerio de Educación presenta al Congreso Nacional de la República de Venezuela en sus sesiones de 1961*, Caracas, 1961, p. 97; article in *La República*, Caracas, July 29, 1962; and Rómulo Betancourt: *V Presidential Message, 12th March 1963*, Imprenta Nacional, Caracas, 1963, p. 64.

administration work on the establishment of another university in Barquisimeto, in Lara State, was far advanced.

A major change in the university situation was brought about by the provisional government through the enactment of the University Autonomy Statute. This law gave to the universities then functioning complete control over their own affairs, and provided that they should be run by boards chosen by faculty members and students. The statute likewise made it impossible for the government to send police or soldiers into university grounds without explicit request from the university authorities.

The Universidad de Oriente was a favorite project of the Betancourt regime. On June 26, 1959, the Ministry of Education issued a decree establishing the organizing commission of the Universidad de Oriente. A week and a half later the members of the commission were named. The group was headed by Dr. Luis Manuel Peñalver, a physician, leading figure in Acción Democrática, and member of the faculty of the Universidad Central in Caracas. The university was formally inaugurated on May 29, 1960.

The Universidad de Oriente was the first institution of higher learning to be established in eastern Venezuela, and was designed to serve the needs of the states of Sucre, Anzoátegui, Monagas, Nueva Esparta, and Bolívar. The university has campuses in four different places in eastern Venezuela. The schools of biology, chemistry, agronomy, geology, and mines and petroleum were established in Cumaná, capital of the state of Sucre. The basic course of two years, which is required of all students, is also given in Cumaná, and the already existing Oceanographic Institute and Fisheries School in Cumaná were incorporated into the new university. The school of medicine was established in Ciudad Bolívar, and in Jusepín, in the state of Monagas, in an abandoned oil camp turned over to the university by the Creole Petroleum Corporation were set up the schools of geological and mining engineering, agriculture, zoology, veterinary medicine, and petroleum engineering. Barcelona, in the state of Anzoátegui, was the home of the school of industrial engineering.[8]

Rafael Pizani, who was Minister of Education at the time of the establishment of the Universidad de Oriente, described the institution at the ceremony of inauguration of the university:

"It will now open up all of the possibilities which technical and scientific education present the man of our time, and for this reason the Universidad de Oriente is established as a center of higher technical education.

". . . This university was not born of political needs or complacency; it is being established as something unique among the universities of Latin America. This university has not begun by establishing classical studies, which are those most easily and inexpensively organized. It has begun appropriately with research institutes, a really new method in the history of the founding of universities, but not with just any institutes, but with those which are most urgently required by the country. The Oceanographic Institute can be said to be the nucleus of the university; and the schools that now begin to function or are already functioning open a new panorama for Venezuelan higher education which will be limitless."[9]

Table VIII shows the number of students registered in the national and private universities from the last year of the dictatorship through the year 1962 to 1963.

President Betancourt reported in his fifth annual message to Congress on March 12, 1963, that there were approximately 35,000 students in Venezuelan universities at that time. He noted that the total increase in students in all of the nation's educational institutions from primary school through the universities had been 818,000, or a rise of more than 90 per cent over the 1957 to 1958 school year.

Bitter partisan politics among the student bodies of the universities and many secondary schools, particularly in Caracas, have dis-

TABLE VIII

ENROLLMENT IN VENEZUELAN UNIVERSITIES, 1957-58 TO 1960-61

Year	*National Universities*	*Private Universities*	*Total*
1957-58	8,188	2,082	10,270
1958-59	13,618	2,508	16,126
1959-60	18,658	2,634	21,292
1960-61	21,194	3,115	24,309
1962-63	—	—	35,000

Sources: Memoria que el Ministerio de Educación presenta al Congreso Nacional de la República de Venezuela en sus sesiones de 1960, Imprenta Nacional, Caracas, 1960, p. 171; same for 1961, p. E-365; and mimeographed sheet "Alumnos, profesores y planteles por ramas de educación clasificados en oficiales y privados: Año Escolar 1960-61."

turbed the educational situation of Venezeula since the overthrow of the Pérez Jiménez regime. The difficulties go back to the days of the dictatorship. During that period the Communists were less violently persecuted in the universities than were members of other parties. As a result, they were able to carry on an intensive propaganda campaign among members of other political groups among the student body. Their proselytizing was particularly successful among the student members of Acción Democrática, who were the most severely persecuted of all.

After the overthrow of the dictatorship, the Communists were able to capitalize on the progress that they had made under Pérez Jiménez. They were favored by a sympathetic attitude on the part of the Junta de Gobierno during 1958, and by the "respectability" of the Communists and the unlikelihood that any other group could attack them openly. During this period, the Acción Democrática student leaders continued to work closely with the Communists. In April, 1960, the student chiefs of AD were the principal founders of the Movimiento de Izquierda Revolucionaria. The Communists and MIR members dominated the students of the Universidad Central and many of the important secondary schools of the capital and several major cities of the interior. After the break between the MIR and Acción Democrática, the MIR and the Communists attempted to mobilize students under their control against AD and the government that it led.

This campaign reached a climax in October and November, 1960, when riots of secondary and university students in Caracas, Maracay, and Valencia were organized by the extreme Leftists. While these were going on, the MIR and the Communist party issued a call for a popular insurrection against the Betancourt government and also sought to launch a revolutionary general strike. These moves failed, but for several days the students, barricaded in the campuses of the Universidad Central in Caracas and Maracay and in the University of Carabobo in Valencia, continued to defy the government. In Caracas, they hid behind university autonomy to use the university as a base from which to fire on police and soldiers who could not enter the campus.

The riots of the last months of 1960 represented a high-water mark of extreme Leftist influence among the students. In elections held among students throughout the country in the early months of 1961, the extremists suffered severe setbacks. Although they continued to control the Students Federation of the Universidad Central, the Copei student group won a greater degree of support than it had ever received before. In 1962 an anti-Communist governing board was elected in the Universidad Central; however, the Communist-MIR coalition continued to control the student body. Because of this, the government closed the Universidad Central for a month before the December, 1963, general election.

The extreme Left lost control of the student bodies of the interior universities, which were captured by the Copeyanos or by Copei-AD alliances. They also were defeated in most of the important secondary school student bodies that they had dominated just after the fall of Pérez Jiménez.

The political situation among the secondary school and university students preoccupied government educational authorities and the leaders of the democratic regime. President Betancourt, at the inauguration of the Universidad de Oriente, underscored the government attitude when he said: "The generation to which I belong, the generation of '28, underwent its apprenticeship of bars and prisons in the jails of Juan Vicente Gómez. And the student body which was the vanguard of the struggle against tyranny in December, 1957, and in the struggle of the 23rd of January, was being loyal to that historical tradition. But now that there functions in Venezuela a democratic regime, now that in our country we are working to bind up Venezuela's wound left by the abominable past, it is inconceivable that there continue actively in the schoolrooms political maneuvering, and even less that teaching posts be used for purposes of political proselytism, and a great deal less that entire faculties of the universities be controlled by minority political parties of a totalitarian philosophy which do not cater to Venezuelan interests but rather to the strategies and tactics of a foreign power."[10]

The intrusion of partisan politics into the high schools and universities had a demoralizing influence in many cases on the studies of the students. This was offered as a partial explanation for the large number of failures in the secondary schools of Venezuela.

Another aspect of this situation was the charge frequently made in the Universidad Central in Caracas and in scattered secondary schools in various parts of the country that professors and teachers belonging to the Communist party and the MIR were discriminating against Copei and AD students in their classes.[11] Whether or not these charges were valid, they undoubtedly had a demoralizing effect in the educational institutions in which they were made.

President Rómulo Betancourt perhaps best summed up the accomplishments and weaknesses of the educational efforts of the government in his message to Congress on March 11, 1961:

"Education, as an element in economic and social development and as a creative source of a democratic conscience, has merited special attention from the constitutional government. Conscientious citizens were alarmed by the extent of our illiteracy, by the masses of children without schools, and more than this, by the disorientation of our young people, deprived of training to participate usefully in the development of the country. . . .

"Quantitatively, the increase in our educational facilities has been excellent. If one were to make a cold judgment, one would have to say that one of the major defects is excessive growth, because expansion was carried out frequently without regard to quality; but this is explained by the urgency of correcting a bad situation. Now there are more than 1.45 million children and young people attending our schools, high schools, technical institutions, and universities, of which the great majority are maintained by the funds of the state. . . .

"This signifies a net increase of 600,000 students over the figures for the last year of the dictatorship 1957 to 1958. To achieve this, it has been necessary to open 5,000 schools, 51 high schools, and 100 institutions of vocational education, and practically to double the capacity of the universities.

"The conditions of the buildings in which the official schools function are not satisfactory, particularly in the primary educational system.

"The fundamental weakness of our primary education, and in general of the whole educational system, is its excessive intellectualism, its lack of relation to the needs of our national life. . . .

"However, the increase in university students must bring us satisfaction, because the job of training the professional people and technicians whom the country requires falls principally to the universities. In this educational field, it is also necessary to study a policy that will tend to raise the quality of teaching and research. . . .

"The success of an educational system is measured by its final results. Among these, beside the training of qualified professional people, must be the creation of a feeling of social responsibility, of a spirit of cooperation and mutual aid, inculcation of the values that constitute the historical patrimony of the people. . . . Such are the objectives of democratic education, and the acquisition of proper values by the student converts the man of the street into a citizen. . . .

"Our educational system is far from having achieved the appropriate objectives . . . because there does not exist an atmosphere conducive to fulfilling creative work, because many past governments had no interest in education and the teachers lacked stimulation and the influence indispensable for fully carrying out their tasks. Now the democratic regime places the school within the reach of all, respects the teachers, and encourages them to carry out a rewarding job."

Chapter Twenty-One
Housing, Public Utilities, and Roads

Perhaps the most popular saying in present-day Venezuela is the statement, "Everything is still to be done in this country." There is a great deal of truth in this idea. The distribution of income is very uneven, and the standard of living generally low. A large part of the Venezuelan people live very much as did their forefathers two or three centuries ago.

Thus, the Betancourt government had to launch development programs for practically all aspects of the country's economic and social life. Not only was there an acute housing shortage, but the basic social services of a contemporary civilized community were missing or inadequate. Paved streets, sewers, sanitary water supplies, medical and hospital services, were all greatly in demand. Very few small towns and villages had anything but the most rudimentary water and sewerage systems; almost none had electricity or more than one or two paved streets; medical facilities were poor or nonexistent. Even in the major cities large sections had dirt streets without sidewalks, and were without adequate sanitation facilities or electricity.

Such substandard conditions prevailed, largely because no previous administration except the Acción Democrática regime of the late 1940's had been concerned about the needs of the provinces. Attention focused on Caracas, where governments were made and unmade and where the foreign visitor was likely to form his impression of the country. In contrast, the Betancourt government turned its primary attention to the interior of the republic. The President, in a speech at the University of Carabobo on September 1, 1959, summed up his administration's attitude in this regard: "the men who are now by the will of the nation governing its destinies are convinced of the need for regarding Venezuela as a nation with a vast and unaided provincial interior, as I have said more than once. We are not trying to create a fight between Caracas and the provinces. What we are attempting is to develop in every way, economically, socially, the Venezuelan provinces, so that we do not continue to be a nation deformed in structure, with a macrocephalic city and with a provincial interior which is economically, socially, and culturally backward. The government over which I preside will attempt to rectify this error by developing the whole nation." [1]

In carrying out this aspect of its program, the Betancourt government assigned an important role to the state governments. Although the appropriate national ministries and independent agencies spent sizable parts of their budgets on programs of rural health, sanitation, water supplies, and electricity, the state governments, which usually are in a position to know better than the national officials the most pressing needs of their regions, spent most of their funds on community services and on education. In many cases the results were little short of spectacular.

One of the most depressing aspects of life for the average Venezuelan is the dwelling in which he lives. The rural folk and a large part of the city people make their homes in tiny, primitive, unhealthy shacks without any modern conveniences.

The Banco Central de Venezuela in its 1960 annual report estimated that the country's housing shortage amounted to over 600,000 dwellings:

". . . The results of the survey mentioned in our report of 1959 showed that between the census of 1950 and 1959 the population had increased by 2,167,000 people. Thus, taking account of the size of the average family, about 5.5 persons, this increase indicated a need for 390,000 new dwellings. It can be said that the supply did not meet the need for new homes, since it would have been necessary to build 518,000, taking into consideration the deficit already existing in 1950, which was 125,000, and new construction provided only 61 per cent of the needs. Thus, the deficit is estimated at 250,-

000, which, in comparison with the situation in 1950, indicates a worsening of the problem.

"On the other hand, in 1950 there existed in Venezuela 408,000 ranchos; this can be considered a precarious type of dwelling . . . there exists a patent necessity for adequate housing for 42 per cent of the Venezuelan population."[2]

The Cámara de Construcción (Chamber of Construction), the trade association of the Venezuelan construction industry, in its annual report for 1960, estimated the housing deficit as even greater than that indicated by the Banco Central. The Chamber of Construction calculated that in 1958 there was a deficit of 780,000 housing units, and that there was need for 70,000 new dwellings each year to meet the increase in population. Because of the crisis in the private building industry during the economic crisis of 1960, however, the total housing deficit had increased by the end of that year to approximately 800,000 units.[3]

The condition of many of the existing dwellings is distressing. The 1950 census showed that 61 per cent of the country's houses had no wells or piped water supply, and 38 per cent had thatched roofs, 70 per cent had walls of adobe or similar materials, and 52 per cent had dirt floors. As President Betancourt remarked, "From this we deduce that between 60 per cent and 70 per cent of the houses of Venezuela are not adequate from a health point of view."[4]

The country's housing crisis has been spiraling over the decades for a variety of reasons. Not only did the development of the petroleum industry attract much larger numbers of people to the urban centers than were accommodated in the oil camps built by the operating companies, but also the concentration of most of the public works expenditures of a succession of governments, particularly the Pérez Jiménez dictatorship, in the capital city, swamped Caracas with people looking for employment in these projects. Furthermore, the neglect of the rural portions of the country by all governments except the two led by Acción Democrática meant that little was done to improve rural housing, and that substandard housing conditions in the agricultural regions impelled people to seek to improve their lot by moving to the cities. Nor was the Venezuelan banking system adapted to providing adequate credit for private housing efforts. Long-term mortgages were unknown, credit for housing being of only two to three years' duration rather than the fifteen- to thirty-year loans characteristic of the United States.

Various aspects of the Betancourt government's program were designed to overcome the country's huge housing shortage; however, this was one of the least successful of the government's activities. Although public housing projects were numerous, there was a decline in private construction during the first half of the Betancourt administration. Not until the middle of 1961 did the housing situation begin to improve significantly.

The government's Banco Obrero, or Workers Bank, was the core of the public housing efforts of the Venezuelan government. It was first established in 1928 to operate in cities and towns with a population of more than 5,000, but its policies varied with different administrations.

The first major efforts of the Banco Obrero occurred during the government of President Isaías Medina Angarita (1941 to 1945), when the principal accomplishment was the replacement of the El Silencio slum area in the center of Caracas with a large white collar workers' project. The Acción Democrática administration of the late 1940's changed the Banco Obrero's policy by concentrating most of its efforts in the provinces, and building principally individual homes instead of large apartment projects.

During most of the nine-year dictatorship following the fall of President Gallegos, the efforts of the Banco Obrero were exceedingly modest. However, in 1956 and 1957 the Pérez Jiménez regime constructed huge multiple dwelling projects in Caracas and some of the principal cities of the interior. There were ninety-seven of these *bloques,* or housing blocks, in Caracas alone, with apartments for 180,000 people. The Banco Obrero spent 700 million bolívares on its Caracas projects.[5] Although these huge projects of the dictatorship period were spectacular, they were highly unsatisfactory as a solution to the housing problem. They were generally buildings of more than ten stories, and in many instances had no elevator service and in some instances no running water. People were forcibly moved into them from the rancho slums on the hills around the city, and after the fall of the dictatorship many thousands of families moved out again. One of their principal objections to the bloques was that they lacked all spirit of a community and were so large and impersonal that the new occupants found themselves very unhappy living there. On the other hand, the huge housing blocks tended to strengthen the already strong tendency of the rural population to drift to the cities. Many more people came into Caracas than could possibly be housed in the bloques.

Under Betancourt, the policies of the Banco Obrero changed once again. As during the first Acción Democrática regime, the organization placed its emphasis on building single family units or small apartment buildings in the interior cities of the republic. In some cases, the activities of the Banco Obrero extended even to the smaller towns.

President Betancourt stated his government's policy for the Banco Obrero in a speech on April 15, 1959: "The Instituto Agrario Nacional and the Banco Obrero are also constructing houses in rural areas. The Banco Obrero is constructing them throughout Venezuela and is changing its policy. Hitherto, in the thirty years that the Banco Obrero has existed (from 1928), 75 per cent of its construction has been concentrated in this macrocephalic city of Caracas, and only 25 per cent in the provinces. This must be reversed, because if not, a city will continue to grow which we well know does not have the conditions required for a manufacturing center, since its land is very costly and it does not have water. It should be a government and commercial city. . . . We are not going to abandon the city of Caracas, not at all, but the situation must be reversed in which more than 60 per cent of the budget is spent in one city, thus multiplying its problems, as has occurred in the capital of the republic." [6]

The shifts in the policy of the Banco Obrero are clearly demonstrated in Tables IX and X. The first shows the types of housing

TABLE IX

Types of Housing Units of the Venezuelan Banco Obrero, 1958 to 1960

Year	*Number of Houses*	*Number of Apartments*	*Total*
1958	100	774	874
1959	2,385	673	3,058
1960	5,363	702	6,065

Source: Compiled from Banco Central de Venezuela: *Memoria correspondiente al ejercicio 1960*, Caracas, 1960, p. 329.

TABLE X

LOCATION OF HOUSING OF THE VENEZUELAN BANCO OBRERO, 1958 TO 1960

Year	*Federal District*	*Interior*	*Total Number of Units*
1958	774	100	874
1959	943	2,115	3,058
1960	1,104	4,961	6,065

Source: Same as Table IX.

developed by the Banco Obrero during the provisional government and Betancourt's first two years.

Table X shows the location of Banco Obrero housing in the country during the three years following the overthrow of the Pérez Jiménez dictatorship.

The year 1960 was a record year for the Banco Obrero. Only in 1954 and 1957 did it construct a greater number of housing units. In addition, the Banco had developed a program of loans to individuals to construct their own homes. In many cities, the granting of these loans was coordinated with a program of state and municipal governments for attacking the problem of slums within their jurisdictions.

By the middle of 1961 the Banco Obrero was concentrating about one fourth of its construction activities in Caracas and three fourths in the provinces. There were at that time large projects under way in Maracaibo, Barquisimeto, Valencia, and Maracay in the center and northern part of the country, and Barcelona and Puerto La Cruz in the eastern part.

President Betancourt, in his fifth annual message to Congress on March 12, 1963, noted that the Banco Obrero had completed 2,600 housing units and had started building 2,300 more during 1962. It had given loans for private construction of 330 more units, and had loaned some 25 million bolívares to the Ministry of Health's Sección de Vivienda Rural to construct 5,500 houses. He noted that in the first four years of his administration the Banco Obrero had either built or contributed toward the construction of 27,000 housing units.

The lending program begun by the Urban Housing Loan Board (Fondo de Crédito a la Construcción de Viviendas Urbanas), established in 1961, had made loans of 123 million bolívares in 1962 for the construction of approximately 6,000 housing units. The Betancourt government's contribution to resolving the urban housing shortage during its first four years in office had been 33,000 units, a very small percentage of the estimated national deficit of 700,000 to 800,000 units.

One of the major problems of the Banco Obrero under Betancourt was the administration of the housing developments already in existence when the constitutional government came to power. These problems arose in part from the great discontent of the occupants of the bloques built during the Pérez Jiménez administration. They arose also from the fact that during the provisional government all of the tenants of these projects were excused from paying rent by the officials of the Banco Obrero. The Betancourt regime found it a difficult and slow procedure to build up a feeling of community solidarity among the Banco Obrero tenants and to get them to pay the rent due.

Characteristic was the situation in the huge 23 de Enero project in Caracas, which houses 130,000 people. The great majority of the people in this project were used to an entirely different way of living before they moved into the housing blocks. They were accustomed to a semirural life, even in the Caracas slums, to having their dogs and their chickens and maintaining their small gardens. The Banco Obrero employed twenty social workers to try to help the people to adapt to their new surroundings. These workers started with those who were most susceptible to change, the youngsters under eighteen, who accounted for more than half of the population of the 23 de Enero project. Play groups and clubs were started with the children, and sports organizations were organized among the adolescents. Through these clubs, the social workers were able to approach the mothers, to discuss the problems of their children and of the environment in which they were living. Mothers' clubs were formed, and as a final step it was possible in some parts of the project to establish community clubs to undertake a variety of self-help projects. Some made gardens in their blocks, others planted trees and bushes, and others concentrated on cleaning up the grounds in the vicinity. This physical improvement of the environment reflected a psychological change that had come over the people who carried them out.

One basic problem of administration after February, 1959, was the fact that the management of the Banco Obrero had few records of who lived in its projects, or who had paid rent and who had not. To remedy this situation, officials of the bank made house to house visits in some of the large projects, particularly in Caracas; and to their surprise, they found that more than half of the people with whom they talked paid up their current rent on the spot, and paid as much as a year's back rent as well. The Banco Obrero administration then made a careful study of the tenants who had not paid. In about 10 per cent of the total, the main reason for non-payment was unemployment. By the end of President Betancourt's term most of the residents of the Banco Obrero's housing developments throughout the country were paying their rent more or less regularly.

In 1961 the bank began a campaign to try to get the people to buy their apartments, as provided for in the basic law of the institution. Since down payment of 10 per cent of the value of the apartment is called for by the law, and most Banco Obrero tenants do not have such funds, the bank evolved three different types of monthly payments. Straight rental involves no purchase of an apartment, but 10 per cent down payment toward purchase may be spread over five years, a part of it being added to the rent each month during this period. By the end of 1962 half of the Banco Obrero tenants in Caracas were becoming owners of their apartments.

The Banco Obrero administration under Betancourt was also anxious insofar as possible to get the tenants to run their own projects. In one of the lower middle class projects in Caracas they succeeded in turning the complete local administration over to a tenants' committee.

Unlike preceding governments, the democratic administration evolved an ambitious program for doing away with the rural slums which are so characteristic of Venezuela.

Various parts of the government participated in the attack on inadequate rural housing; however, the most significant of these was the Sección de Vivienda Rural, or Rural Housing Division, of the Directorate of Malariology and Environmental Sanitation of the Ministry of Health and Social Assistance. In Venezuela the Directorate of Malariology is an appropriate agency for such work, for it has nearly won a two-decades-long war against malaria, which until a few short years ago afflicted a large proportion of the population of the country. The peasant is traditionally suspicious of city people, but officials of the directorate have won the full confidence of the rural people, and are willing to cooperate in a self-help housing program.

The Vivienda Rural works on the principle of helping the peasants to help themselves in constructing decent houses. This has been made possible by a close study of the problem of rural housing in Venezuela. Since the Vivienda Rural was established in March, 1958, its architects have developed model houses which are adapted to the Venezuelan countryside because they are built of local materials, suit the climate, and cost relatively little. The Vivienda Rural first surveys the housing needs of a community, then conducts meetings to explain the program and to enlist the people's cooperation with it. Only after such cooperation has been assured does the Vivienda Rural provide aid toward construction. Under one plan, the beneficiaries are provided with the materials and the technical direction necessary for building their houses, as well as with long-term loans to cover the costs. Under a second plan, the peasant is provided with materials and technical assistance, but receives no financial help.

By the middle of Betancourt's term of office, the visible accomplishments of the Vivienda Rural program were modest. Between March, 1958, and May, 1961, only 2,629 houses had been completed under the credit plan, and 1,298 more were under construction, or 3,927 in all; 178 communities had benefited from the program. Another 785 houses had been built under the second plan. The total number of houses either built or under construction by the end of May, 1961, was therefore only 4,712.[7] However, by the end of 1962 more than 10,000 rural houses had been built, according to Betancourt's fifth annual message to Congress.

Among the other agencies that participated in the Betancourt government's rural housing program were the Instituto Agrario Nacional and the various state governments. Complete figures on their contributions were not obtainable, but there is no doubt that several thousand additional houses were built in each year by the agrarian reform authorities and the state governments.

As in most other countries, the private building industry in Venezuela in recent decades has engaged principally in constructing middle-class and upper-class dwellings. Typical are the dwellings in the many "better" residential areas of Caracas, the *urbanizaciones*, or subdivisions.

During the Pérez Jiménez dictatorship, a private housing boom was one of the essential elements of the Venezuelan economy. A great deal of speculation in land and construction took place in this boom. Sizable fortunes were made in the mere buying and reselling of land, and in construction of luxury apartment buildings for speculative purposes. This boom was made possible largely by the vast government expenditures on the construction of public buildings in and around Caracas, by the corruption of the Pérez Jiménez dictatorship, and by the secondary effects of the oil boom of the middle 1950's. The corruption was curtailed and the oil boom slackened under the provisional government in 1958, but the Caracas construction business was maintained by the Plan de Emergencia of the interim regime. However, when this plan was officially ended in August, 1959, the Betancourt government shifted much of its expenditure on housing from the capital to the provinces, provoking a serious crisis in the construction industry of Caracas.

The decline in private construction in the Distrito Federal and the part of the state of Miranda bordering on the capital was 22 per cent between 1959 and 1960. The situation is made even clearer by the fact that only 30 per cent of the building permits taken out by private contractors in the Distrito Federal in 1960 were actually used. It is worth noting that private construction rose 12 per cent in the same year in the provincial cities of Valencia and Barquisimeto.[8]

The Betancourt regime took energetic steps to deal with the crisis in private construction during 1961. The most fundamental move, taken in August, was to establish the Fondo de Crédito a la Construcción de Viviendas Urbanas, as a means of financing relatively long-term mortgages for private purchases of houses. The total amount of this fund was 200 million bolívares, of which 75 million bolívares came from a loan that the government had just received from the Export-Import Bank of the United States; the other 125 million was subscribed by the oil companies operating in Venezuela. As established in Decree No. 611 of August 11, 1961, the fund was to be directed by a five-man board of directors, three to be named by the President of the Republic and one each to be nominated by the oil companies and the Chamber of Construction.

The decree provided that the fund was to give loans not exceeding 100,000 bolívares per loan, in return for mortgages not to exceed 70 per cent of the value of the house to be constructed. The loans were normally to run for ten years, though under exceptional circumstances loans of less than 30,000 bolívares could run for as long as fifteen years. The loans were to carry 7 per cent interest, a low rate for Venezuela. They were not to be granted directly by the fund, but rather through existing private mortgage banks or through the Banco Obrero. The bank extending a loan was to be granted a voice and a vote in the board of directors of the fund on decisions affecting its loans.[9] One purpose of the new fund was to remedy a basic institutional weakness, the lack of long-term mortgage credit. It was hoped that the fund's operations would stimulate private mortgage banks to grant comparable loans.

By the end of 1961, the fund had granted loans amounting to 70 million bolívares on 5,000 dwellings. President Betancourt had also announced that when the original 200 million bolívares of the fund had been exhausted, the government intended to provide it with more money to continue its operations.[10]

In August, 1961, the government also established a Savings and Loan Commission for the purpose of laying the bases for a system similar to that of building and loan societies prevalent in the United States. A loan of $10 million was received from the Development Loan Fund of the United States to aid the commission's work.

The efforts to stimulate private construction begun by the Betancourt administration were effective. The construction industry expanded by 20 per cent during 1962, after two years of decline. Its growth continued through the remainder of the Betancourt regime.

Besides these official efforts to encourage the private construction industry, significant work in this field was done by nongovernmental groups. Eugenio Mendoza, the country's leading industrialist, organized a firm called FINCA, which has as its purpose the provision of housing for rent or sale to employees of his various manufacturing enterprises. In addition, he organized the Fundación de la Vivienda Popular, which established the Banco Hipotecario de la Vivienda Popular, with a beginning capital of 10 million bolívares. The purpose of this new mortgage bank was to build low-cost housing on a nonprofit basis. To assure that it will not be used for purposes of private profit, the Fundación agreed that the Banco Hipotecario's stock would be placed in the hands of philanthropic institutions.[11]

As essential as the construction of houses was the provision of adequate water supplies and sewerage systems. The principal instruments of the national government in this field were the Instituto

Nacional de Obras Sanitarias (INOS) in towns of 5,000 people or more and the Ministry of Health in rural areas.

The INOS during the first year of the Betancourt administration constructed sewers for nineteen towns, with a total population of 104,000 inhabitants. In addition, studies were made for thirty-two other localities. It was contemplated that during the balance of the Betancourt administration, improvements and extensions would be made in the sewerage systems of forty-one of the fifty-one towns and cities in which the INOS administered these services. In addition, twenty-six new towns which had grown large enough to come within the jurisdiction of the INOS were to receive sewerage services.[12]

The extent of the work of the INOS on water supply and sewerage systems in 1960 and 1961 was noted by President Betancourt in his annual message to Congress on March 11, 1961. The INOS in 1960 amplified and improved twenty-eight existing water supply systems and twenty-three existing sewerage systems, increasing the population served by the organization by 133,000 people. In 1961 water supply systems were augmented or constructed in fifty-nine cities and towns, as the President informed Congress in March, 1962. According to Betancourt's fifth annual message to Congress on March 12, 1963, the urban population served by INOS water supply had increased from 1958 to 1962 from 1.8 million to 2.45 million by the latter year, approximately 60 per cent of all urban residents received water from the INOS. In 1963 it was planned, with the help of loans from the Inter-American Development Bank and the Export-Import Bank of the United States, to increase the number of people served with water by the INOS to some 4.1 million. Between 1958 and 1962 the urban population served by INOS sewers had risen from 1.1 million to 1.5 million.

Some of the individual projects completed by the INOS during the Betancourt regime were of major importance. One of these was the Quebrada Seca Dam, near Caracas, which has a capacity of 11 million cubic meters, enough to relieve the water scarcity problem in the capital which had existed for several years. Subsequently, the Lagartijo Dam, with a capacity of 80 million cubic meters, was completed, resolving the water supply problem of Caracas for several decades, at least. In the oil-producing area of Zulia, the INOS also completed the Pueblo Viejo Dam, which brought water to many thousands of people who had never had enough before. It also finished building a water pipeline from the mainland to Margarita Island in the state of Nueva Esparta, which had previously had a severe water shortage.[13]

In July, 1960, the construction of rural water supplies and sewers was taken over from the INOS by the Ministry of Health. When it assumed this job, it was hampered by a lack of plans, and one of its major tasks during the first year or so was to make requisite studies and draw up feasible projects. By the end of 1960 it had concluded one hundred and ten preliminary studies in eighteen states and one federal territory, seventy-six field studies on a more advanced level, and had completed some fifty-one plans for rural water supply construction.[14]

By the end of 1960 the Ministry had constructed fourteen rural water supply systems, providing water for 23,840 inhabitants, and the state governments had built two hundred and fifty-one rural water supply systems, an increase of 46 per cent over the previous year's accomplishments in this field. However, the President noted in his March, 1961 annual message to Congress that 60 per cent of the population of Venezuela still lacked sanitary water supplies.[15] By the end of 1960 the Ministry of Health had under construction seventeen other water supply projects serving 44,670 people. In fifteen other towns in various parts of the country deep wells had been dug by the Ministry, but facilities for bringing water to individual homes were still to be installed. In 1961 more than two hundred rural water supply systems were constructed and put into operation. By the end of 1962 the number of people served by rural water supplies of the Ministry of Health had increased from 629,000 to 890,000. By that time, 73 per cent of the people in towns of between 500 people and 5,000 were being provided with water.

Some indication of the impact of the government's water-sewerage program was the fall in the incidence of diarrhea. Deaths from this disease had fallen from 163 per 100,000 in the 1949 to 1957 period to 96 per 100,000 in 1962.[16]

The Ministry of Health adopted a system for building individual toilets where a locality had no sewerage system. In 1959 the Ministry built some 15,951 such toilets, and in 1960 it built 22,844.[17] Unspecified additional numbers were built by the state governments.

In many cases, particularly in rural projects managed by the state governments, it was possible to evoke a good deal of cooperation among the peasants benefiting from the installation of water and sewerage facilities. The author visited several villages where the local residents had with their own unpaid efforts dug the trenches necessary for water and sewer pipes, or under supervision had built towers to hold the town's new water supply. There was live interest on the part of the small town and village dwellers in getting these sanitary facilities.

Essential to bringing the benefits of modern civilization to the outlying parts of the country was the construction of highways and roads into the interior. The elaboration of a National Highway Development Plan was one of the first projects of Cordiplan, the planning agency of the Presidency of the Republic. The principal objectives were to connect the country's most important towns and to open up new areas that had been economically isolated from the rest of the country. In March, 1963, President Betancourt reported to Congress on the progress in road construction which the government had made during its first four years. Between 1959 and 1962 it had built some 1,990 kilometers of road, had paved 4,144 kilometers, and had improved 4,831 kilometers. As a result, there were 15,700 kilometers of national highways at the end of 1962, of which 8,900 were paved. In 1958, only 40 per cent of the nation's highways had been paved. The President announced that the National Highway Development Plan was substantially completed by the end of 1962, and that funds which had been used on highway construction would henceforth be diverted to other uses.

Probably more important than these trunk highways to the average Venezuelan peasant are the rural roads that the Betancourt regime undertook to build. By the end of 1962 the national and state governments had built some 5,000 kilometers of such roads, and 3,600 kilometers more had been reconditioned, according to Betancourt's fifth annual message to Congress.

A great deal of work on farm-to-market roads was done by the state governments in collaboration with the Ministry of Agriculture. In the state of Anzoátegui, for example, the local government built during 1960 fourteen projects of this nature, totaling 129 kilometers.[18] In the same year, the state government of Táchira constructed twenty-seven roads, totaling 127 kilometers, started nine other projects, totaling 103 kilometers, and repaired fifty-eight others, amounting to 189 kilometers.[19]

These rural roads were usually unpaved; but they served a very important purpose in making it possible for the peasants to earn some income and to improve their living conditions enough so that they were willing to stay in the country and make their contribution to the nation's economy.

Programs were also carried out in several states to rehabilitate the capital cities and other important towns. These programs involve the paving of streets in outlying wards and the provision of basic public services in these parts of the cities and towns. In most cases, this is the first time that any government has taken an interest in the living conditions in these neighborhoods.

Mention should be made likewise of the national government's special program launched at the end of 1961 to provide basic public services to all of the country's county seats. This project was the subject of close study by the Cordiplan in consultation with the appropriate ministries and independent agencies. Every county seat was surveyed to determine deficiencies in streets, water supplies, sewers, and schools.

Beginning with the budget of 1962 the Betancourt government allocated funds to provide all of these towns with all the basic modern services. The proposals of Cordiplan were for this job to be completed by the end of the Betancourt administration. A loan of $20 million was received from the Export-Import Bank of the United States to aid the completion of this program.[20]

One final aspect of the Betancourt regime's work to create modern living conditions in the interior of the republic, and particularly in the rural areas, was the program for providing electricity. The role that the national government's electrical firm CADAFE played in this program was discussed in Chapter 16. In the rural parts of the country the work of the state governments was even more important than that of CADAFE. The state regimes established a large number of small diesel engine electric systems to meet the needs of the peasants until CADAFE was able to extend its network to include these areas. For example, the state of Táchira constructed nine such electric plants and repaired twenty-two others during the year 1960, and also wired homes in forty-seven localities.[21] In the same year, the state government of Anzoátegui constructed small electric plants in eleven localities in the state.[22]

In his fifth annual message to Congress in March, 1963, President Betancourt noted that installed electric power in Venezuela in 1962 amounted to 122 per cent of what the country had had in 1958. He also noted that whereas 29.4 per cent had been generated by publicly owned plants and 70.6 per cent by private ones in 1958, 45.5 per cent was produced by public facilities and 54.5 per cent by private ones in 1962.

These programs for providing transportation facilities and essential public services are an essential part of the Venezuelan Democratic Revolution. One fundamental objective of these programs is to improve the standards of living of a large segment of the population. Together with the agrarian reform they are also designed to slow down the migration of the rural population to Caracas and other urban centers where they would constitute a burden on the economic and social development of the whole nation.

Chapter Twenty-Two

Health, Social Welfare, and Prison Reform

The Venezuelan Democratic Revolution has affected virtually every aspect of Venezuelan society. Less spectacular than its efforts in the fields of agrarian reform, economic development, and education, but nonetheless important, are its programs to improve health conditions, to better social services, and to reform conditions in the nation's penal system.

Dr. Arnaldo Gabaldón, one of the country's outstanding scientists, served as Minister of Health and Social Assistance throughout the Betancourt regime. He was one of the leaders in the highly successful campaign to eradicate malaria, a disease which had for centuries sapped the energies of the Venezuelan people. To aid him in promoting the development of the country's health services, the Betancourt administration increased considerably the budget of the Ministry, until it amounted to 9 per cent of the total budget.

Without political ambitions, Dr. Gabaldón was concerned, not with producing spectacular results, but with establishing a solid basis for future work in the fields of public health and general medicine. He emphasized the necessity of building up a corps of trained people who will be able to provide the citizens of Venezuela with the services they have needed for centuries.

Speaking before the Second Venezuelan Congress of Public Health in 1961, he stated: "I have been convinced since my youth that in order to progress in our field, it is necessary to have properly trained personnel, capable of understanding and carrying out the work that is required. If it is remembered that no less than 756 million bolívares are spent by the Venezuelan state annually on medical attention and that these funds are not producing the results expected, the necessity is apparent for our personnel to develop a better understanding of the proper procedures and to have the ability to put them into practice with enthusiasm and energy. The role played by the general practitioners and medical education centers where they are trained is of great importance. This explains our efforts to aid the functioning of the departments of preventive and social medicine in the medical schools and the development of courses for training health personnel on all levels . . . at the present time, by means of our ample program of scholarships, more than 5 per cent of the Venezuelan medical profession receives postgraduate training within the country or abroad. . . . It constitutes the essential basis which will permit an improvement of the health of the Venezuelans with increasing rapidity."[1]

An example of the training efforts of the Ministry under Dr. Gabaldón was its program in 1960. The Ministry subsidized one hundred and eighty-three physicians in postgraduate work in Venezuela, and one hundred and twenty Venezuelan physicians studied abroad under the Ministry's auspices. These included sixty-one in the United States, thirty-two in Great Britain, nineteen in Mexico, eleven in Argentina, and the rest in twelve other countries.[2]

To increase the efficiency of the Ministry's operations, Dr. Gabaldón reorganized it, in close collaboration with the Commission of Public Administration and with Cordiplan. A new Directorate of Personnel was established, and various other alterations were made in the administrative organization of the Ministry.[3]

Minister Gabaldón also reoriented the Ministry in the interests of placing more emphasis on the work of creating an environment conducive to good health. A new Directorate of Malariology and Environmental Sanitation was given control of the malaria eradication campaign, as well as of the new housing program undertaken by the Ministry in 1959.

Although budgetary constraints inhibited moves to start construction of many large new hospitals, the government of President Betancourt was able to continue work on hospital buildings already under construction. For example, it went on with the construction of a large 600-bed hospital near the city of Barcelona, capital of the eastern state of Anzoátegui. In his fifth annual message to Congress on March 12, 1963, President Betancourt announced that in its first four years his administration had increased the number of hospital beds in national government hospitals from 19,636 to 23,700.

The Betancourt regime centered its attention on the construction of small health centers in the rural areas. These are of two kinds. The *medicaturas rurales* are attended by a physician, have a few hospital beds, and treat outpatients. The state governments with the national administration cooperated in setting up these institutions, twenty of which were established in 1960, for example. In the same year, buildings for at least thirty-four medicaturas rurales were built.[4]

In addition to these, the states constructed numerous medical centers of a more primitive kind, the *dispensarios*. These are staffed by a nurse and some untrained personnel. Figures for the country as a whole are not available, but the work of the state government of Anzoátegui in this field is perhaps characteristic. During the 1959 to 1960 fiscal year, eight new dispensarios were opened by the state, as well as five new medicaturas rurales.[5]

President Betancourt in his message to Congress in March, 1963, cited a speech by Dr. Pastor Oropeza, one of the country's leading physicians, indicating the results of the government's health program. Dr. Oropeza noted: "The number of births in hospitals during the 1949 to 1957 period was 40,000. During the 1959 to 1962 period the number reached 150,000. . . . The vaccinations for children during the 1949 to 1957 period was 55,305 per year. During the 1959 to 1962 period the number reached 130,000 per year. . . . Infant mortality during the 1949 to 1957 period was 85 per 1,000 children born alive. The average has come down to 56 per 1,000. . . ."

One other program of the Ministry of Health that received special attention from the Betancourt government was the school lunch project. In December, 1959, some 72,650 school children were receiving free lunches, and by December, 1962, this number had increased to 180,000. During the first four years of the Betancourt government, some 235 new school dining rooms were opened per year, compared with a total of 334 such dining rooms constructed during the preceding thirteen years.[6]

The work of the semiofficial Consejo Venezolano del Niño (Venezuelan Childrens Council) and other agencies which concern themselves with the problems of minors is of tremendous importance in present-day Venezuela, for about half of the Venezuelan people are eighteen years of age, and over 55 per cent are under twenty-one. Family ties tend to be weak, and it is not unusual for a woman to have children by several men, none of whom is her legal husband. Many children are abandoned.

The Consejo was established in 1936; however, at the end of the dictatorship, the budget of the Consejo Venezolano del Niño was only about 16.6 million bolívares. During the year of the provisional government and the first year of the Betancourt regime, the funds of the Consejo and of the institutions that it supported were greatly augmented. Its budget rose to some 46.1 million bolívares in 1959 and to 57.4 million in 1960. One hundred and thirty new institutions were established during this period, supplementing the seventy that existed in 1957.[7]

In 1960 President Betancourt named a prominent physician, Dr. Edmundo Fernández, as president of the Consejo Venezolano del Niño. Under Dr. Fernández' administration, the policy of the Consejo was altered. He felt that the increase in the institutions of the Consejo had been too rapid between 1958 and 1960, and that the organization did not have sufficient trained personnel to staff these organizations adequately. Dr. Fernández therefore sought to consolidate the institutions already in existence rather than to increase their number further, and organized programs for training new personnel. In addition, he established the Instituto de Orientación Profesional, an organization which tests youngsters under the care of the Consejo to determine their aptitudes and indicate the trades or professions for which they should be trained. The Instituto thus helps to get the children started on an appropriate career but also aids in building up the supply of trained personnel in the country.

The Consejo engaged in a wide range of activities. In 1961, for example, scholarships enabled 654 children to attend boarding schools, and a considerably larger number received financial help to purchase school books, uniforms, and other needs. In addition, 25,862 families received a subsidy from the Consejo to help support their many offspring. Numerous families able to take in homeless children also received small subsidies from the Consejo through its placement service. A total of 4,700 children were in Consejo nursery schools, and 8,658 children attended Consejo kindergartens.

A total of 43,319 children used the Consejo's recreation parks. These parks have sports facilities, and children may join supervised groups in arts and crafts, chess and checkers, and some academic subjects.

The Consejo also administers institutions which handle juvenile delinquents. Indeed, to many people in Venezuela, the Consejo Venezolano del Niño is thought of principally in this connection. In addition to its work in the institutional field, the Consejo drew up a revision of the Minors Law, governing the treatment of children.

Finally, the Consejo helps to maintain a number of organizations which are not directly dependent upon it. These include a number of private institutions operated by the Roman Catholic Church and by charitable organizations.

According to President Betancourt's fifth annual message to Congress, a total of 254,000 minors were taken care of directly by the Consejo in 1962, an increase of 134,000 over the previous year. In addition, a total of 60,000 children were taken care of by foster families who received financial aid from the Consejo.

The Betancourt regime also sought to make it possible for workers to have cheap seaside and mountain vacations. As a result of the increase in collective bargaining after the fall of the Pérez Jiménez dictatorship, more and more workers enjoyed paid vacations in Venezuela; however, the majority did not make enough money to go away for their holidays. In its concern over this fact, the Betancourt regime took some preliminary steps to provide facilities for low-cost vacations at the beach. Early in his administration President Betancourt dedicated a seaside vacation colony, Ciudad de Los Caracas, 50 kilometers from the capital; however, until the middle of 1961 the rates at Los Caracas were too high for most urban workers. A solution was found by Carlos Behrens, a former leader of the Federación Campesina and an important figure in Acción Democrática. As director of the Instituto Nacional de Recreación para los Trabajadores, in charge of the administration of Los Caracas, he undertook to reorganize the administration of the seashore resort. Furthermore, he initiated the policy of signing direct contracts with unions and with employers whose workers were covered by collective agreements, providing that the workers should be able to spend their vacations in Los Caracas.

In announcing this policy, Behrens stated "There are 569 contracts covering 800,000 workers in 2,500 firms in the country. This means that on any given day several thousand workers are on vacation. If we can reach agreements with trade unions and business firms, Los Caracas can be continuously filled with vacationing workers. If it is full all year round, the costs of maintenance will be lower, and in consequence prices can be reduced."[8]

Subsequently, the Instituto established a second vacation resort in the western state of Zulia. It also made arrangements for workers to spend low-cost vacations at the chain of government-owned tourist hotels.

Another problem that the Betancourt regime attacked promptly was the antiquated prison system, still based on the concept of punishment rather than rehabilitation of the criminal. It took time to codify a new law; however, in July, 1961, a new Law of Prisons was passed and signed by the President.

Under the new system, all of the prisons and penitentiaries of the country now have work programs and provide for teaching the prisoners trades or agriculture so that they can come out as skilled workers, with a much better chance than before of making a living and staying out of trouble.

Even before the new prison law was passed, the Betancourt regime had established primary schools in all of the prisons, and by the middle of 1961 there was a six-year school in every prison and penitentiary in Venezuela. The new law also adopted the fundamental principle of segregation of offenders by type. Hardened criminals are kept apart from first offenders, youthful offenders apart from older ones. An effort was also made to segregate the mentally ill, and a small hospital for the criminally insane was established, which by September, 1961, had some eighty inmates. In January, 1962, a new psychiatric hospital was opened in the San Juan de los Morros penitentiary, with a capacity of one hundred prisoners.

The work program established in the prisons was organized under an autonomous organization, the Caja del Trabajo Penitenciario. The reason for this was that the Caja undertook to sell some of the products turned out in the prisons, and it was felt that this job could be undertaken better by an organization not directly associated with prison administration. The purpose of the work program, however, was to re-educate the prisoners, not production for commercial purposes.

A social welfare program for the prisoners and their families was placed in the hands of a special subdivision of the Ministry of Justice's Directorate of Prisons. It tried to take care of their families, sought to get work for their wives, attempted to get scholarships for their children, and tried to get jobs for the convicts upon their release.

The government further tried to improve the living conditions of the prisoners. For one thing, it introduced a system of paying them something for their work. For another, libraries, theater groups, musical ensembles, and the like were organized in each of the prisons and penitentiaries of the country. Sports programs were also established.

In the state of Barinas, an agricultural colony was established. This is designed as a place to which the prisoners can go in the last years of their terms to work a plot of ground, under minimal guard. When they finish their terms, they are given plots of land of their own. Their families are brought to this colony even when they are still serving their sentences.

Another innovation introduced by the Betancourt regime was a parole system. To qualify, a person with less than a five-year sentence must complete three fourths of his term, have a certificate from the prison psychiatrist that he is in good mental health, and another certificate that he is not a major risk to society. Prisoners with sentences of more than five years can qualify after serving two thirds of their sentences.

The Betancourt regime also attempted to improve the quality of personnel employed in the prison system. Considerable numbers of technical and administrative employees were given scholarships to study abroad. These included prison psychologists, sociologists, and economists. Also, one architect was given a grant to go abroad to study prison construction. Most of the scholarships were given for study in Belgium, because the teachers of criminology in both the national university in Brussels and the Catholic university of Louvain are people who are also prison directors.

Personnel in the lower echelons of the Venezuelan prison system have received a one-year training course since the advent of the Betancourt regime. To take this course, they must have finished the third year of secondary school. Emphasis was placed on recruiting young and capable men to the prison service. Most of those who graduated from the first course in the middle of 1961 were from twenty-one to twenty-five years of age.

Much needed new penal institutions constructed under the Betancourt regime included two general prisons in Valencia and Maturín, a new women's house of detention near Los Teques, and a new building for youthful offenders near Barquisimeto.

The thorough-going nature of the attempt to transform Venezuelan society which was made by the revolutionary democratic regime is shown as much by its activities in relatively unspectacular fields as in its handling of more widely publicized problems. Thus, it greatly augmented the health services available in the rural areas, in conformity with its general policy of giving special attention to the needs of the provinces and the rural population in particular. The government also greatly expanded and began the process of improving the quality of services available to the less fortunate among the country's youth. Finally, the reforming zeal of the regime carried over into the field of penology, with the introduction of modern penal principles and the improvement of the living conditions of the inmates of penal institutions.

Part Four

Significance of the Venezuelan Democratic Revolution

Chapter Twenty-Three

The Balance Sheet of the Revolution

The most obvious observation that one can make about the Venezuelan Democratic Revolution concerns the magnitude of the programs that were launched in order to transform Venezuela, to convert the country into a modern nation with a balanced economy, a relatively equitable distribution of wealth, and a democratic political system. It set out to abolish the conditions of life and the patterns of thought that made it possible for a long series of military dictators to rule the country. It sought to transform the semidependent economy in which the majority of the people lived under the primitive conditions of several centuries ago.

Through its agrarian reform program, the Betancourt government began a massive redistribution of the national wealth. Through its projects for economic diversification and industrialization, the regime sought to develop new wealth and establish a balanced economy. Through its education, housing, and health efforts, and its program for providing basic social services to the rural people and the residents of towns and cities, the Betancourt government attempted to develop the country's human resources, and to raise the standards of living of its people.

The regime's oil policies as well as the industrialization program were designed to develop a greater degree of national independence in the economic field. Finally, through its handling of the armed forces and its general political policies, the Betancourt administration tried to establish the basis for a stable democratic form of government in Venezuela.

In carrying out its various programs, the government of the Venezuelan Democratic Revolution had certain advantages. These put it in a relatively favorable situation when compared with some of the other Latin American countries that are faced with more or less the same problems as Venezuela.

First of all, the country has been receiving and will probably continue to receive, for many years, a sizable income from the oil industry. This petroleum income meant that in spite of the temporary economic and financial crisis that marked the first years of the Betancourt administration, the regime could count on relatively large resources for financing its various reform and development efforts.

In the second place, the regime had the advantage of being led by two political parties which were well disciplined, well led, and which knew what they wanted and how they wanted to achieve their ends. The leaders of the Venezuelan Democratic Revolution were seasoned by long political experience, but were not so old as to have lost willingness to experiment and a feeling of enthusiasm for the fundamental changes that they were trying to bring about in Venezuelan life.

Finally, the Betancourt regime was fortunate to come to power at a time when the policies of the United States in its relations with Latin America were undergoing a decided alteration for the better. As a result, the Venezuelan democratic government had the benefit of receiving considerable moral, political, and financial support from the United States, particularly after the inauguration of President John F. Kennedy.

These advantages were partly offset by a number of serious handicaps which made the path of the regime a rough one and in some ways limited the effectiveness with which the administration was able to carry out its objectives.

The first such handicap was the economic-financial crisis that marked the first half of the Betancourt administration. Arising largely from circumstances created by the Pérez Jiménez and provisional regimes, this crisis limited considerably the financial resources available to the government, and forced it to spend large sums on projects that probably it would not otherwise have favored.

The second major handicap that the government of the Venezuelan Democratic Revolution faced was the recalcitrance of its political opposition. The Right-wing opponents of the regime refused to give up their belief that the Betancourt government was "Communist" and that it should be overthrown by the time-honored but presently discredited means of the military conspiracy and *coup d'état*. The Left-wing opposition, for its part, made little secret of the fact that it repudiated political democracy and would overthrow the Betancourt government by insurrection in the streets or guerrilla warfare in the mountains if the opportunity to do so presented itself. This type of opposition made it exceedingly difficult for the Betancourt regime to be as simon-pure in preserving full civil liberties as its leaders would have liked. Even the democratic opposition frequently tended to go to extremes and to skirt on the edge of subversion in pressing its dissidence with the administration.

A third difficulty of the Betancourt regime was the necessity to continue to spend too large amounts on the armed forces. Although under Betancourt the military item became for the first time only the third largest part of the budget, it continued to be necessary to spend impressive sums on the military. This remained the case not only because the regime did not want to run the risk of creating widespread discontent among the soldiers, sailors, and airmen, but also because of the genuine military dangers to the regime arising from action by disgruntled and displaced elements of the old Pérez Jiménez dictatorship, and from possible armed attacks on the government by the Movimiento de Izquierda Revolucionaria and the Communist party, with the backing of the Cuban regime of Fidel Castro.

As this is being written, the indications are that the Venezuelan Democratic Revolution will be successful. Its first administration, that of Rómulo Betancourt, made substantial progress in its economic and social programs. Its success in completing its term of office—the only time in Venezuelan history in which a democratically elected regime had done so—gave rise to hope that democratic stability might become a reality.

The agrarian reform got well under way during Betancourt's term of office. Although the leaders of the revolutionary democratic government had no illusions about completing the process of land distribution in a few years, let alone training fully the new landowners to use their land efficiently, they made a start on both under Betancourt. In the central part of the republic, the land redistribution program basically altered the pattern of ownership. A somewhat less dramatic impact was felt in the area around Lake Maracaibo and in the mountain states. The small holding was on the way to becoming typical in Venezuelan agriculture by the end of the Betancourt regime.

The Betancourt regime's program of industrialization also made very marked progress. Through a policy of protection for important branches of manufacturing, coordinated with the lending policies of the Corporación Venezolana de Fomento, the textile industry became capable of producing all but a small percentage of the country's needs, and the food-processing and metallurgical industries made important progress to the same end. By the end of the Betancourt administration, the country was also self-sufficient in automobile assemblies, pharmaceuticals, basic steel, and fertilizers.

Besides stimulating the growth of privately owned industries in many fields, the democratic government went ahead with the development of state enterprises in the field of heavy industry. It proceeded with the building of the steel and petrochemical plants, and undertook the establishment of an aluminum factory, in conjunction with the Reynolds Aluminum Company as a minority stockholder. It also pushed energetically the construction of a nation-wide government-owned electricity network to serve as a basis for further widespread industrial development.

During the Betancourt administration the basis was laid for a new nationalist policy for dealing with the country's principal source of foreign exchange, petroleum. The policy of giving no further concessions was firmly established. The organization late in 1960 of the Corporación Venezolana del Petróleo laid the foundations for a Venezuelan government-owned sector of the nation's oil industry, and opened the possibility for the gradual and orderly taking over of the industry by the government without disrupting it as a source of foreign exchange.

The most spectacular progress made by the Betancourt government was in the field of education. School attendance rose dramatically, and the government undertook to change the orientation of the nation's educational system to conform more closely to the needs of a rapidly developing economy and society.

The number of students in the primary schools doubled during the Betancourt regime. Teacher training facilities were increased several times over, and a program for giving on-the-job training to uncertificated teachers was established. The staff and physical facilities of the university system were greatly expanded, and enrollment increased by more than 300 per cent.

At the same time, the lower and middle ranks of the educational system were modified so as to put more emphasis on training students for their future employment. The new Universidad de Oriente was given a technological and scientific emphasis. Likewise, through the Instituto Nacional de Cooperación Educativa, a system of apprenticeship and training-within-industry was set up with the cooperation of the nation's industrial employers.

In the political field, too, the Betancourt regime made progress against very great odds. It quelled many attempts of both Right- and Left-wing totalitarians to overthrow it by force. The three powers of government functioned normally, the three democratic political parties existing in February, 1959, continued to operate, and were joined by several more. Although some constitutional guarantees had to be suspended for considerable periods, there was more political freedom in Venezuela under Betancourt than in almost any other period in the country's history, and more than existed contemporaneously in most other Latin American countries.

Finally, an indication of the success of the government of the Venezuelan Democratic Revolution was its ability to keep a majority of the people behind it. Although the Venezuelan Constitution does not call for off-year elections during the five-year presidential term, there are various other indications that the Betancourt regime in fact maintained the support of the people. One of the earliest and most objective pieces of evidence was the outcome of the series of elections in popular organizations which took place during the Betancourt administration. The great majority of these polls were won by Acción Democrática and its ally in the government, the Partido Social Cristiano Copei.

Almost all of the elections in peasant organizations during 1961, for example, were won by Acción Democrática, a small minority by the Copei, and of the three opposition parties, only the Unión Republicana Democrática was able to muster any significant following among the peasants. Even a split of some top peasant leaders from AD in 1962 did not seriously weaken the party's position in the countryside.

The results in the trade union elections were similar, though the predominance of the government parties was not so great. Acción Democrática and the Copei won from 75 per cent to 80 per cent of the trade union elections held in 1961, and in subsequent years the percentage of the government parties rose continuously. In most of the professional organizations of lawyers, doctors, architects, and the like, Acción Democrática had the largest single following throughout the Betancourt period, with the Copei being the second largest in most cases.

In the organizations of students, where the two government parties were relatively weak after the Movimiento de Izquierda Revolucionaria broke away from Acción Democrática in 1960, they gained strength in the second half of the Betancourt administration. Student elections in the Universidad Central in Caracas showed a marked increase in the support for the Copei, which became the largest single political group among the students. In most of the provincial universities, the government parties were able to gain at least a small majority among the students.

There were indications that the sway that the Left-wing opposition had over the citizenry of Caracas at the time of the 1958 election declined at least somewhat during the Betancourt regime. Trade union election results there were one indication of this. The failure of the Left-wing opposition parties to mobilize support among the residents of the government housing blocks and the slums on the hills of Caracas in its various mass demonstrations against the government was another indication of the decline of support for the URD, the MIR and the Communist party. One such failure was evident on July 26, 1961, eighth anniversary of the Castro movement, which the extreme Left had hoped to use as occasion for a demonstration against the regime, but there was virtually no response to their calls for such a manifestation. Even more striking was the inability of the extreme Left to cause any serious disturbance during the visit of President John F. Kennedy to the country in December, 1961.

The most conclusive evidence of the ability of the revolutionary democratic forces to keep the support of the Venezuelan citizenry was the outcome of the election of December 1, 1963. The Acción Democrática candidate, Raúl Leoni, won an unquestionable victory, and Rafael Caldera, nominee of the Copei, came in second among nine candidates.

Although the Venezuelan Democratic Revolution has so far been successful, a number of serious weaknesses may be noted in the way the Betancourt government carried out its programs. For one thing, the government did not publicize adequately the things that it achieved, and so, failed to give to its revolution the spirit of a crusade. In the nature of the case, the regime had to tackle a vast number of small projects, most of them in the interior of the country. A casual observer, Venezuelan or foreign, was likely to be unaware of what was being done. As a result, there was honest belief on the part of many people who might otherwise have been favorably disposed toward the government that "this government isn't doing anything."

Partly the failure sufficiently to publicize its achievements was a reflection of the personality of the principal leader of the Venezuelan Democratic Revolution. Rómulo Betancourt has a personal abhorrence of anything approaching demagoguery. This is at once one of his principal elements of strength and a weakness. On the positive side, it led to Betancourt's having a reputation for veracity and forthrightness, which inclined people to believe what he said. On the negative side, however, he sometimes played down situations and acts that might have been dramatized to good purpose.

The failure to give adequate publicity to achievements was demonstrated in many ways. There was little attempt to proclaim the accomplishments of the regime by the simple procedure of putting up signs on the schools, factories, and hospitals built by it, pointing out that they were built by the constitutional government; nor were such signs put up in towns that were supplied with sewerage or water systems by the democratic regime.

In its dealing with foreigners, too, the revolutionary democratic administration showed this same lack of concern with manifesting itself in the best possible light. There was no central office established where visiting newspapermen or researchers could go to arrange appointments and otherwise facilitate their work.

Finally, the Betancourt administration lost opportunities to mobilize the people behind the regime by dramatizing its activities on public occasions. Although large public meetings were held on some public holidays, in which government officials expounded on their government's achievements, there was little effort to mobilize on a mass scale the enthusiasm and energies of the followers of the regime for its principal projects. For instance little attempt was made to enroll young people on a large scale for educational, community development and other programs.

Government officials and political leaders with whom the author discussed this problem protested that a large-scale publicity campaign would be too costly, and that the government could better use its funds in other directions. Nevertheless, a modest expenditure might have produced valuable results.

This lack of adequate publicity had detrimental effects both within Venezuela and outside. Within the country it meant that the regime did not capitalize sufficiently on the enthusiasm of the government's supporters. The Betancourt regime did not rely enough on the possibilities of enlisting voluntary cooperation, largely independent of the government apparatus. If there had been a better publicity campaign accompanying the regime's various programs, this might have been possible.

Of course, propaganda can be carried too far. Mass mobilization, in which really voluntary participation all but disappears, is one of the hallmarks of all totalitarian regimes. Undoubtedly fear of such ersatz popularity was one of the factors making the leaders of the Venezuelan democratic regime hesitate to use methods of modern publicity to a greater degree than they did. Nevertheless, it is the author's opinion that the Betancourt administration could have publicized itself to a greater degree without running the risk of being criticized for using totalitarian tactics.

Another weakness of the Venezuelan democratic regime was the excessive bureaucracy and red tape which characterized it. This was in large part an inheritance from the Pérez Jiménez dictatorship and the provisional government, which greatly inflated the number of government employees. Furthermore, the democratic regime had to face a situation of considerable unemployment and it had no wish to turn thousands of government employees into the streets, to become plotters or rioters against the regime.

Nonetheless, the fact (which the author was able to verify) remained that under Betancourt there was an excessive number of government employees who had little to do and were eating up precious funds which might well have been used for better purposes. This was particularly the case in the central government offices in Caracas. The blight of bureaucracy was less noticeable in the state governments than in the federal administration in Caracas. Much might have been gained in terms of efficiency if there had been greater decentralization of the various programs, if a greater responsibility had been turned over to the state governments.

A third weakness of the Betancourt regime was political jealousy or rivalry among the various parties which participated in the administration. This was particularly noticeable as long as the Unión Republicana Democrática was part of the government, but it continued on a lesser scale after the URD had passed over to the opposition.

The Betancourt administration faced all of the disadvantages of any coalition government. There was sharp negotiation among the parties concerning the allocation of posts in the public administration. As long as there were three parties in the government, each of them was supposed to receive approximately equal treatment in this regard. There were bitter controversies in various states and in some national ministries when one party or the other felt that one of its rivals was getting preferential treatment in patronage.

The problem was particularly acute with regard to the Unión Republicana Democrática. It was intensified because at least a part of the URD was largely out of sympathy with the way in which the government was proceeding. Furthermore, many of the URD leaders had little understanding of the meaning of a multi-party regime, and of the need for solidarity among partners in a coalition. As a result, there were frequent violent attacks upon the government, its policies, and its leaders in the URD press while that party was still in the coalition.

Even after the URD left the government late in 1960, tiffs were not infrequent between the remaining partners in the regime, Acción Democrática and the Copei. Crises occurred from time to time in the state governments, largely over the division of government jobs among the partners. Sometimes these problems broke into the press in the state capitals and in Caracas.

One of the fields in which these problems were of most crucial importance was the agrarian reform. There existed notable lack of coordination among the three principal agencies upon which the success of the reform depended: the Instituto Agrario Nacional, the Banco Agrícola y Pecuario, and the Ministry of Agriculture. Although the granting of land by the IAN was supposed to be accompanied by adequate loans from the bank and by technical assistance and other help from the Ministry of Agriculture, seldom were the operations of the three institutions synchronized. One of the principal reasons for this lack of coordination in the fulfillment of the agrarian reform was the fact that the different institutions were under the control of different political parties. Another reason for the lack of coordination was the bureaucratic unwieldiness of having the essential parts of the same operation under three administrative heads; however, the political problems involved were of key importance in preventing the President from overcoming these bureaucratic handicaps.

It seems to the author that the agrarian reform would be likely to progress a good deal faster than it has if the granting of land, credit, and technical assistance to the beneficiaries of the agrarian reform were placed in the hands of a single government body. Thus, when it was decided to expropriate a given piece of land, prompt decisions could be made concerning needs and procedures.

Another serious criticism of the agrarian reform is that in many cases it sought to do too much. The officials of the Instituto Agrario Nacional felt that they must provide not only land but housing, marketing facilities, and other aid for the beneficiaries. In only one project, along the Pan American Highway in the state of Mérida, was homesteading procedure attempted, although there is undoubtedly a large amount of government-owned land not too far from main highways which could have been thrown open for peasant settlement by anyone willing to cultivate it. Such a procedure would have obviated many of the problems which gave rise to complaints among the agrarian reform beneficiaries.

One other serious criticism might be made of the social programs of the Betancourt government. Too little attention was paid to the housing problem. Although the work of the Banco Obrero in the urban parts of the country continued at a rate which averaged better than that achieved under the dictatorship, and a new program of rural housing was launched, too little was done. In view of the rapid rate of increase in the population, the housing efforts of the democratic government were hardly adequate to keep up with the growth in the number of people needing homes. The regime was not able to make more than a small beginning in overcoming the shortage of more than 700,000 houses which is generally agreed to exist. However, there is no doubt that the basis for greater progress in the housing field was established during the Betancourt regime. A more orderly process of construction was instituted in the Banco Obrero, and the rural housing program of the Directorate of Malariology and Environmental Sanitation of the Ministry of Health was founded. Furthermore, the government succeeded in obtaining several loans abroad to be used principally on the nation's housing efforts.

In the economic sphere, the author is dubious about one aspect of the Betancourt regime's program to overcome the economic crisis that it faced within a year after coming into office. This was the emphasis of the government upon balancing its budget at all costs. Simple Keynesian economics would demonstrate that severe cutting of the government budget, particularly in a country in which the whole economy is as dependent upon the government's finances as is the case in Venezuela, could not help but have a depressing effect upon the economy. Certainly, the experience of 1960 and 1961 indicates that such a depressive effect was felt. President Betancourt took steps to reverse this late in 1961, when he launched a sizable public works program and began to put to use the substantial foreign loans that his government had negotiated; but meanwhile, unwise economic policies had caused serious damage.

Finally, it may be argued that the fact that it was necessary to suspend some constitutional guarantees over a considerable period of time was a partial defeat for a government such as that of Rómulo Betancourt. This regime was pledged to carry out a social revolution in a democratic manner. Therefore, any restriction on democracy would indicate that the government was falling short of its aspirations and its intentions. It must be underscored, however, that the suspension of guarantees was forced by serious attempts of the Left-wing opposition to overthrow the regime, or to provoke Right-wing military elements to do so. It should also be emphasized that the suspension of guarantees had little effect on the functioning of the three powers of government, and that the opposition had a wide range of legal activity open to it in spite of the suspension of guarantees. Nonetheless, it is to be lamented that such action had to be taken.

On balance, the Betancourt government was successful in planning for and carrying out the kinds of economic development and social reform programs that were promised by President Betancourt and Acción Democrática before and during the 1958 election campaign. For those who look for perfection, there is much to criticize in what the Betancourt regime did or left undone; however, when one considers the vastness of the problems involved in the Venezuelan Democratic Revolution, the achievements of the Betancourt regime far outweighed its errors of omission and commission.

Chapter Twenty-Four

The Role of the Venezuelan Democratic Revolution in America

The significance of the Venezuelan Democratic Revolution should be appraised against the background of Latin America as a whole. The area in general is in process of upheaval and rapid change. The question in most of Latin America is not whether there will be a revolution, but rather what direction the revolution will take. The issue is whether the revolution will be under democratic or totalitarian leadership.

There are several facets to the movement for basic change in Latin America. In the first place, it is a revolt against traditional class and race relationships, inherited for the most part from the European conquest of America. It is an effort to destroy the entrenched power of the landed aristocracy, whose ancestors, as soldiers or favorites of royalty, received title to their holdings directly or indirectly from the Spanish or Portuguese crown. With the land, the crown usually granted control over the Indians who worked on it. Their descendants, and those of the Negro slaves who were in many places brought in to work the land when the Indians were killed off, have continued to work it under semiservile conditions.

Basic to this revolt against traditional class and race relations is the drive for an agrarian reform, the redistribution of the holdings of the large landowners. A part of it, too, is the impetus toward an expanded and more varied educational system to facilitate social mobility as well as to provide a labor force which can better serve a changing economy.

Another aspect of the Latin American revolution is its characteristic as a revolt against poverty, ignorance, and ill health, which are in large part the consequences of an underdeveloped economy. Incomes are very low in most of the area, illiteracy ranges from 10 per cent to 90 per cent in the various Latin American countries, and much of the population suffers from endemic diseases as well as infirmities caused by malnutrition.

The circumstance that creates a revolutionary situation in the mid-twentieth century, after four and a half centuries of oppression, is not the existence of these substandard conditions, but rather the fact that the people of Latin America are in increasing degree aware that these conditions were not decreed by the Almighty, but are the work of human society. The masses are therefore determined to change that society.

One fundamental way in which the Latin Americans seek to overcome these handicaps is through economic development, and particularly through industrialization. Every government in Latin America is now convinced of the necessity for building manufacturing industries to produce at least the basic consumers' goods needed by its citizenry. In addition, the larger countries—Mexico, Colombia, Venezuela, Peru, Chile, Argentina, and Brazil—have established heavy industries, including steel plants and heavy chemical firms.

A third factor in the Latin American revolution is the growth of nationalism. Like nearly every other part of the world, Latin America has been deeply influenced by nationalistic ideas. This development is the natural result of economic changes that have been under way in Latin America for three quarters of a century. With the development of modern mining and plantation industries, of railroads and other means of fast transportation and communication, and the mushrooming of a variety of manufacturing industries, there have developed middle groups in the Latin American countries. These new classes lie somewhere in between the traditional aristocracy and the agricultural laborers and peasants who were the lower classes.

The ideas of nationalism appeal particularly to these new middle groups that have appeared in Latin American society in the last two or three generations. For the two numerically significant classes of traditional society, nationalism had little appeal. The landed aristocracy felt little in common with the great masses of the people, and felt more at home with people of its own level of wealth and culture in Europe than with its co-nationals. On the other hand, the predominantly Indian or Negro peasantry was parochial in its outlook and its loyalties, and in many cases was even unaware that the nation existed. The middle groups are "middle" not only in an economic sense but often in racial and cultural terms as well. They are not accepted by the old aristocracy, some of whose blood they nonetheless have running in their veins. And in many cases they tend to despise the peasantry, some of whose blood they also possess. They do not have the loyalties of either of the old classes.

To the middle groups, nationalism has real meaning. The nation is a concept in which they can have passionate faith. Nationalism thus has taken on some of the aspects of a crusade in most of the Latin American countries. The nationalists seek to make the sovereignty of their republics more meaningful than it has been hitherto. They see that the very high degree of dependence of their countries on a small number of export products sold to a handful of countries —80 per cent of Chile's exports being copper, 90 per cent of Venezuela's, petroleum, 90 per cent of Guatemala's, coffee, and so on— limits the effective sovereignty of their nations. It makes them subject to pressure from their customers which can effectively limit the political independence of the Latin American countries.

The nationalists have therefore sought to diversify their national economies. They also seek to limit the control of foreign enterprises over vital parts of these economies, such as public utilities, railroads, steel plants, and petroleum fields.

The fourth aspect of the revolution in Latin America is the struggle for democracy. This is a fight against the tradition that has been all too consistent in many of the Latin American nations, of alternation between periods of military or civilian dictatorship and periods of chaos. It is a struggle against the domination of politics by the military; it is a fight to establish stable, democratic regimes. The struggle for democracy is probably the weakest aspect of the Latin American revolution. It is what many Latin Americans would be willing to sacrifice if they felt that by doing so they could achieve the other objectives of the revolution.

The totalitarians present an attractive program to those who are anxious to get on with the Latin American social and economic revolution. They promise a change in traditional class and race relationships in the most drastic possible manner, through the confiscation of the property of the old aristocrats and even their physical liquidation.

Moreover, the totalitarians are in a position to point to several countries as examples of how rapid economic development can be achieved. They can show how the Soviet Union grew from a relatively minor industrial power to the world's second largest in about one generation. They can use Communist China as an example of a contemporary underdeveloped nation which is making spectacular progress in the drive toward industrialization. Naturally, the Communists and other totalitarians do not discuss the tremendous tolls in terms of both exploitation and tyranny of the totalitarian methods of economic development. Indeed, they discount these, or when possible, they deny them completely.

Furthermore, the absolute and unmitigated opposition of the Communists and most other totalitarians to the United States stirs those Latin American nationalists who since World War II have felt growing frustration and disillusionment with the United States and its policies toward their part of the world.

In addition, as long as the totalitarians are not in power, they picture themselves as the most stalwart of democrats. They have stressed the need for "unity" against whatever dictatorship happened to be in power in any given country. Sometimes they have combined such an appeal with active cooperation with the current dictator by having two Communist parties functioning, one in favor of the regime, one opposed to it.

At first blush it is surprising that the totalitarians have not made more progress in Latin America. In part, their considerable failure is explained by the fact that the Latin American people are more sophisticated than they are sometimes considered to be. The people of Latin America have frequently been able to see through the demagogic postures of the totalitarians. No matter how attractive the totalitarians' appeals may seem to be, Latin American public opinion is often able to discount them and to understand the real implications of a totalitarian victory.

Thus, large numbers of Latin Americans have not been fooled by the democratic protestations of the Communists and other totalitarians. The Latin Americans' dislike for dictatorships has not been confined to opposition to the current regime in power in their own country, but has extended to the kind of government that the totalitarians would establish as well.

Likewise, large segments of Latin American public opinion have not been misled by the Communists' nationalistic pretensions. They are alienated by continuous Communist praise of the Soviet Union, they still remember the attempts of Latin American CP'ers to wrap the Soviet Union flag around themselves when it was popular to have close association with the U.S.S.R. during World War II.

As a result of these and other factors, the totalitarians have so far succeeded in achieving government positions in only a handful of the Latin American countries, and in all these cases but that of Castro's Cuba, they have been ousted from the government before they were able to consolidate their control on the country in question.

If they have so far been relatively unsuccessful, the totalitarians should not be underestimated, however. There has developed in recent years a sizable fringe element in Latin American political life which may perhaps best be described as the "Jacobin Left." This element favors most of the programs of the Latin American revolutions, but has become disillusioned with political democracy, and seeks to achieve the other aims of the revolution by means of violence and dictatorship. In recent years these elements in Latin American politics have tended more and more to ally themselves with and even to merge with the Communists.

The development of the Jacobin Left has been favored by a growing feeling of desperation over the slowness of social change and economic development in Latin America, as well as by disenchantment with the United States as the chief world exponent of political democracy. In spite of the pretensions—honest pretensions—of the United States to be the great leader of democracy against totalitarianism throughout the world, this posture was not reflected in United States policy in Latin America from the death of Franklin D. Roosevelt until the inauguration of John F. Kennedy. Quite to the contrary, in almost every case, the United States gave moral and material support to the dictators who plagued the hemisphere during those years. It refused to see or understand the vital nature of the struggle of Latin American democrats against the traditional kind of dictatorship in the area.

Furthermore, the United States failed to understand the tremendous preoccupation of the Latin Americans with economic development. During most of this period, this country was niggardly in the extreme in its aid programs to Latin America, and it refused even to discuss the problem of stabilizing the demand for and prices of Latin American export products. It showed little or no concern for the fact that as a result of declines in prices of Latin American exports after the Korean War the area lost about $1 billion a year in income.

Getulio Vargas and the political movement that developed around him were perhaps the first evidence of the Jacobin Left. As dictator of Brazil two decades ago, Vargas launched his country on a process of economic development and social change which still continues, but he did so with utter contempt for political democracy.

In the late 1940's and early 1950's, Perón did the same thing, though, unlike Vargas, Perón attempted to develop an ideology to justify his regime to history and to his fellow Latin Americans. He aspired to form a hemisphere-wide political movement of which he would be the supreme chief. His message to the rest of Latin America was that political democracy was largely a protective device of the entrenched interests, and that if the Latin American aspirations of nationalism, economic development, and social change could be achieved through a totalitarian regime, the lack of freedom would not be noticed by the rank and file citizen.

In recent years the Jacobin Left has tended to unify behind the figure of Fidel Castro. He seemed to be a romanticist, which Perón was not, he did not have the taint of the militarist, which handicapped Perón, and he was not an Argentine and therefore was not subject to the suspicion that any strong Argentine ruler always excites among the people of neighboring countries.

Whatever Fidel may have become subsequently, when he came to power, his appeal was certainly not that of the orthodox Communist. Indeed, he insisted quite correctly that he was not a party-line Communist. Yet, only a few months after seizing control over Cuba, Castro began to attempt to rally the people of Latin America around him on the basis of a simple proposition: The long overdue Latin American revolution can be achieved only by a totalitarian dictatorship and through alliance with the enemies of the United States. Or, conversely, it cannot be achieved through political democracy or with the tolerance of the United States.

When Castro finally came out in 1961 and proclaimed himself and his movement to be an integral part of International Communism, he made a serious mistake insofar as his appeal to the rest of Latin America was concerned. He drew upon himself much of the unpopularity and suspicion that the Latin American Communists had justly earned among the citizenry of the area. Nevertheless, although Fidel Castro's popularity in Latin America undoubtedly declined drastically from 1960 on, and particularly after he proclaimed himself a Communist, the influence of the Jacobin Left, which still looks more or less to Castro for leadership, should not be underestimated. The challenge that Castro threw out both to democratic revolutionaries in Latin America and to the United States remains to be answered.

It has not yet been shown that economic development sufficiently rapid to bring measurable benefits to sizable segments of the population in a short time is possible in Latin America through democratic processes. The rate of increase in national income in the Latin American countries fell drastically after 1955 and amounted to only 1 per cent per capita by 1960. If the rate of development can not be drastically increased in the 1960's, the chances of democracy in Latin America will be dim. Democratic regimes are at a certain disadvantage. They are not in a position to enforce the totalitarian practice of long-time suppression of consumers' demands in favor of capital accumulation. They cannot move people around at will. They have to entice their citizens into choosing the activities that are most advantageous to economic development, without force.

Nor has it been proved that necessary social changes can be achieved through democracy. Even in countries in which democracy is more or less strongly entrenched, the old privileged elements often continue to exercise great influence through their economic power, through their relations with the armed forces, and even through their prestige with a considerable segment of the voting public. They use this influence to thwart needed social and economic reforms.

Finally, it remains to be shown that rapid economic development and social change can be achieved with the help or even the tolerance of the United States. Although the changes in United States policy brought about by the Kennedy administration offer some hope that such is the case, the program of the Alliance for Progress is as yet too young for one to pass judgment on it. Nor does one know what the Johnson administration will do with this program.

The Venezuelan Democratic Revolution represents one answer to the totalitarian challenge. Although it did not begin as such, since the movement antedates Castro or even Perón, the course of recent events has made Venezuela the principal testing ground for those who wish to prove that Fidel, the Jacobin Left, and the Communists are wrong. In a sense, the rivalry between Cuba and Venezuela in Latin America is comparable to the contest between Communist China and India in Asia.

Rómulo Betancourt and other Venezuelan leaders tried to bring about a revolution by consent. Betancourt rejected all pressure urging him to deal with his opponents by the simple device of the firing squad, so much in vogue in Castro's Cuba. The Venezuelan democratic regime initiated an agrarian reform by law, with compensation for the former landowners instead of confiscation, and with freedom for most of the peasants to manage the land as they saw fit, whether as individual landholdings or cooperatives.

Furthermore, the Betancourt regime elicited the cooperation of most elements of the community. It set out to industrialize the country by pooling and coordinating the efforts of the government and private investors, domestic and foreign. It sought to get industrial peace not by government fiat but by genuine collective bargaining. It called forth the cooperation of national and state governments, of the trade unions, of the peasants organizations, and of civic groups to develop programs for providing the people of the interior with the basic social services of a modern nation. However, as we have noted earlier, more might have been done to mobilize rank and file citizens in carrying out specific programs.

Although a nationalist government, the Betancourt regime did not carry its nationalism to the point of xenophobia. It established the basis for a gradual transfer of the petroleum business to national control without disrupting the export and production patterns of the industry. It arranged loans for economic development, under conditions established by Venezuela, from foreign firms, the United States government, and international financing agencies. It rejected the idea put into effect by Castro of cutting off established economic relations with the United States and Western Europe and throwing its economic fortunes completely into the hands of the Soviet Union bloc.

The end result that the Betancourt regime tried to achieve is also very different from that of the totalitarians. The objective sought by Acción Democrática is a mixed economy, in which there will be extensive government planning, particularly for purposes of economic growth and social welfare, and in which many of the basic industries of the nation—electric power, petroleum, steel, petrochemicals, and aluminum—will be in the hands of the state; however, most other manufacturing, practically all commerce, and most agriculture will be in the hands of private entrepreneurs. There is no desire on the part of the leaders of the Venezuelan Democratic Revolution to establish a system in which all phases of the economy are run by an official bureaucracy and the only employer is the state.

Above all, the present leaders of Venezuela want the future society to be a democratic one. They believe firmly in the right of the majority of the voters to decide in an orderly fashion who should rule the country; and in the right of the minority to continue peacefully to agitate to become the majority. They seek once and for all to end the role of the armed forces as the maker and destroyer of governments; at the same time they reject the totalitarian concept of the right of a self-chosen elite to rule "in the name of the people."

The United States will have a key role in the success or failure of the Venezuelan Democratic Revolution, and hence in the fate of the attempt to carry out a democratic change throughout the hemisphere. There should be little doubt that if the Venezuelan Democratic Revolution fails, the chance of victory over the totalitarians in other parts of Latin America will be greatly reduced.

Although the record of the United States in Inter-American affairs in the first fifteen years after World War II was appalling, the administration of President Kennedy came to grips with the problems facing the hemisphere. Through the Alliance for Progress program, enunciated by President Kennedy a few weeks after taking office, and organized into a hemispheric multilateral project by the Punta del Este Conference in August, 1961, the President of the United States sought to take the lead in a hemisphere-wide program for economic development and social change under democratic principles.

The Alliance for Progress calls not only for extensive planning for economic development but also for a much vaster effort than ever undertaken in the past, with greatly augmented United States aid to this process. At the same time, it requires those nations participating in the program to carry out basic reforms such as land redistribution and the establishment of more equitable tax systems.

During his visit to Venezuela in December, 1961, President Kennedy not only made clear his support for the democratic Latin American revolution but also showed his understanding of the key role that Venezuela plays in that development. In his speech at the La Morita agrarian reform project, he said, among other things:

"Now, today, in 1961, it is our obligation to move ahead and to bring to fruition the conception that along with national independence and individual liberties goes the well-being of the people themselves. We do not merely talk of slogans of democracy and freedom.

"It is our function here in this hemisphere in 1961 to make it possible for all the people not only to be free but to have a home, to educate their children, to have a job for themselves and their security, and that is what we are determined to do.

"Economic security, the bringing of a better life to all of our people, must now in the 1960's, be the principal object and goal of the Inter-American system. And what is happening here today at La Morita in pursuit of that goal symbolizes the gigantic new steps that are now being taken. . . .

"We will be partners in building a better life for our people. And here in Venezuela the meaning of the new Alianza para el Progreso is being demonstrated, for you have made a transition from depressive dictatorship into a free life for the people of this country, to progressive democratic rule under the . . . great democratic statesman of the Western Hemisphere—your distinguished President, Rómulo Betancourt.

"And one of the first goals of the new spirit of this hemisphere must be the elimination of tryranny from the north to the south until it is a hemisphere that Simón Bolívar once predicted of free men, of free countries, living under a system of liberty. . . .

"Today eighty-six families will receive their titles to their own homes under a program which has already settled 38,000 families on 3,800,000 acres of land.

"This is your program—the program of your progressive far-seeing Government—and the people of my country will share in this program by making available more loans to build rural homes and more credits to finance your crops.

"This program is at the heart of the Alianza para el Progreso.

From now on real progress is impossible unless the benefits of increased prosperity are shared by the people themselves. I do not hold the view which some now preach that the only way we can make economic progress is through dictatorship. I believe the reverse. . . ."[1]

A day later, in neighboring Colombia, President Kennedy again indicated his grasp of the basic issues in Latin America, and of his determination that the United States help resolve them:

"In our time the veil has again been torn asunder. The millions of our people who have lived in hopeless poverty—patiently suffering hunger, social injustice and ignorance—have now glimpsed the hope of a better and more abundant life for themselves and their children. And they do not intend to be thrust back into the darkness.

"La Alianza para el Progreso is designed to transform this hope into reality. It calls for a vast and immediate effort on the part of all American nations to satisfy the basic needs of our people for work and land, for houses and schools. It expects within the next ten years—the decade of development—to be well on the way toward satisfying those needs. . . .

"The leaders of Latin America, the industrialists and the landowners are, I am sure, also ready to admit past mistakes and accept new responsibilities.

"For unless they are willing to contribute their resources to national development, unless they are prepared not merely to accept, but initiate basic land and tax reforms, unless they take the lead in improving the welfare of the people of your country—then that leadership will be taken from them and the heritage of centuries of Western civilization will be consumed in a few months of violence."[2]

These speeches, and the program that President Kennedy launched in the Inter-American sphere, represent a fundamental change in attitudes by the United States. If it materializes in actual deeds, the democratic revolutionaries in Latin America will have a better than even chance to win out over their totalitarian adversaries.

Venezuela is in a particularly advantageous position to take a leading part in the Alianza para el Progreso. Through Cordiplan it elaborated the kind of long-range projects for economic development that are called for in the Punta del Este agreements. It has a far-reaching agrarian reform in progress, and the leaders of the revolution are disposed to carry out a tax reform along the lines foreseen in the Alliance.

In a very real sense, the future of all of Latin America rests on the success or failure of the Venezuelan Democratic Revolution. If the programs set in motion by the Betancourt regime to industrialize the country, to redistribute the land, to provide the people with the educational facilities and social services that they need and want, are successful, and if they can establish more firmly the country's national independence, the chances for democracy throughout Latin America will be greatly strengthened.

Events in Venezuela are being closely watched in the neighboring countries. At the present moment, Acción Democrática stands as the most influential representative of a group of parties that are seeking to carry out a democratic reform program in their respective countries. Every success of Acción Democrática is a success for the Peruvian Apristas, the members of the Movimiento Nacionalista Revolucionario of Bolivia, of Liberación Nacional of Costa Rica, and several other parties of the same type.

The Venezuelan revolution is significant, too, because of the participation of the Catholic Social Copei party in the process. The alliance of Copei and Acción Democrática symbolizes cooperation throughout the hemisphere between the national revolutionary and Christian Democratic parties. Upon these two groups of political parties rests most of the burden of bringing about the necessary social changes in a democratic environment.

The success of the Venezuelan Democratic Revolution is of great significance not only for the Latin Americans but also for the United States. If democracy perishes in Latin America, the world position of the United States will be greatly weakened. The people of the United States must realize, as President Kennedy did, that the best assurance for democracy in this country is the existence of strong and progressive democracies in the countries that share the hemisphere with us. The success of the Venezuelan Democratic Revolution can go far toward assuring that the United States will have such neighbors.

Notes

Chapter One

1. Rafael Caldera: "Interpretación sociológica de Venezuela en la hora de América," speech given in Quito, Ecuador, September 2, 1960 (mimeographed).
2. *Ibid.*

Chapter Two

1. Rómulo Betancourt: *Venezuela: Política y petróleo,* Fondo de Cultura Económica, Mexico, D.F., 1956, pp. 236-237.
2. *Ibid.*, p. 246.
3. *Ibid.*, p. 246.
4. *Ibid.*, p. 252.
5. *Ibid.*, p. 253.
6. *Ibid.*, p. 259.
7. *Ibid.*, pp. 314-315.
8. Figures in preceding chapters given by Betancourt, pp. 326-327.
9. *Ibid.*, p. 340.
10. *Ibid.*, p. 328.
11. Corporación Venezolana de Fomento: *Cuadernos de información,* May-June, 1950, cited by Betancourt, p. 328.
12. Betancourt, p. 405.
13. *Ibid.*, pp. 401-404.
14. *Ibid.*, pp. 306-307.
15. Ramón Fernández y Fernández: *Reforma agraria en Venezuela,* cited by Betancourt, p. 353.
16. Cited by Betancourt, p. 352.
17. *Ibid.*, pp. 357-358.
18. *Ibid.*, p. 300.
19. *Ibid.*, p. 358.
20. *Ibid.*, p. 340.

Chapter Three

1. Rómulo Betancourt: *Venezuela: Política y petróleo,* Fondo de Cultura Económica, Mexico, D.F., 1956, p. 498.
2. *Ibid.*, p. 560.
3. *Ibid.*, p. 671.

Chapter Four

1. New York *Times*, January 13, 1960. *The Quarterly Review* of the Bank of London and South America, in its issue of January, 1961, estimated the debt left by the dictatorship of 4.5 million bolívares, which, when converted at the legal exchange rate of 3.35 to the dollar, would amount to slightly less dollars than indicated by the *Times*.

Chapter Five

1. Estado Aragua, Organismo Regional de Desarrollo Comunal: *Programa de realizaciones*, Julio de 1961.

Chapter Six

1. The philosophy and program of Acción Democrática is presented in capsule form in *La cartilla del militante*, published by Acción Democrática as a handbook for its members (Caracas, 1958).

Chapter Seven

1. Article by G. García Ponce, 'Sobre la discusión política en la Conferencia del P.C.V. en Caracas," in *Principios* (Communist magazine), Caracas, May, 1961, p. 22.
2. Quoted in *El Nacional*, Caracas, July 19, 1961.

Chapter Eight

1. Rómulo Betancourt: *Mensaje del Presidente ante el Congreso Nacional, 11 Marzo 1961*, Imprenta Nacional, Caracas, 1961.
2. *Alas de la democracia*, Imprenta Nacional, Caracas, 1959, p. 12.
3. *Ibid.*, p. 14.
4. *Bien definida posición*, Imprenta Nacional, Caracas, 1960, pp. 6-7.
5. Rómulo Betancourt: *Inabatible espíritu de servicio público*, Imprenta Nacional, Caracas, 1960.
6. Rómulo Betancourt: *Una voluntad al servicio de la nación—Mensaje del Presidente Betancourt a los Venezolanos el 16 de Julio de 1960*, Imprenta Nacional, Caracas, 1960, pp. 11-12.
7. *Bien definida posición*, p. 60.

Chapter Nine

1. Speech of Rómulo Betancourt, reprinted in *Defendemos nuestra democracia*, Caracas, 1960, p. 17.
2. *La República*, Caracas, July 20, 1961.
3. Rómulo Betancourt: *Bajo una política de nuevo signo*, Imprenta Nacional, Caracas, 1961, p. 10.
4. Speech of Betancourt, reprinted in *Defendemos nuestra democracia*, p. 18.

Chapter Ten

1. Rómulo Betancourt: *Dos años de gobierno democrático*, Imprenta Nacional, Caracas, 1961, p. 401.

2. *Ratificación de principios teóricos y de orientación programática normativos de Acción Democrática,* Acción Democrática Secretaría Nacional de Prensa y Propaganda, Caracas, 1958, p. 20.
3. There were a few pro-Communist delegates also present at this conference, largely as a result of the influence of the URD in the arrangements committee.

Chapter Eleven

1. Rómulo Betancourt: *V Presidential Message, 12th March 1963*, Imprenta Nacional, Caracas, 1963, p. 25.
2. *Ibid.*, p. 27.
3. *El Mundo,* Caracas, July 27, 1961.
4. Betancourt, p. 27.
5. *International Commerce,* Washington, D.C., November 25, 1963.

Chapter Twelve

1. *El Nacional,* Caracas, August 25, 1961.
2. Ministerio de Agricultura y Cría: *Reforma agraria: Informe de la Sub-Comisión de Economía,* Caracas, Volumen II, Tomo I, pp. 45-46.
3. *Ibid.*, p. 47.
4. *Ibid.*, p. 47.
5. Rafael Caldera: "Interpretación sociológica de Venezuela en la hora de América," speech in Quito, Ecuador, September 2, 1960 (mimeographed).
6. Instituto Agrario Nacional: *Ley de Reforma Agraria,* Caracas, 1960, Article 74.
7. *Frente a problemas del campo venezolano,* Imprenta Nacional, Caracas, 1959.
8. *Jornada,* organ of Confederación de Trabajadores de Venezuela, Caracas, October 9, 1963.
9. *Jornada,* August 15, 1963.
10. *Jornada,* October 9, 1963, and *International Commerce,* Washington, November 25, 1963.

Chapter Fourteen

1. *Jornada,* organ of Confederación de Trabajadores de Venezuela, Caracas, August 15, 1963.

Chapter Fifteen

1. Rómulo Betancourt: *Confianza en el presente y el porvenir de Venezuela,* Imprenta Nacional, Caracas, 1959.
2. Rómulo Betancourt: *Ante las perspectivas de un Nueva Año; Visión realista en la alocución presidential en el Palacio de Miraflores el 31 del Diciembre de 1959,* Imprenta Nacional, Caracas, 1960.
3. *La República,* Caracas, August 2, 1961.
4. *El Nacional,* Caracas, July 28, 1961.
5. Peter Wenzl: "El clima económico de Venezuela" (mimeographed), p. 4.
6. *El Nacional,* Caracas, August 1, 1961.

7. Rómulo Betancourt: *Dos años de gobierno democrático,* Imprenta Nacional, Caracas, 1961, p. 402.
8. Rómulo Betancourt: *Mensaje presentado al Congreso por el Presidente de la República Señor Rómulo Betancourt durante sus sesiones ordinarias de 1962,* Imprenta Nacional, Caracas, 1962.

CHAPTER SIXTEEN

1. Rómulo Betancourt: *Confianza en el presente y el porvenir de Venezuela,* Imprenta Nacional, Caracas, 1959.
2. Speech by Rómulo Betancourt, published in *CVF–15 Años de una labor patriótica,* Imprenta Nacional, Caracas, 1961, p. 33.
3. Rómulo Betancourt: *Dos años de gobierno democrático,* Imprenta Nacional, Caracas, 1961, p. 279.
4. *Ibid.,* p. 280.
5. *Ibid.,* p. 279.
6. *Ibid.,* p. 132.
7. "CADAFE en Marcha hacia la electrificación de Venezuela," in *Boletín de la CVF,* May 29, 1961, p. 114.
8. *Ibid.,* pp. 114-115.
9. *Ibid.,* p. 115.
10. Betancourt, *Dos años de gobierno democrático,* p. 282.
11. Rómulo Betancourt: *Mensaje Presidencial, 12 de Marzo de 1962,* Imprenta Nacional, Caracas, 1962, p. 51.
12. Banco Central de Venezuela: *Memoria correspondiente al ejercicio anual 1960,* Caracas, 1961, pp. 300-303.

CHAPTER SEVENTEEN

1. George Wythe: *Industry in Latin America,* Columbia University Press, New York, 1946, p. 145.
2. Banco Central de Venezuela: *Memoria correspondiente al ejercicio anual 1960,* Caracas, 1961, p. 121.
3. *OPEP–Organización de Países Exportadores de Petróleo,* Caracas, 1961, p. 90.
4. Banco Central de Venezuela, *Memoria correspondiente al ejercicio anual 1960,* p. 90.
5. Acción Democrática: *Tesis petrolera, Caracas,* 1958.
6. *CVP: Corporación Venezolana del Petróleo,* Imprenta Nacional, Caracas, 1961, p. 16.
7. Rómulo Betancourt, Message to Congress in May, 1961, in *A.D.,* Caracas, May 13, 1961.
8. *CVP: Corporación Venezolana del Petróleo,* p. 17.
9. Betancourt Message to Congress, in *A.D.,* May 13, 1961.
10. *El Nacional,* Caracas, September 14, 1961.
11. *CVP: Corporación Venezolana del Petróleo,* p. 24.
12. *Ibid.,* p. 25.
13. *Ibid.,* p. 23.
14. *El Mundo,* Caracas, September 13, 1961.
15. Article IV, Resolution #2 of Baghdad Conference, published in *OPEP: Organización de Países Exportadores de Petróleo,* p. 14
16. *Ibid.,* pp. 12-14.

17. In 1962 Indonesia and Libya also joined OPEC, thus bringing within its ranks countries responsible for 93 per cent of the world's oil exports. The U.S.S.R. and Colombia were the only significant exporters remaining outside.
18. *La República,* Caracas, September 15, 1961.
19. Rómulo Betancourt: *Dos años de gobierno democrático,* Imprenta Nacional, Caracas, 1961, p. 404.

Chapter Eighteen

1. Speech by Rómulo Betancourt on first anniversary of his administration, in *Dos años de gobierno democrático,* Imprenta Nacional, Caracas, 1961, p. 199.
2. Rafael Caldera: "Interpretación sociológica de Venezuela en la hora de América," speech given in Quito, Ecuador, on September 2, 1960 (mimeographed).
3. *Jornada,* organ of Confederación de Trabajadores de Venezuela, Caracas, October 9, 1963.
4. Betancourt, pp. 49-50.
5. Rómulo Betancourt: *V Presidential Message, 12th March 1963,* Caracas, 1963, pp. 77-78.

Chapter Nineteen

1. *Memoria que el Ministerio de Educación presenta al Congreso Nacional de la República de Venezuela en sus sesiones de 1961,* Caracas, 1961, pp. E-36, E-37.
2. *Ibid.,* p. E-4.
3. *Ibid.,* p. E-163.
4. *Ibid.,* p. 70.
5. Rómulo Betancourt: *Mensaje del Presidente ante el Congreso Nacional, Caracas, 11 Marzo 1961,* Imprenta Nacional, Caracas, 1961, pp. 67-68.
6. *Progresos en la educación oficial* (*1958-60*), Caracas, February, 1960.

Chapter Twenty

1. *Memoria que el Ministerio de Educación presenta al Congreso Nacional de la República de Venezuela en sus sesiones de 1960,* Caracas, 1960, p. 90.
2. *Memoria que el Ministerio de Educación presenta al Congreso Nacional de la República de Venezuela en sus sesiones de 1961,* Caracas, 1961, pp. 52-53.
3. Interview with Guido Olivares, head of the factory literacy campaign in Caracas, July 22, 1961.
4. Article by Juan Ramón Bucce in *A.D.,* Caracas, September 13, 1961.
5. *Memoria que el Ministerio de Educación presenta al Congreso Nacional de la República de Venezuela en sus sesiones de 1961,* p. 63.
6. Article by Juan Ramón Bucce in *A.D.,* Caracas, September 13, 1961.
7. *V Presidential Message, 12th March 1963,* Imprenta Nacional, Caracas, 1963, p. 65.
8. *Memoria que el Ministerio de Educación presenta al Congreso Nacional de la República de Venezuela en sus sesiones de 1961,* pp. 115-116.

9. *Así nació la Universidad de Oriente,* Imprenta Nacional, Caracas, 1960, pp. 15-16.
10. *Universidad de Oriente: Almácigo de porvenir,* Imprenta Nacional, Caracas, 1960.
11. Editorial in *La Esfera,* Caracas, July 25, 1961.

CHAPTER TWENTY-ONE

1. Rómulo Betancourt: *Dos años de gobierno democrático,* Imprenta Nacional, Caracas, 1961, p. 105.
2. Banco Central de Venezuela: *Memoria correspondiente al ejercicio anual 1960,* Caracas, 1961, p. 321.
3. *La Esfera,* Caracas, July 31, 1961.
4. Rómulo Betancourt: *Viviendas para todos; Definición de una política,* Imprenta Nacional, Caracas, 1959, p. 6.
5. Article by Victor Alba in *La Esfera,* Caracas, July 31, 1961.
6. Betancourt, *Dos años de gobierno democrático,* p. 45.
7. Ministerio de Sanidad y Asistencia Social: *Venezuela: Rural Housing Program Activities,* Maracay, May, 1961.
8. Banco Central de Venezuela, *Memoria correspondiente al ejercicio anual 1960,* pp. 316-317.
9. *La Esfera,* Caracas, August 17, 1961.
10. Speech by Rómulo Betancourt, published in *Ante el IV Congreso de los Trabajadores, Los Caracas, diciembre de 1961,* Caracas, 1961, p. 17.
11. *El Nacional,* Caracas, July 17, 1961.
12. Betancourt, *Dos años de gobierno democrático,* p. 299.
13. *Ibid.,* pp. 400-401.
14. Ministerio de Sanidad y Asistencia Social: *Año 1960: Memoria y Cuenta,* Caracas, 1961, pp. 473-475.
15. Betancourt: *Dos años de gobierno democrático,* p. 461.
16. Rómulo Betancourt: *V Presidential Message, 12th March 1963,* Imprenta Nacional, Caracas, 1963, p. 69.
17. Ministerio de Sanidad y Asistencia Social, *Año 1960: Memoria y Cuenta,* p. 454.
18. *Mensaje que presenta el ciudadano Doctor Rafael Solórzano Bruce, Gobernador del Estado Anzoátegui a la Asamblea Legislativa del Estado en sus sesiones ordinarias de 1961,* Barcelona, 1961, p. 29.
19. *Mensaje que presenta el ciudadano Edilberto Escalante, Gobernador del Estado Táchira a la Asamblea Legislativa del Estado en sus sesiones ordinarias de 1961,* San Cristóbal, 1961, p. 12.
20. Rómulo Betancourt: *Mensaje presidencial, 12 de Marzo de 1962,* Imprenta Nacional, Caracas, 1962.
21. *Ibid.*
22. *Mensaje que presenta el ciudadano Doctor Rafael Solórzano Bruce, Gobernador del Estado Anzoátegui a la Asamblea Legislativa del Estado en sus sesiones ordinarias de 1961,* p. 29.

CHAPTER TWENTY-TWO

1. *II Congreso Venezolano de Salud Pública,* Caracas, 1961, p. 23.
2. Ministerio de Sanidad y Asistencia Social: *Año 1961: Memoria y Cuenta,* Caracas, 1961, p. 12.

3. *Ibid.*, p. 18.
4. *Ibid.*, p. 234.
5. *Mensaje que presenta el ciudadano Doctor Rafael Solórzano Bruce, Gobernador del Estado Anzoátegui a la Asamblea Legislativa del Estado en sus sesiones ordinarias de 1960*, Barcelona, 1960, p. 30.
6. Rómulo Betancourt: *V Presidential Message, 12th March 1963*, Imprenta Nacional, Caracas, 1963, p. 70.
7. Interview with Edmundo Fernández, President of the Consejo Venezolano del Niño, Caracas, August 31, 1961.
8. *El Nacional,* Caracas, July 20, 1961.

Chapter Twenty-Four

1. New York *Times,* December 17, 1961.
2. *Ibid.*, December 18, 1961.

Bibliographical Note

Much of the material in these pages comes from personal observation and conversations with more than six hundred people during the author's various visits to Venezuela. Those interviewed included politicians of all of the parties, civil servants, industrialists, trade union leaders, military men, priests, and various foreigners resident in or knowledgeable about Venezuela.

Most of the printed sources consulted were Venezuelan and in Spanish, and are not easily accessible in this country. Of fundamental importance was the collection of speeches by President Rómulo Betancourt during the first two years or more he was in office. This is entitled *Dos años de gobierno democrático* and was published in 1961 by the Imprenta Nacional in Caracas. Also cited are pamphlets containing other speeches by Betancourt and other government officials, published by the Imprenta Nacional since 1959, as well as pamphlets published by Acción Democrática and the Movimiento de Izquierda Revolucionaria.

For the chapter on the Acción Democrática government of the 1940's the author relied heavily on a book by Rómulo Betancourt, *Venezuela: Política y petróleo*. This was published by the Fondo de Cultura Económica of Mexico City in 1955, when Betancourt was in exile in Puerto Rico.

Of great importance for statistics and details on government operations were reports of various government departments and institutions. Most outstanding are the annual reports of the Banco Central of Venezuela, which have invaluable information on all aspects of the nation's economy. Other useful annual reports were those of the Ministries of Health and Education, the Corporación Venezolana de Fomento, and CADAFE. Of considerable interest also were the annual reports of various governors to their state legislatures. Finally, the annual messages to Congress of President Rómulo Betancourt in 1962 and 1963 contain much valuable information.

Venezuelan periodicals consulted include weeklies such as *A.D.* and *Combate,* official publications of Acción Democrática; *Copey,* the official organ of the Partido Social Cristiano Copei; *U.R.D.*, issued by the Unión Republicana Democrática; *Tribuna Popular, Gaceta,* and *Tiempos,* published at various times by the Partido Comunista de Venezuela; and *El Campesino,* organ of the Federación Campesina de Venezuela. Also of value were the monthly "theoretical" organs of the Movimiento de Izquierda Revolucionaria and the PCV, entitled *Pensamiento Revolucionario* and *Principios,* respectively; and the monthly *Política,* an unofficial organ of AD.

The author also used a number of Caracas daily newspapers. Of these, *La Esfera* and *El Mundo* represent the Right-wing opposition to the Betancourt regime, although they also carry articles by AD and Copei members. *El Nacional* is an independent journal carrying articles by people of almost all shades of opinion; *La República* is the semiofficial organ of Acción Democrática. *The Caracas Daily Journal,* the city's only English-language daily, is noncommital politically.

A full list of the sources to which reference has been made can be gathered from the text and footnotes. A reader who is interested in going further into various aspects of recent events in Venezuela may find several books in English of some use. These include Edwin Lieuwen's *Arms and Politics in Latin America* (Praeger, New York, 1960), which goes at some length into the problem of the tradition of military interference in politics in Latin American countries, including Venezuela. Tad Szulc's *Twilight of the Tyrants* (Henry Holt, New York, 1959) includes a study of the rise and fall of the Pérez Jiménez dictatorship, as does *The Struggle for Democracy in Latin America* (Macmillan, New York, 1961), written by the present author and Charles O. Porter. Finally, the reader might be interested in the extensive biographical sketch of Rómulo Betancourt appearing in the present author's *Prophets of the Revolution* (Macmillan, New York, 1962).

Several periodicals in the United States cover more or less adequately the news coming from Venezuela. Most complete is the monthly *Hispanic American Report,* published by Stanford University. Among the daily newspapers, the New York *Times*, the *Christian Science Monitor*, and the Washington *Post* probably have as good day-to-day coverage as any in this country. Journals of opinion such as *The New Leader, New America, The Nation, New Republic,* and *The Progressive* on the Left, and *National Review* on the Right, sometimes carry articles on Venezuelan affairs.

Index